Point & Click OpenOffice.org!

Point & Click OpenOffice.org!

Robin 'Roblimo' Miller

Upper Saddle River, NJ • Boston • Indianapolis • San Francisco
New York • Toronto • Montreal • London • Munich • Paris • Madrid
Capetown • Sydney • Tokyo • Singapore • Mexico City

The publisher offers excellent discounts on this book when ordered in quantity for bulk purchases or special sales, which may include electronic versions and/or custom covers and content particular to your business, training goals, marketing focus, and branding interests. For more information, please contact:

U. S. Corporate and Government Sales
(800) 382-3419
corpsales@pearsontechgroup.com

For sales outside the U. S., please contact:

International Sales
international@pearsoned.com

This Book Is Safari Enabled
The Safari® Enabled icon on the cover of your favorite technology book means the book is available through Safari Bookshelf. When you buy this book, you get free access to the online edition for 45 days. Safari Bookshelf is an electronic reference library that lets you easily search thousands of technical books, find code samples, download chapters, and access technical information whenever and wherever you need it.

To gain 45-day Safari Enabled access to this book:

- Go to http://www.prenhallprofessional.com/safarienabled
- Complete the brief registration form
- Enter the coupon code 9BDJ-P83E-ZN8F-ZHDZ-9HFP

If you have difficulty registering on Safari Bookshelf or accessing the online edition, please e-mail customer-service@safaribooksonline.com.

Visit us on the Web: www.prenhallprofessional.com

ISBN 0-13-187992-8

Text printed in the United States on recycled paper at R.R. Donnelley & Sons in Crawfordsville, Indiana.

First printing, November 2005

Library of Congress Cataloging-in-Publication Data

Miller, Robin, 1952-
Point & click Openoffice.org! / Robin 'Roblimo' Miller.
p. cm.
Includes bibliographical references and index.
ISBN 0-13-187992-8 (alk. paper)
1. OpenOffice.org (Electronic resource) 2. Integrated software. 3. Business–Computer programs. I. Title: Point and click openOffice.org!. II. Title.
HF5548.4.O57M54 2006
005.5–dc22

2005024236

Table of Contents

Foreword

Over the last decade, open source has continued its meteoric ride to the top; with Web servers like Apache and operating systems like Linux and BSD Unix, open source's development and continued growth has profoundly impacted the software marketplace.

For years, Microsoft Office has been the undisputed champion of the "productivity" suite. But recently, some critics have accused it of being bloated and overly complex—not to mention expensive! Sun's acquisition of StarOffice, and its subsequent release as OpenOffice.org, was met with derision from some pundits, who said going up against Microsoft Office was a fool's game.

Yet, look where we are now: OpenOffice.org has reached the point where the development and user communities are growing by leaps and bounds. And recent efforts by corporations, institutions, and other groups to find ways to get their work done without having to pay more software licensing fees have given OpenOffice.org the opening it needs to really take off.

Robin's book comes at the perfect time. With the extremely popular 2.0 release, more people will discover OpenOffice.org's incredible value. A book like Robin's is important because it helps people master the OpenOffice.org tools they need to get things done. And that's ultimately what software should be about—the tools to get things done. OpenOffice.org is one of the best tools around for the business of doing business—and it is ready, willing, and able to work for you.

Jeffrey Bates
VP Editorial Operations, Co-Founder Slashdot.org

About the Authors

Robin 'Roblimo' Miller (www.roblimo.com) is editor-in-chief of OSTG, one of the world's leading online tech news publishers. He has written extensively about computers and the Internet for Slashdot, Linux.com, NewsForge, Time New Media, *Online Journalism Review*, *Web Hosting Magazine*, the *Washington Post*, the *Baltimore Sun*, and many other Web sites, newspapers, and magazines. He is one of modern interactive journalism's creators and has served as an Internet business consultant to several Fortune 500 companies and many Internet entrepreneurs. He has also authored *The Online Rules of Successful Companies* (Financial Times Prentice Hall 2002) and *Point & Click Linux* (Prentice Hall 2004).

Bruce Byfield (Chapter 11, "Sharing Files Between OpenOffice.org and Microsoft Office") is a course designer, instructor, and computer journalist whose work has appeared on both NewsForge.com and the Linux Journal Web site.

Daniel Carrera (Chapter 6, "Slick OpenOffice.org Writer Tricks") is a long-time OpenOffice.org volunteer, user, and advocate who has written dozens of articles about OpenOffice.org.

Lalaine "Lizza" Capucion (Chapter 5, "OOo Calc: Spreadsheets and More," and Chapter 9, "Make Calc Spreadsheets Dance for You") is a freelance writer, editor, and abstractor/indexer who has been creating and working with sophisticated spreadsheets since 1993.

Rob Reilly (Chapter 3, "OOo Impress: Slide Shows That Will Impress Almost Anyone," Chapter 8, "OOo Impress: Smooth, Sophisticated Slide Shows," and Chapter 10, "OOo Database 'Front End': Your Free Pass") is a consultant, speaker, and freelance writer who has set up countless databases for clients—and loves to wow audiences with sophisticated slide presentations.

Linda Worthington (Chapter 7, "Draw: Not Your Father's Drawing Board") is a writer and graphics artist who maintains several sections of the official OOo Users Guide.

Introduction

OpenOffice.org is free, open source software.

The OpenOffice.org logo.

"Free" in this case is more a matter of philosophy than price. I explain free and open source software concepts at greater length in Chapter 12, "OpenOffice.org as a Community Effort." For now, just know that, despite being free, OpenOffice.org is an easy-to-use, professional-quality office software suite that consistently wins rave reviews.

This wealth of features is why this book is laid out the way it is, with lots of short chapters that each cover one OpenOffice.org feature. The accompanying Flash videos—on the second CD in the back of the book—follow the same pattern. Almost all the videos are less than 10 minutes long, and each one covers a single task or a group of simple tasks. Instead of getting a headache from trying to learn too much at once, you can read a few pages, watch a few minutes of video, and then immediately use what you just learned.

This friendly learning style is appropriate for OpenOffice.org, which is called by its nickname OOo instead of its formal name, throughout most of this book.

In fact, let's start using the "OOo" nickname right now. OOo is friendly software you can use while wearing shorts and sandals just as easily as when you're wearing business attire, so we might as well treat it like a friend from the start.

Not Just Friendly But Practical

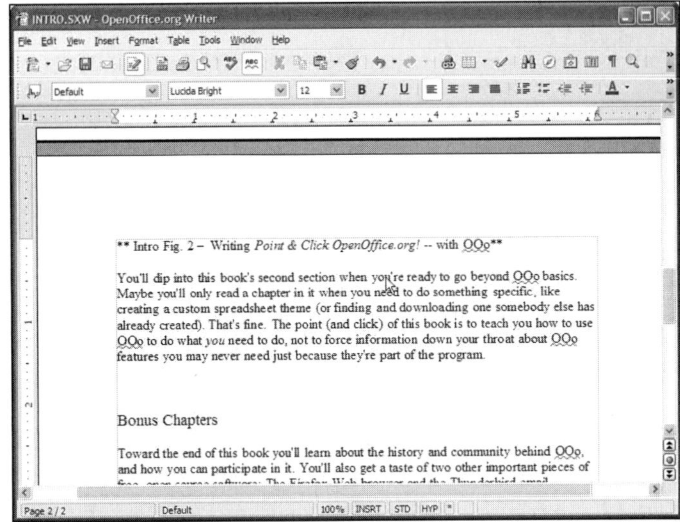

An author's view of OpenOffice.org.

This book was written with OOo. Prentice Hall edited with Microsoft Office, but I did my final revisions in OOo—and saved them in Microsoft's .doc format. The fact that this book got completed and you're reading it is proof that OpenOffice.org users can share files with Microsoft Office users. It's also proof that OOo is all the office software an author needs.

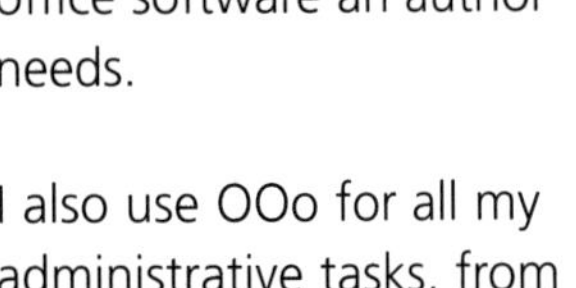

I also use OOo for all my administrative tasks, from filling out purchase orders to creating and editing spreadsheets. I make and give slide presentations with OOo, and I use it to view slide presentations sent to me in Microsoft's PowerPoint format. OOo has been my primary office software choice since 2001. It serves me well. And by following the simple instructions in this book and on the CD, you will soon join me—and millions of other people around the world—in using OOo to

- Write, edit, save, print, and share text documents
- Make, alter, and resize graphics
- Design, edit, save, print, and share spreadsheets
- Create, edit, and display slide shows
- Build, edit, and use simple databases
- Read, edit, save, print, and share Microsoft Office files

Bonus Chapters

The Firefox logo.

The Thunderbird logo.

At the end of this book you'll get a taste of two other important pieces of free open source software: The Mozilla Project's Firefox Web browser and the Thunderbird email program. These two programs have received rave reviews in media ranging from *eWeek* to the *Wall Street Journal*.

And now, having said all that, it's time to install and start using OpenOffice.org, one of the world's finest and most versatile pieces of office software.

Section I

OpenOffice.org Basics

Chapter 1

First Things First

If you run Windows, you can install OOo from the CD included with this book. But OOo is constantly being improved, so you may want to check the OpenOffice.org Web site for the latest downloadable version and install that one instead.

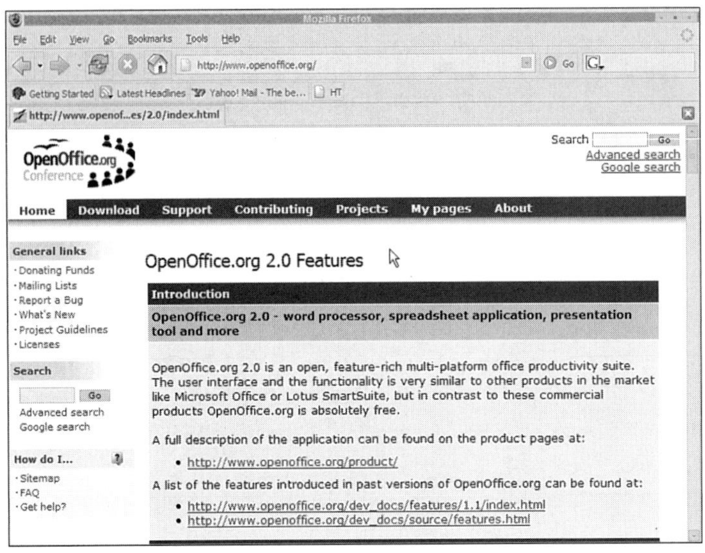

The OpenOffice.org Web site.

The CD also contains a version for Linux. However, if you're a Linux user, your best bet is to check your distribution's download repository for binary files made to integrate directly with your favorite "flavor" of Linux. This will make installation easier and smoother.

Since development of OOo for Mac OS X was lagging behind the Linux and Windows versions when I wrote this book—over three months before it was published—Mac users should check both the OpenOffice.org Web site and the NeoOffice.org Web site to see which one is more up-to-date. NeoOffice currently looks like the best bet; it integrates smoothly with the Mac OS X structure, while the "main" OOo Mac version requires X11 knowledge to get going.

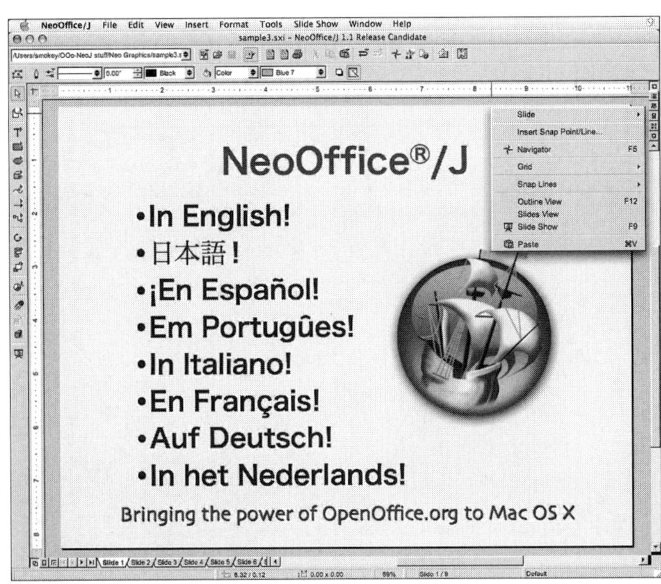

NeoOffice.

Once you get OpenOffice.org installed, though, it *works* almost exactly the same on any operating system. What you learn from reading this book and watching the videos is applicable no matter what kind of computer you use.

Installing OpenOffice.org

Windows users: Open the OOo-Windows folder on the CD. Click on the OOo-install file to start your installation.

Linux users: Copy the OOo-Linux folder to your hard drive. Follow standard procedures to extract the OOo tar.gz file in that folder. Then, install the RPM files you'll see after extraction. Or, use the binary version you downloaded from your distribution's repository and install OOo the same way you install any other binary program in your distribution.

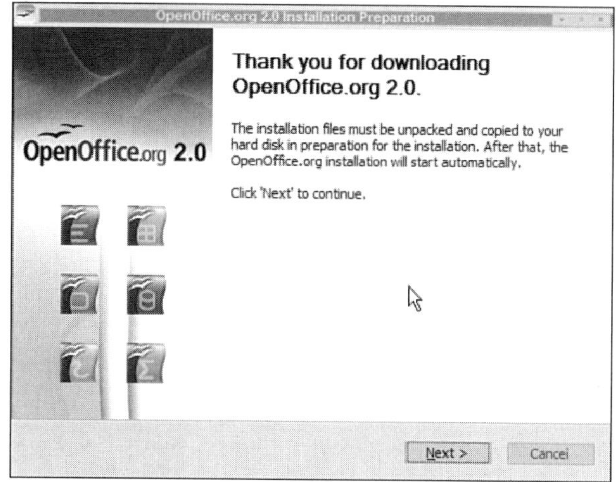

OpenOffice.org Windows installer.

Mac OS X users: If you choose NeoOffice—which is highly recommended—"unstuff" NeoOffice like any other program.

The setup procedure is approximately the same in Windows, Linux, and Mac OS X.

Right now, let's concentrate on the Windows version.

In Windows, double-click the OOo-install file to start the installation.

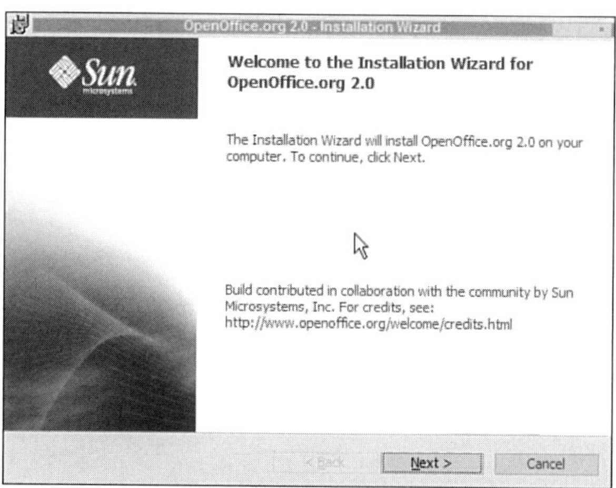

The OOo Windows Installation Wizard.

The next window (not shown) asks you to select the folder where OOo will install itself. The default location is fine for virtually all standard Windows setups. (Do not change this if you do not know what you are doing!) Once you accept the default file location, click Unpack and the program will prepare to install itself. It will check to see if you have enough free hard drive space for OOo. If there is not enough space, you need to cancel the installation and delete some old, unused programs or possibly use the Windows defragmentation utility so your hard drive can more efficiently use its space. Either way, once you get through this step, you'll come to the actual Installation Wizard.

Click Next and you'll see an "Accept the license" agreement window—and because this is open source software, its license is much more generous toward software users than typical proprietary software licenses. Read the license and then click to accept it.

After you've accepted the license, the next screen asks for your name and organization. Filling in these blanks is optional, as is your answer to whether you want all users of your computer to have access to OOo or whether you want to keep it for yourself.

Next, select a setup type. You should go with the default Complete installation.

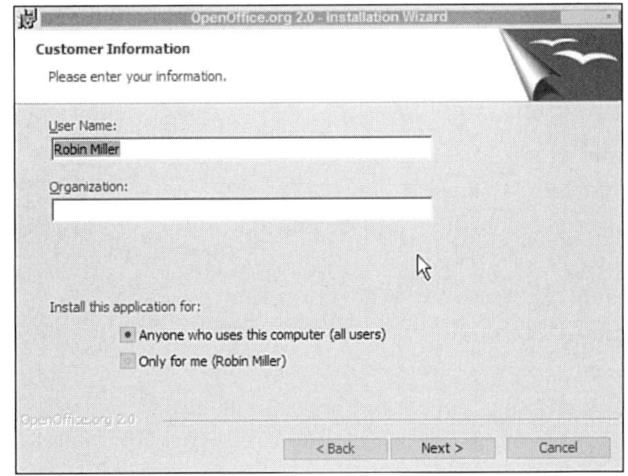

The Customer Information window.

Your next choice is whether you want OOo to automatically open Microsoft Word documents, Microsoft Excel spreadsheets, or Microsoft PowerPoint presentations. Click all three boxes if you're serious about using OOo all the time, and then click Next.

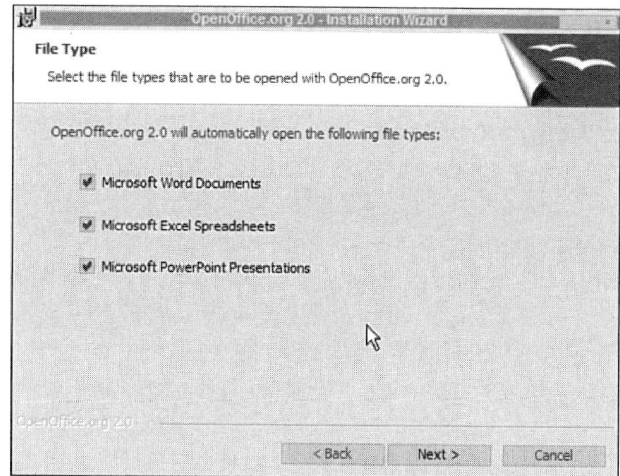

The File Type window.

Now you're ready to actually install the program. Click Install, and away you go. Installation time depends on your computer's speed, but it won't be more than a few minutes. The next window you see says "Installation Wizard Completed," and the only choice you have is to click Finish.

That's it. No reboot is needed. OpenOffice.org is now installed on your computer.

Setting up OpenOffice.org

The first time you run OOo, you're asked to read and agree to the license. You must scroll through the license text window before you click I Agree. The other request the software makes is to register it online. This is optional. You can decline to register, click Next, and move on without any problem. If you do decide to register, you'll find yourself on a Web page with a survey form full of questions that can help guide OOo's future development directions.

You can probably provide better feedback if you register and fill out the survey after you've been using the software for a few weeks than you can when you first try it, so it's probably a good idea to skip registration for the moment.

Seeing Some Action

You make things happen in OOo by clicking the mouse buttons. Throughout this book, "click" means a left-button click, and "right-click" means a right-button click. If you have a scroll wheel, you can use it to scroll.

Some commands are given using keystroke combinations, such as holding down the Ctrl key while you press the F1 key. This combination would be shown as Ctrl-F1. You will also learn, as you go along, that *keyboard shortcuts* exist for almost every "point-and-click" mouse command in OOo. For example, instead of clicking the Spellcheck icon, you can press the F7 key to open the Spellcheck window.

You can get a complete list of keyboard shortcuts by selecting Tools > Customize—and this shows you another bit of jargon you'll see in this book. Tools is a menu—in this case at the top of your OOo window. When you click Tools, a menu drops down, and one of the choices on it is Customize. The command Tools > Customize is shorthand for "First select Tools, and then select the Customize menu option." The videos make this clearer; some actions are easier to *show* than to *tell*.

Another action you might read about is the mouseover. This is what happens when you move the mouse cursor over a word or button and something happens. One example of this is the little text box that appears next to any button (also called an icon) if you move the cursor over it but don't click it. That text box tells you what that button (or icon) does.

Buttoning up—35 Times

Thirty-five buttons appear on almost every OOo screen. Others appear only when you're working with text in Writer, a spreadsheet in Calc, a picture in Draw, or a slide show in Impress.

Lots of buttons!

Here's a complete list of the 35 "basic" buttons and what they do. You don't need to memorize them, but it's nice to have an idea of what they all do—and to have a page you can come back to if you forget what one is for, and the little mouseover text box doesn't tell you enough to jog your memory.

Here are the buttons from left to right, starting with the top row:

New opens a new, blank text document window.

Open opens an existing document. When you click it, you see a dialog box like the one shown here. (It looks different in Linux and NeoOffice for Mac, but it works the same.)

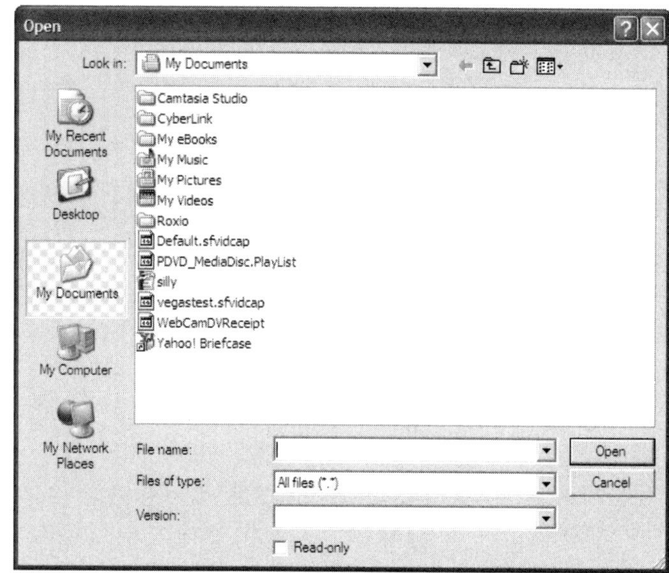

The Open dialog box.

Save saves the document you're working on.

Document as E-mail turns your current document into email and sends it to recipients you select, using whatever email program you choose. (The first time you click this button, you're led through a simple dialog that sets up a link between OOo and your email program.)

Edit File changes a read-only document or database table into one you can edit. This works only when you have a read-only file open in your OOo window.

Export Directly as PDF automatically saves a copy of your document as a PDF file exactly as it appears on-screen.

Print prints your document exactly as it appears on-screen. (The first time you click this button, you go through a simple printer setup and selection dialog.)

Page Preview shows how your document will look as a printed page or as a PDF file before you print it or turn it into a PDF.

Manual Spellcheck checks the spelling of every word in your document or the spelling of a word or group of words you highlight before clicking this button.

AutoSpellcheck is the utility that makes the squiggly lines under misspelled words. It's on by default when you install OOo. Click this button, and this feature turns off. Click again, and it's back on.

Cut removes highlighted text from the current document but saves it to the clipboard so that you can copy it someplace else if you want.

Copy copies your selection to the clipboard but doesn't cut it out of the current document.

Paste inserts whatever you most recently cut or copied where the cursor is now, either in the original document or in another one. If you want to save the selection in a format other than the original one, click the little arrow to the right of the clipboard symbol to see several choices.

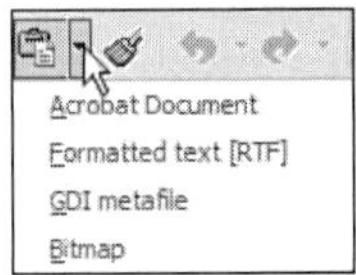

The Paste dialog box.

Format Paintbrush is an interesting button. Suppose you have something like a headline in a particular size and font, and you want to make another group of words into a headline that's the same font size and style. You first highlight the words whose style you want to apply to the second group of words, and then click this button, and then highlight the second group. (This is a lot easier to do than to describe.)

Undo untypes the last word you typed or unselects your last format change. When you click this button, whatever you just did gets undone. Or you can click the little arrow next to the icon and pick which of your recent actions (not necessarily the last one) you want to undo. (You can undo quite a few words or commands if you keep clicking this button.)

Redo is the opposite of Undo. If you unbold a headline, and then you decide you really do want it bold, click this button, and the bold is reapplied. Or retype a word you removed. Again, you can use the little arrow to select a recent action other than your last one.

Hyperlink—Highlight some text and then click this button. You see a dialog box where you can paste in a URL and, voilà! Instant link!

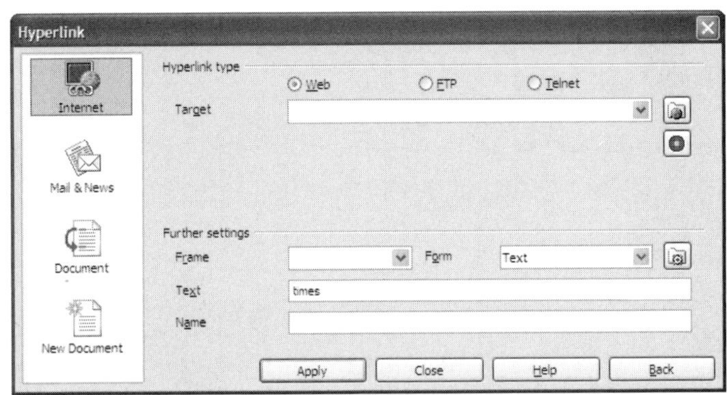

The Hyperlink dialog box.

Table inserts tables in your document, which is a good way to make a multiple-column layout.

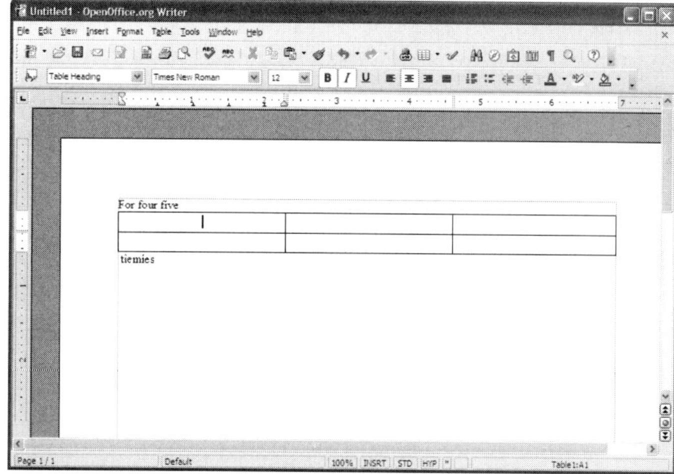

A table.

Show Draw Functions—Did you ever have a sudden desire to add a small heart, a large plus sign, or another simple graphic to a text document? This button helps you do that. It's easier to learn how it works by trying it than by reading an explanation. Experiment a little on your own, and you'll figure it out in just a few minutes.

Find & Replace searches for a word or a string of text and replaces it with something else. This button brings up a pretty self-explanatory dialog box.

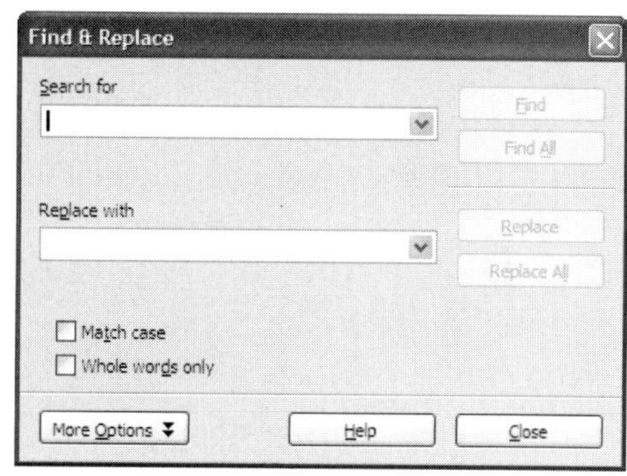

The Find & Replace dialog box.

Navigator—This is an interesting function that lists "classes" of material in your document such as headlines or lists, and gives you a fast way to find them in a large document.

Gallery—Want a slick background? Interesting-looking lines instead of plain ruler-type dividers? Lots of other little pretties to make your document lively, up to and including sound files? You can also create or download additional pieces of clip art (and whatever else you want, up to and including movie clips) and add them to your gallery for easy insertion into your OOo documents.

Data Sources calls up whatever database you've decided to use with OOo. Databases are covered in Chapter 10, "OOo Database 'Front End': Your Free Pass."

Nonprinting Characters—All word-processing programs use "invisible" characters to indicate spaces, line breaks, paragraph ends, and other formatting details. Click this button and you'll see them.

Zoom—Sometimes you need a close-up view of part of your page, especially if you're trying to do something like line up a picture or chart "just so." Use this button and the dialog box it calls up to set your "zoom" level exactly where you want it—and to bring it back to the normal 100% when you're done.

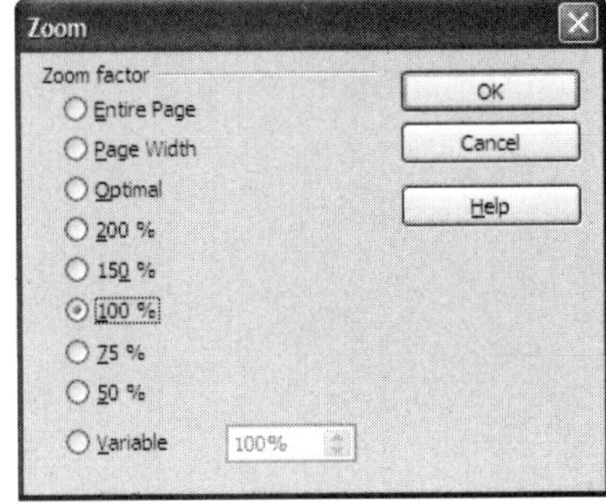

The Zoom dialog box.

Help calls up the complete OOo manual that's built into the program. It's a pretty good manual overall. Use it often, along with this book, and you'll soon become your neighborhood's OOo expert!

Customize Toolbars—Click this arrow or the one below it on the second toolbar line to add or delete buttons and generally change things around on your toolbars to suit yourself. It's probably best to wait until you have a little experience with OOo to see what buttons you use most and which ones you never use before messing with this, but that's up to you.

Styles and Formatting, at the left end of the lower toolbar, opens (or closes) a little window that shows a whole bunch of style and formatting options. This is covered in Chapter 6, "Slick OpenOffice.org Writer Tricks."

The remaining buttons are the group on the right end of the lower toolbar. Here they are from left to right:

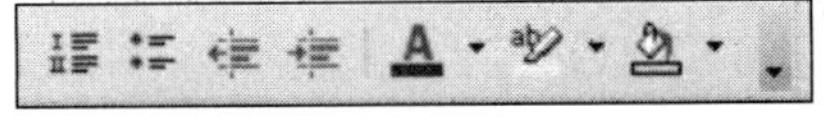

- **Numbering On/Off** puts numbers in front of paragraphs, in order, and indents them slightly.

- **Bullets On/Off** puts bullets (big dots) in front of paragraphs, creating what some people call a "bullet point" style.
- **Decrease Indent** moves the left end of an indented paragraph or line closer to the left margin.
- **Increase Indent** moves a paragraph or line farther from the left margin.
- **Font Color** lets you click the arrow next to the A and change the color of any text you have highlighted (or all the text in your document if you "select all" first).
- **Highlighting** is just like using a highlight marker to make a word or group of words stand out, except that you have 90 color choices instead of just the typical yellow.
- **Background Color** works the same as Highlighting in the version of OOo that was used to write this book. You may want to test this button to make sure its function hasn't changed since then.

Once you have a little experience with OOo, you may want to remove buttons you rarely or never use by selecting Tools > Customize > Toolbars. But for now, it's best to leave them in place.

File Format Confusion

The "native" text file format for earlier versions of OOo and its predecessor, StarOffice, was .sxw, the StarWriter format. OOo 2.0 uses the Open Document Format, developed by the international Organization for the Advancement of Structured Information Standards (OASIS).

The following table shows the standard extensions for documents saved in Open Document Format.

File Type	Extension	MIME Type
Text	.odt	application/vnd.oasis.opendocument.text
Spreadsheet	.ods	application/vnd.oasis.opendocument.spreadsheet
Presentation	.odp	application/vnd.oasis.opendocument.presentation
Drawing	.odg	application/vnd.oasis.opendocument.graphics
Chart	.odc	application/vnd.oasis.opendocument.chart
Formula	.odf	application/vnd.oasis.opendocument.formula
Database	.odb	application/vnd.oasis.opendocument.database
Image	.odi	application/vnd.oasis.opendocument.image
Master document	.odm	application/vnd.oasis.opendocument.text-master

Almost all open source office software released since the summer of 2005 uses this standard file format and its standard extensions (such as .odt and .ods). As of mid-2005, Microsoft had not announced whether it would include the ability to read and write OASIS-approved file formats in its next release of Microsoft Office. A growing number of government agencies around the world are starting to require the use of open, nonproprietary file formats in any software they buy, but Microsoft may stick with its own proprietary formats anyway. For the foreseeable future, it is likely that anyone sharing files with Microsoft Office users will need to save their documents in Microsoft formats. This is a simple task. File > Save As offers many format choices, including both current and older Microsoft-proprietary ones.

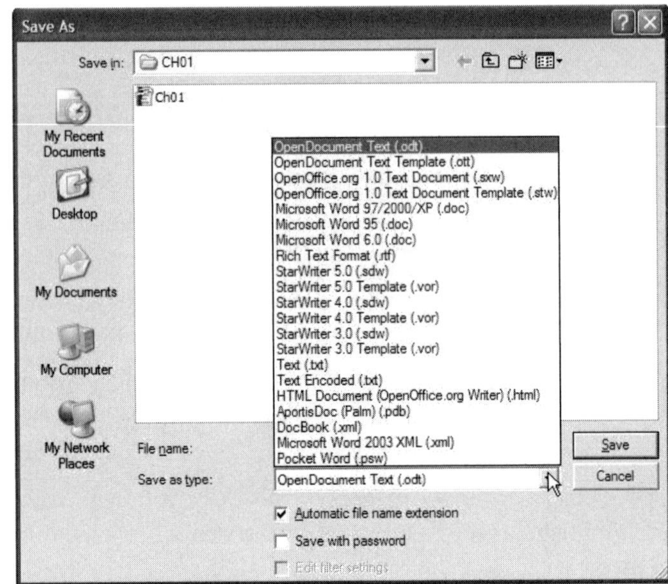

21 OOo file format choices.

Another file choice OOo gives you is to "export" files by using File > Save As > Export. Early versions of OOo 2 (including the one on this book's program CD) offer only two export choices: PDF, which saves your document exactly as it looks when you print it, and XHTML, (currently) the latest format for Web publishing.

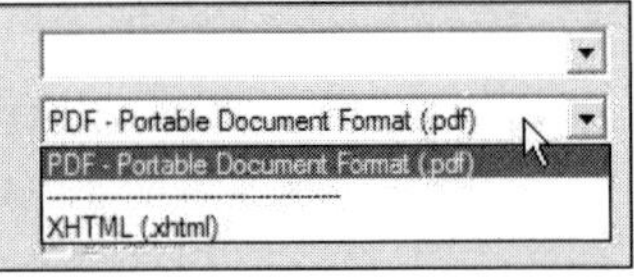

File export choices.

Yes, it would be nice if all the software publishers—including Microsoft—came up with a standard format so that every program could create, open, and edit files created in any other program, but that's as unlikely to happen as all car manufacturers putting the heater controls in the same place. So we deal with the problem as best we can, and OOo—with a total of 23 file-type choices—helps us deal with it better than most office software.

As a general rule, it's best to save your work in the native OOo file format and then resave it in a different format only if you need to share it with friends or coworkers who use OASIS-incompatible software. Note, too, that you need to ask what file formats—or at least what software—your friends use so that you can pick the format that suits them best.

Of course, the best solution is to get as many friends and coworkers as possible to use OOo. Since it's free software, and you now know how to install it and set it up so that you can help them do their own installations, it shouldn't be hard to get at least some of them to switch.

Chapter 2

OOo Writer: Text Documents with Pizazz

When you open OOo Writer, you're faced with the usual blank page.

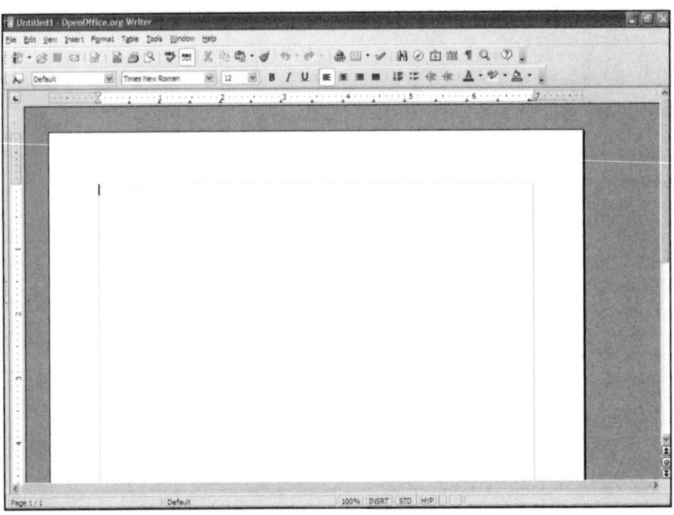

The OOo Writer main screen.

As a fun exercise for this book, I decided to make a little flyer advertising my dog, Terri, as a neighborhood watchdog. Besides barking at strangers—especially strange cats—she loves to watch me work, to the point where she'll stick her nose on my laptop keyboard if I leave it within her reach. "You might as well have her help you with the book," my wife said. "And if she can pick up a little extra cash doing guard duty, that wouldn't hurt, either. She eats *a lot*."

Terri typing.

Entering Text

This is my first try at a flyer for Terri.

Experienced
Guard Dog
Available

Knows the neighbrhood

Florida native; adopted from Manatee County animal services

Keep your property safe from terrorists, squirrels, cats, and other dangers

Email terri@roblimo.com

The first draft of Terri's flyer.

Spellchecking a single word.

It came out pretty bland, didn't it? I'll make it cuter in a minute. But first, I notice that the word "neighbrhood" has a squiggly line under it. This warns of a possible misspelling. Right-click the underlined word, and one or more alternatives appear. I'll choose "neighborhood" as the correct spelling. (If the word that generated the alert is a proper name or for some other reason isn't in the OOo dictionary, you can click Add in the Spellcheck dialog box so that it will be in the dictionary the next time you use it.)

You can also choose the typeface (the font) and size either for the entire document or for a single word or line. Pressing Ctrl-A selects everything in the document. This is the standard "Select All" combination for nearly all popular software. To select a single word or a group of words within the text, highlight the words you want to change by clicking and dragging over the part you want to change.

Jazzing It Up

Next, look at the top-left corner of the OOo window to select the font style and size.

18-point Times New Roman.

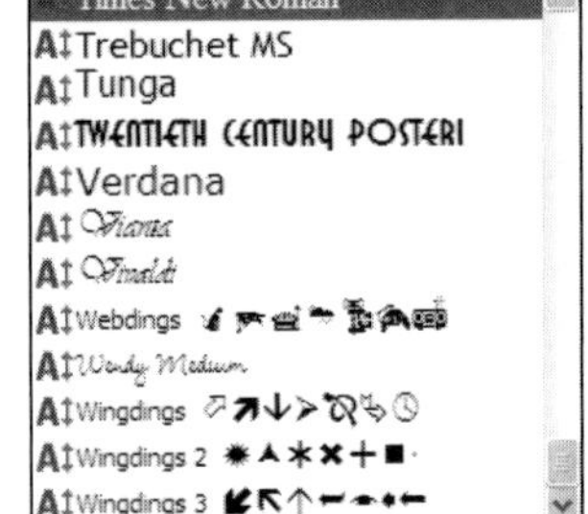

Select from more than 100 fonts.

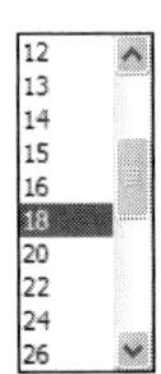

Choose a size between 6 and 96 points.

To the right of where you select font sizes and styles are text-control buttons. The B button makes text bold, the I button makes it italic, and the U button underlines it.

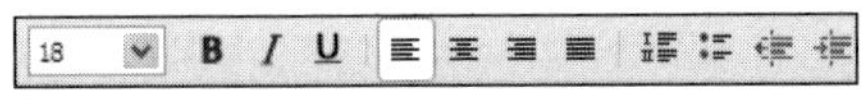

Text format buttons.

The next group of buttons to the right controls layout rather than individual letters or words. The usual (default) style is "flush left, ragged right," which is how I typed in Terri's original flyer text.

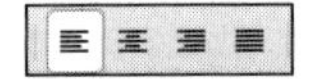

Alignment buttons.

Then I centered the text and made the headline bold and changed it to a larger font size.

Experienced Guard Dog Available

Knows the neighborhood

Florida native; adopted from Manatee County animal services

Keep your property safe from terrorists, squirrels, cats, and other dangers

Email terri@roblimo.com

Centered text with a larger headline.

Here's justified text from another chapter in this book. The spaces between words are automatically adjusted to make all the lines exactly the same length.

> Just because Calc is extremely functional doesn't mean that it has to be boring. We can customize our spreadsheets and make them easy on the eye by selecting any of the font types and sizes we already learned about while using OOo Writer. We can also use all the same text alterations (including bold, italics, underline) and alignments (such as left, right, center, and justified). We can also increase or decrease decimal places, add borders and cell backgrounds, and change font colors—all with just a few clicks of the mouse!

Justified text.

The text in this book is justified, as is the text in most newspapers and magazines. Because early Web browsers didn't do a good job of handling the proportional spacing that justification requires, most material published on the Internet is "ragged right" instead of justified. You may want to consider where and how something you write will be published before you select a text-alignment style (although your choice can be changed with a few clicks after you finish writing).

Adding an Image

Our little flyer looks blah even with centered text and a bold headline. It needs a picture of Terri on guard, looking fierce, to make it an effective sales tool.

To add a picture, select Insert > Picture > From File.

Next, select an image by going to the "Pictures, assorted" gallery. (You may use a different title for the folder where you keep *your* pictures, but you get the idea.)

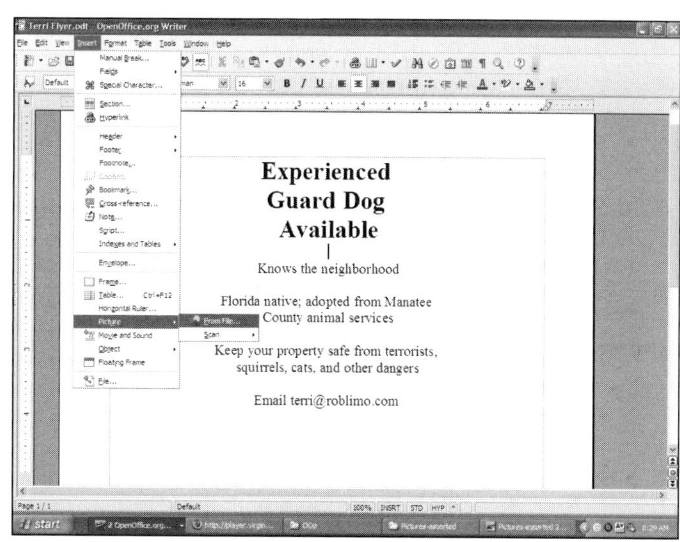

The Insert menu.

Here's a nice shot of Terri alertly keeping a cat from coming over the fence.

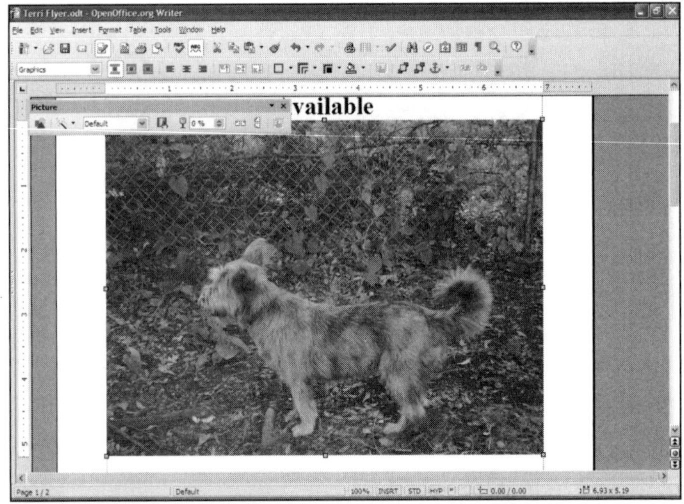

Terri on guard.

Whoa! That picture's way too big. But when I right-click the image, I see the frame alteration menu.

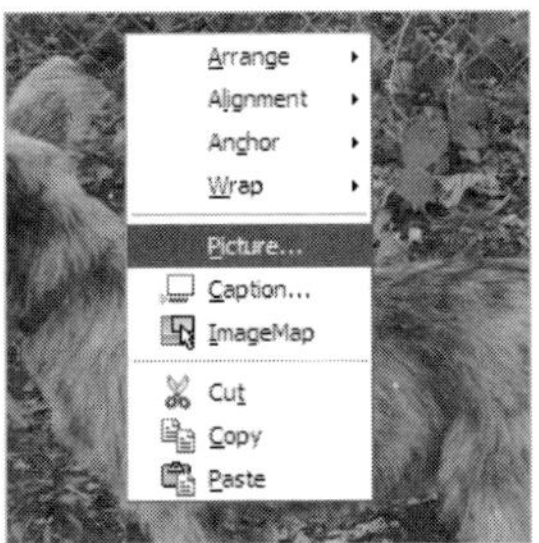

The frame alteration menu.

When I select Picture, I get the Picture dialog box.

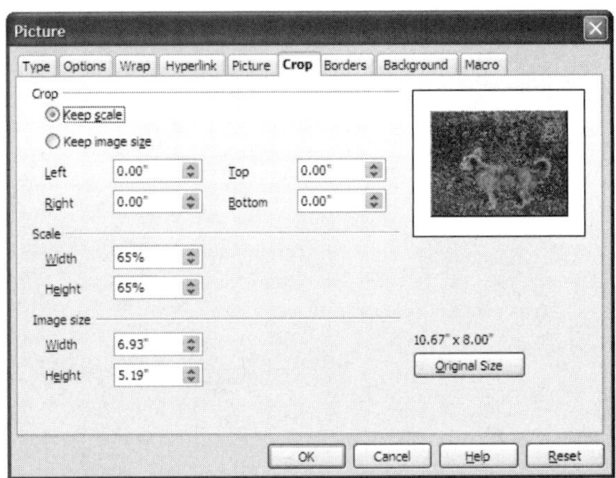

The Picture dialog box.

We can do a lot with this picture. We selected the Crop tab, which also lets us scale the picture to fit our flyer. We did our scaling by setting both the width and height to 30%. This is a crude, "quick-and-dirty" way to alter a picture to fit into a document. We'll cover more graphics manipulations in Chapter 4, "OOo Draw: Documents with Imagination," and we'll get even more sophisticated in Chapter 7, "Draw: Not Your Father's Drawing Board," but this was all we needed for Terri's simple flyer, which ends up looking like this, ready to save and print.

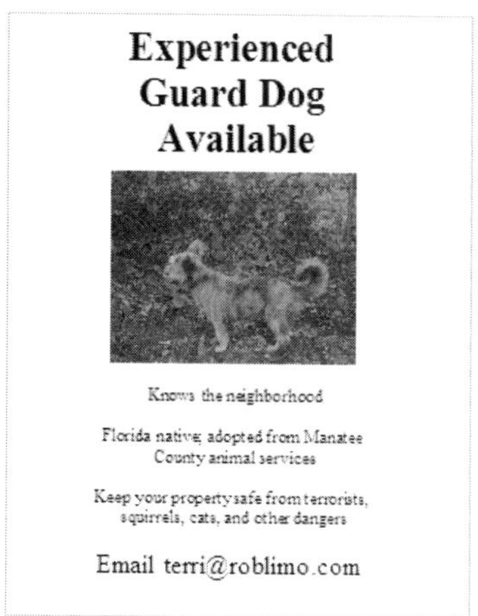

Terri's finalized flyer.

Saving the Document

When you click the Save icon, you see the Save As dialog box.

You can choose where you want to save the document on your hard drive—that is, in which folder. You can either click a folder you already have or click the folder icon at the top of the window (the folder with a star in its corner) to create a new folder.

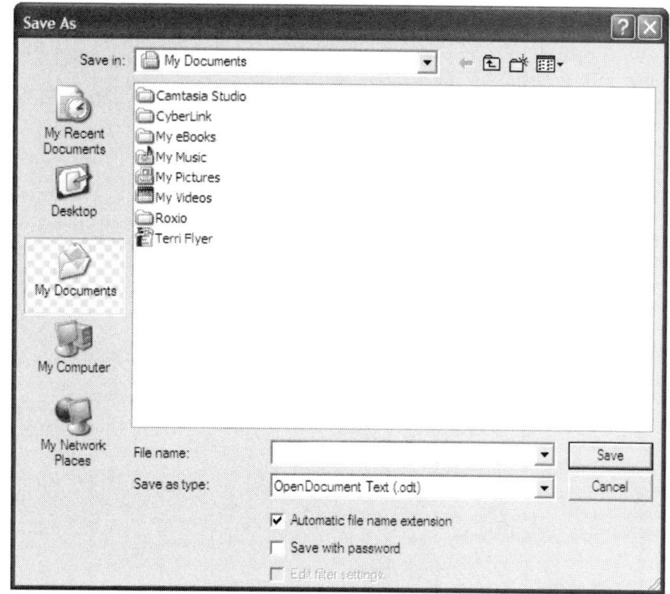

The Save As dialog box.

Next, you need to select a file format. If you want to save this document on your computer and either print it or come back and edit it later, the default Open Document Text (.odt) is your best choice. If you'll publish it on the World Wide Web, you'll want to choose HTML.

If you'll share this document as an electronic file with someone who has only Microsoft Office on his or her computer, you'll want to choose the .doc selection that matches the version of Office the person has, as mentioned in Chapter 1, "First Things First."

Note: Not all versions of Microsoft Office can read or edit documents created in all other versions, but OpenOffice.org can read, edit, and save documents in just about all of them. You can often use OOo as a "translator" program to bridge the gap between different Microsoft Office versions!

Printing It for All to See

Tip: Use the File > Page Preview function before printing, especially on documents with multiple pages, such as this mockup for a neighborhood newsletter. A final glance to make sure that everything displays correctly can often save you a lot of wasted paper.

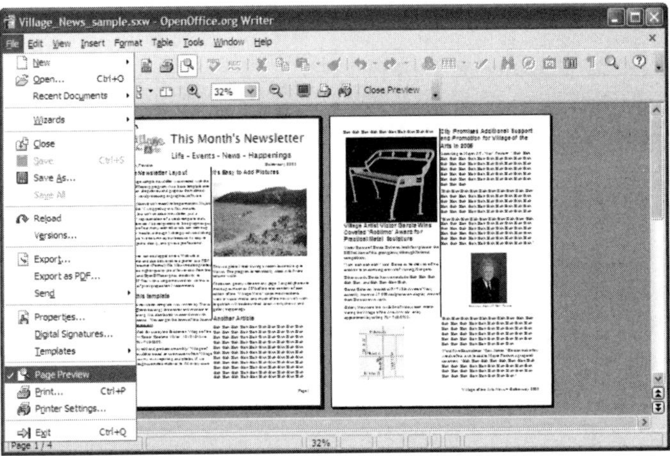

Page Preview.

After that, printing is merely a matter of selecting File > Print or clicking the Printer button.

That's it.

You have now created, altered, saved, and printed a document using OpenOffice.org. Because OOo is an *integrated* program suite, you now know how to save and print any kind of file you create or edit with OOo, not just text documents.

And if you get stuck anywhere at any time while you're using OOo, you have the handy ? help button near the top right of the screen. Click that and you'll see the entire, detailed, built-in OOo manual. It doesn't have every answer to every question, but it has *most* answers to *most* questions.

Beyond that, there's the www.support.openoffice.org Web site. It is *the* place to get the most up-to-date help with OOo. It includes many constantly-updated FAQs, tutorials, and other resources—and a link to the OpenOffice Forum, where you can ask other users for help with any problems you couldn't solve by searching the rest of the material on the site.

Chapter 3

OOo Impress: Slide Shows That Will Impress Almost Anyone

By Rob Reilly

OOo Impress is a replacement for Microsoft's PowerPoint. Even if you're not an experienced presenter, Impress will help you create professional-looking slide shows.

Creating a Slide Show from OOo's Built-in Templates

OOo has a couple of canned presentations you can use. Bring up the templates, add your text, and you have a quick presentation, all ready to go.

Start OOo and select File > New. Choose Templates and Documents from the bottom of the list. Select the "Introducing a New Product" template. The basic slide show outline appears in the main slide-editing window, ready for your customization.

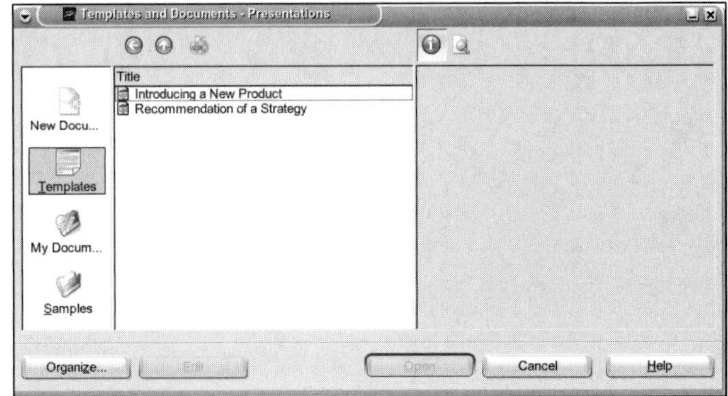

Making a slide from a template.

Highlight the "title" in the middle of the screen, and change it to your own topic. You can select another slide to edit from the slide thumbnails to the left of the main slide-editing window. Each slide has hints that you can replace with your corresponding information.

Introducing a new product.

As you fill in the information for your product, it's a good idea to periodically save your slide show by selecting File > Save As. Give your slide show a name, and make note of the directory so that you can find it again. OpenOffice.org fills in the default file extension of .odp.

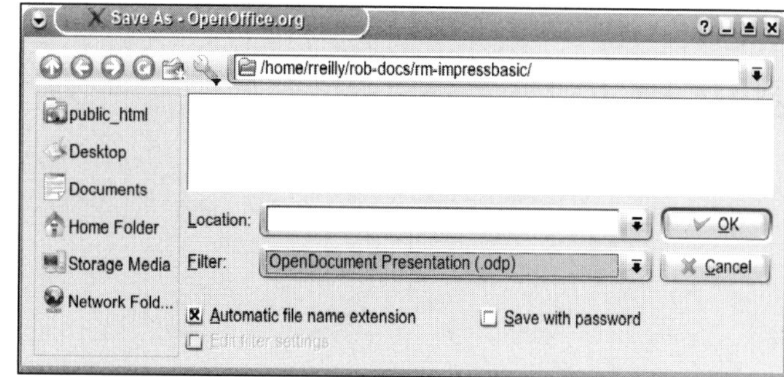

Saving your slide show.

Making Your Own Slide Patterns from Scratch

Perhaps you don't want to use a canned presentation but want to jump in and start building slides from scratch. To do this, select File > New > Presentation. Enable the Empty Presentation radio button. Then click Create to go directly to the main slide-editing screen.

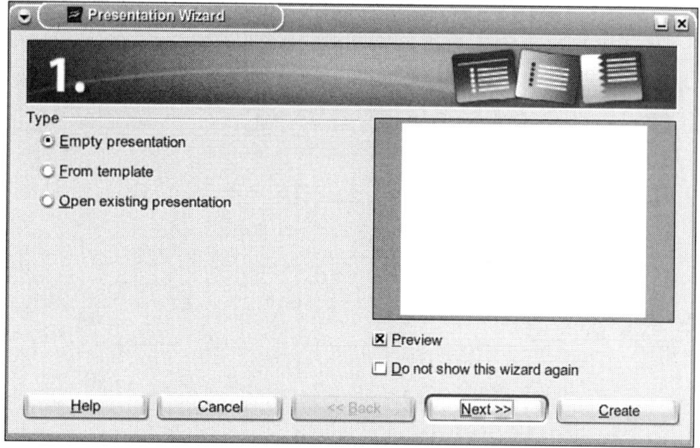

An empty presentation.

The main slide screen has all the controls and menus you could ever wish for in a presentation package.

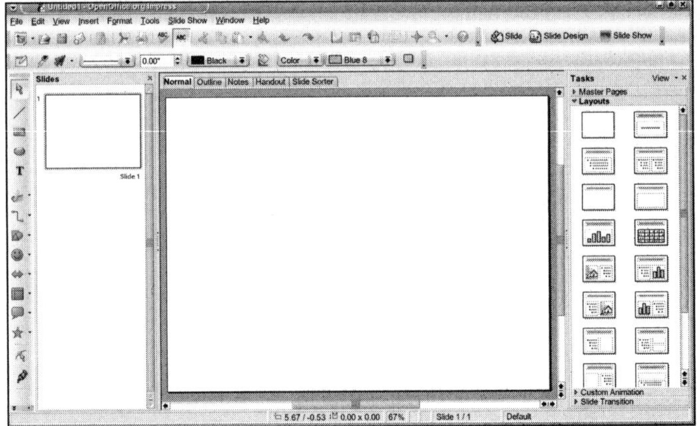

Controls to the left, controls to the right.

Along the left side are the drawing tools you use to add boxes, lines, text, and other objects to your slides. At the top are the menus and toolbars. You can turn the toolbars on and off by selecting View > Toolbar. Active toolbars (the ones that are displayed) have a checkmark next to them.

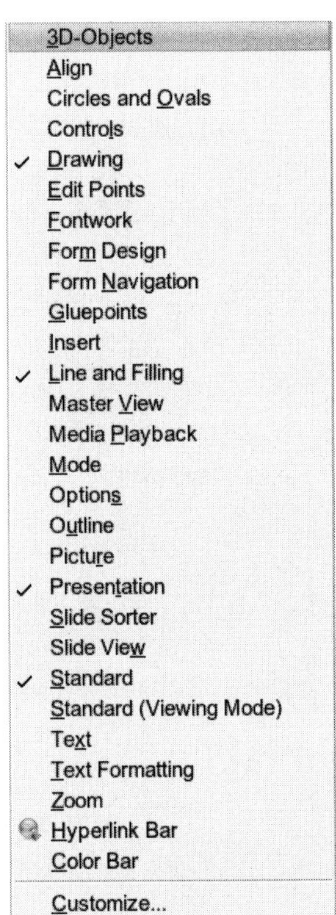

Active toolbars have check-marks next to them.

Click the checked items to turn them off, and click the unchecked ones to turn them on.

The right side of the screen houses the Layouts window, where you can select the type of layout your slide will have. When you click one of the layouts, it appears in the slide-editing window in the middle of the screen.

The bar at the bottom of the screen gives slide status information, such as the cursor coordinates, object size, slide number, and so on.

Basic operations such as opening and saving files are located on the File menu. To view your masterpiece, click the Slide Show button in the upper-right corner of the screen. You can press Ctrl-Z or select Edit > Undo to back up through commands if you make a mistake.

Using the OOo Impress Auto Layout Feature

The auto layout feature is great for making a simple slide show in a hurry.

Start by selecting File > New > Presentation. Enable the Empty Presentation radio button, but this time click Next instead of Create, as you did when you were making a slide show from scratch.

The next screen lets you pick from a couple of available backgrounds. You can add your own backgrounds as you get more comfortable with OOo. You'll see how to do that, as well as use a master slide, in Chapter 8, "OOo Impress: Smooth, Sophisticated Slide Shows." For now, just click Next.

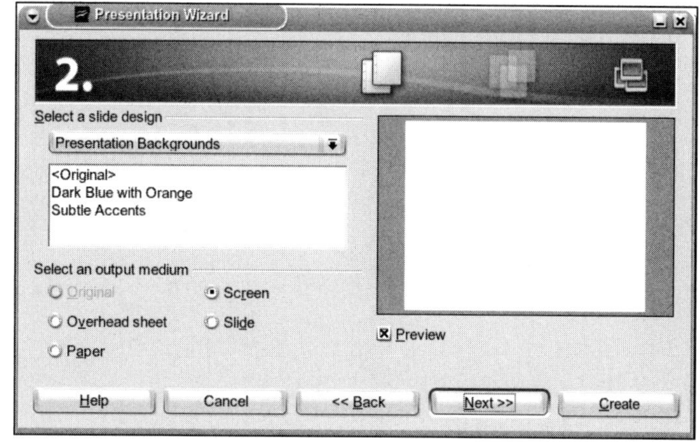

Picking a background.

The slide transition screen is used to smoothly move from one slide to another during your presentation. You can select various fades, slide-ins, cover-ups, and dissolves. You can also change the effect's speed, which is affected by the speed of your hardware.

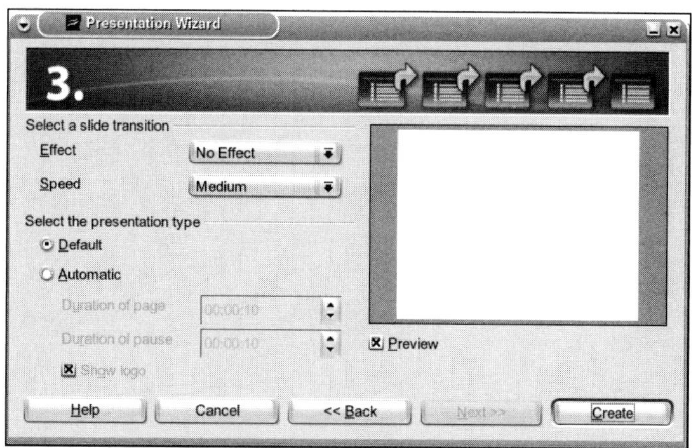

Selecting slide transitions.

Complete the setup of the basic blank slide show by clicking the Create button. The main slide-editing window appears, ready for your customization. You can choose any of the slide layout patterns shown on the right side of the screen. When you click one, the layout is displayed in the slide-editing window, as well as in a thumbnail viewer on the left side.

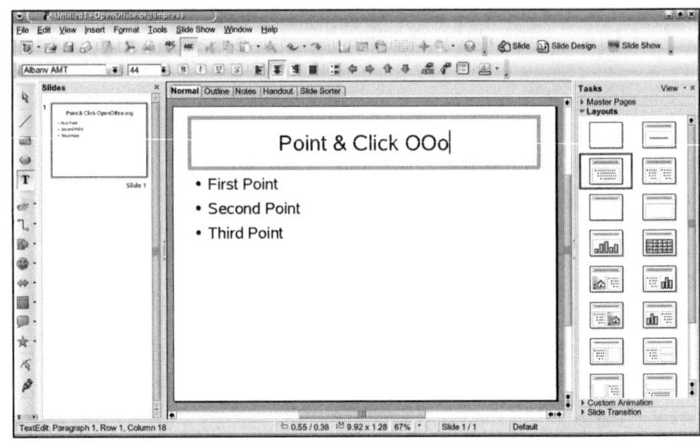

Adding text to a slide template.

Each layout has simple instructions you can click and replace with your own text. Notice that the thumbnail slide gets updated as you add information in the main working screen.

Adding another slide is as easy as selecting Insert > Slide. A new slide appears in the main slide-editing screen and in the thumbnail viewer on the left. The same layout as the previous slide is used by default, but you can change it if you like.

You can even select the blank layout and add your own bullet points or text. The Text tool appears as a T icon on the left side of the screen. Click the T icon and then place the cursor anywhere on the main working screen. Click the screen and start typing. If you want to create more than one line of text, press Enter to go to the next line. When you're done entering text, click the arrow icon, above the T. This puts you back into selection mode, where you can select and manipulate objects that are already on-screen.

Selecting the Text tool.

Once you are back in selection mode, you can right-click an object and do things such as resize it, move it, or even delete the object altogether.

Click the text you just entered; the outline is marked by a series of small green boxes. Move between any of the boxes, and the cursor changes to a thick crossed arrow symbol. You can click to grab the text (or any other object) and move it to a new position in the main working screen. If you mouse over one of the boxes, the cursor changes to a double-ended arrow with a bar, letting you click that handle and make the box bigger or smaller. If you make a text box too narrow, the text wraps automatically to fit. You have to highlight the text to change the font or size.

Before we get into more advanced operations, such as adding graphics to a slide, you should know how to view your handiwork as an actual slide show. Running your presentation is easy. Click the Slide Show icon in the upper-right corner of the screen. Your current slide appears full-sized on the screen.

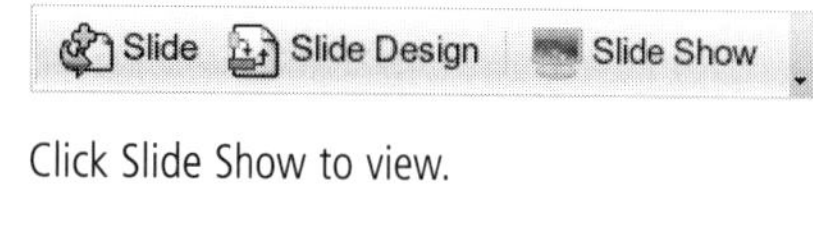

Click Slide Show to view.

You can switch to slide show mode and page through your presentation using the mouse or the Page Up/Page Down keys. The left mouse button moves you forward through your slides, and the right mouse button does the opposite. Press the Esc key at any time to get back to the drawing view.

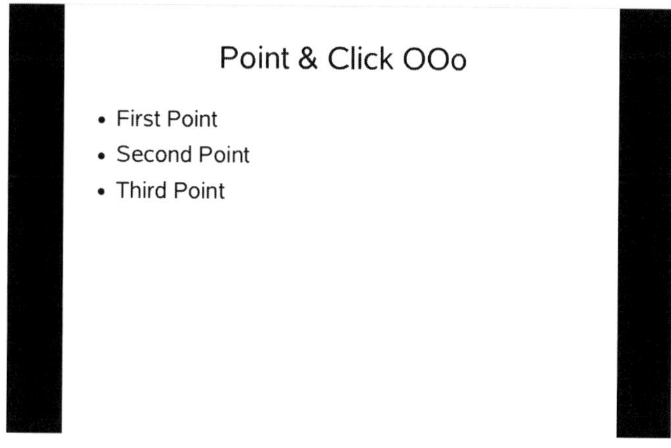

The slide, full-sized but still crude.

Don't forget to occasionally save your slide show while you work.

Adding Graphics to Your Slides

Slide shows are pretty boring with just bullet points and text. It's nice to add a little spice in the form of a picture or two.

Select Insert > Picture > From File. The standard file manager screen appears. That's where you choose the picture you want to use. You can go to a different directory using the arrow keys or common directory names on the left side of the screen. You can also display specific file types (such as .gif and .jpg) by using the Filter dropdown list at the bottom of the window.

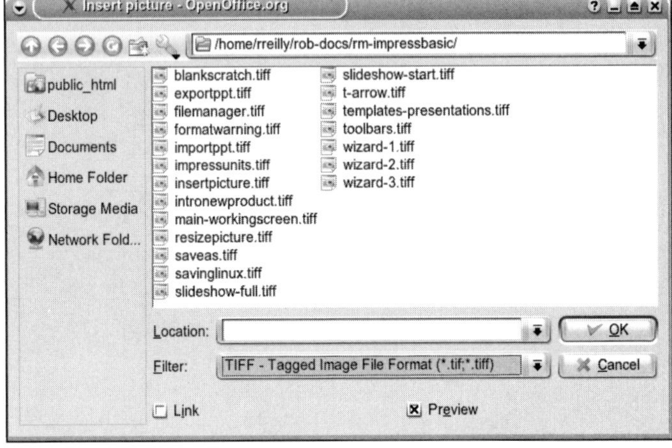

The Insert Picture window.

Choose an image from a directory on your hard disk, and it is inserted full-size into your slide. It also appears, smaller, in the thumbnail viewer at the left.

An inserted image.

To resize the picture, click the picture, hold one of the little green, square handles on the edge of your picture, and slide it to the desired size. Notice that the object dimensions (in the status bar at the bottom) change when you release the mouse button. (The videos show this better.)

Another way to get the same result is to roll the cursor onto the picture and then click and hold to move the picture around on the slide. Combine the resize and move functions to get the picture right where you want it.

Your picture, now smaller.

Advanced graphics functions such as transparencies, alignment tools, and animations are covered in more depth in Chapters 7, "Draw: Not Your Father's Drawing Board," and 8.

Saving Your Slide Show

You can make just a few slides or hundreds. Saving them is exactly the same as saving a text document, except that the default file extension is .odp (Open Document Presentation) instead of the default .odt (Open Document Text) that you saw when you saved a text document in the default OOo format.

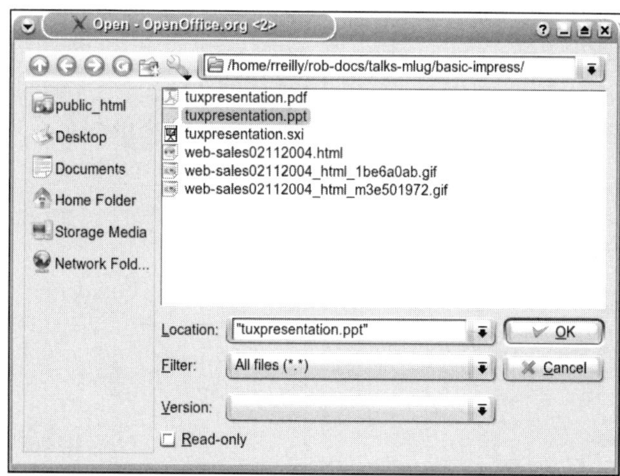

Saving your slide show.

Importing and Editing PowerPoint Slide Shows

PowerPoint native slide shows look the same in Impress as in any other presentation file. Isn't this an interesting opening slide for a PowerPoint presentation?

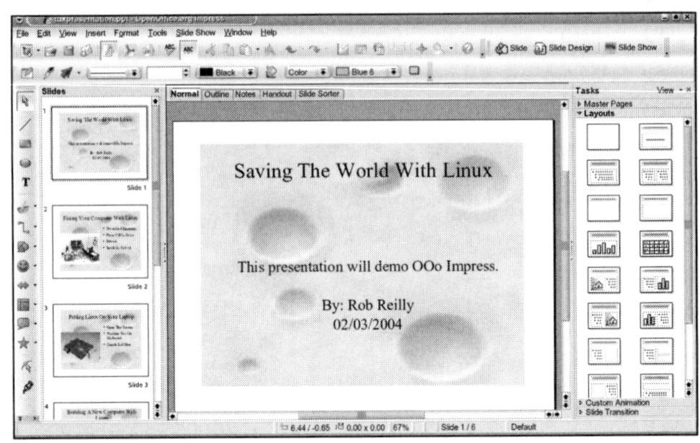

Using a PowerPoint slide to promote Linux.

All the normal functions available in OOo Impress can operate on PowerPoint files, too.

One limitation you might run into with editing PowerPoint files on a Linux machine is with TrueType fonts. TrueType fonts have traditionally been available on Windows machines by default, but TrueType fonts on Linux machines have been problematic because of licensing issues. Many Linux distributions include TrueType fonts on the installation CDs and DVDs, but some versions do not. If your PowerPoint slide show uses an unavailable font, it uses a default that may be unsuitable for your presentation. In that case, you may have to go through the presentation and replace the missing font with a more suitable one.

Exporting Slide Shows to PowerPoint Format

Select File > Save As, and save your slide show as a PowerPoint (.ppt) file.

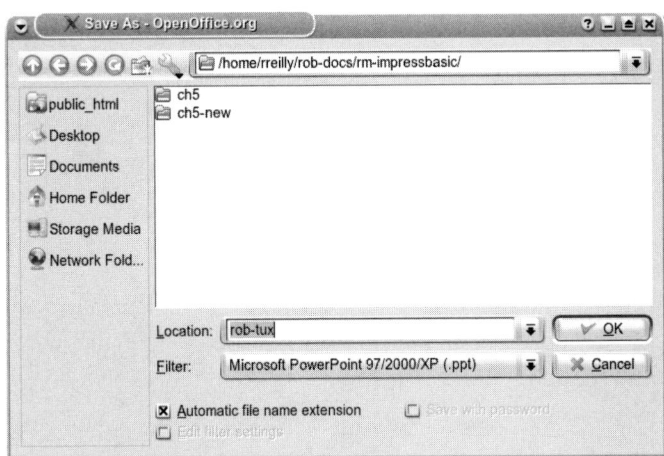

Saving a .ppt file.

OOo usually warns you that you may lose formatting if you save in something other than the native OOo .odp file. You can turn off this warning permanently by checking the "Do not show this warning again" box at the bottom. It might be a good idea to save a few of your OOo presentations in PowerPoint format and then view them with PowerPoint to see if you notice any incompatibilities.

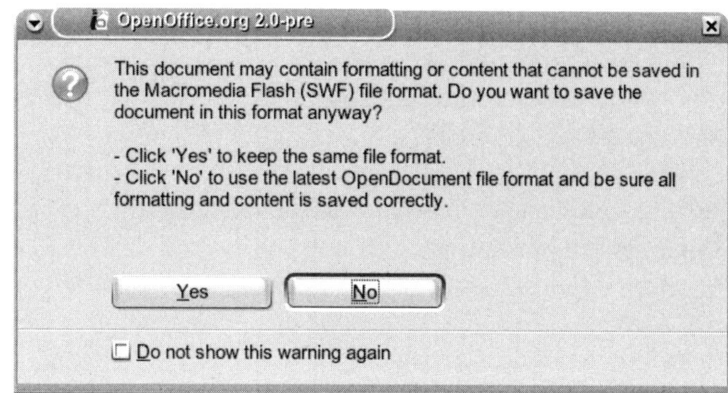

The file export warning.

Complete the file save operation by clicking OK.

Exporting Slide Shows as Flash for Web Viewing

OOo can save your slide show as a Macromedia Flash file so that a colleague or Web surfer can view the entire presentation from any Flash-equipped Web browser. Here's how to do it.

After you've finished creating your presentation, select File > Export. Select Macromedia Flash (SWF) from the Filter dropdown menu. Give your Flash file a name, and click the OK button to complete the operation.

You'll see the "loss of formatting" warning screen again. I usually ignore the warning and just double-check the slide show manually using a Flash-equipped browser such as Firefox.

When viewing the Flash file, the user can advance to the next screen by clicking and can go back to the previous slide by right-clicking.

An interesting—and increasingly popular—use for Flash-delivered slide shows on the Web is for colleagues or clients to view your presentation through their browsers while you discuss it with them in a conference call.

Overcoming (Most) Format Incompatibilities

You might notice several incompatibilities when importing and exporting between Impress and PowerPoint.

As mentioned earlier, TrueType fonts should be correctly installed on your machine, whether Windows or Linux, to head off any unexpected default fonts. This problem has largely disappeared with current distributions of Linux. OOo on a Windows box takes advantage of the TrueType font libraries that are already installed.

Margins may occasionally appear out of whack when you convert from PowerPoint to OOo. You may have to adjust the margins manually to clear things up.

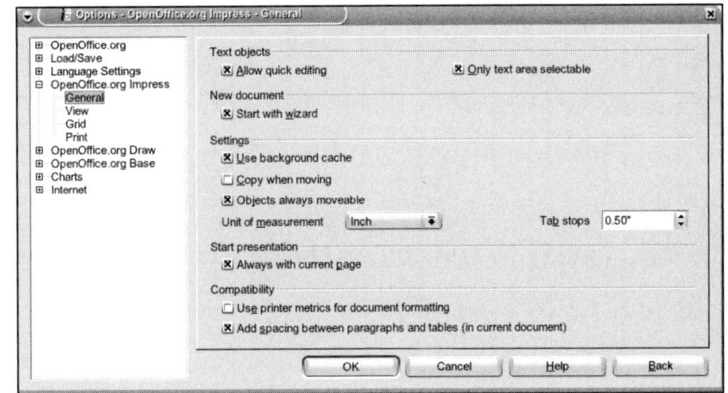

Selecting a unit of measurement for your slide show.

The unit of measure used in your presentation is one of the biggest causes of incompatibility when you work with imported and exported files. You can set the unit type by selecting Tools > Options > OpenOffice.org Impress. This setting appears on the General Options screen. Common measurements such as centimeters and inches can be selected from the Unit of Measurement dropdown menu. You must set your measurement unit type to match the one used to save the original PowerPoint presentation. If you don't know what it is, a few seconds of experimentation will show you the right one.

The Real Secret to Good-Looking Presentations

The best way to learn how to create professional-looking slide shows is to practice. Experiment. Use your imagination. Keep a little notebook (or text file) of techniques that work well for you, along with photos and other illustrations that will make your slides look more interesting than screen after screen filled with text.

Chapter 4

OOo Draw: Documents with Imagination

OOo Draw is a simple program, not really suited for professional graphics people. But it's good enough for at least 90% of the photo manipulation and drawing most of us do most of the time when we're preparing text documents, slide presentations, and other basic "office" jobs that graphics can enliven.

This chapter covers some of the simplest and most popular OOo Draw features. Chapter 7, "Draw: Not Your Father's Drawing Board," covers advanced Draw techniques and tricks, including some you wouldn't expect to find in an Office program—especially one that's free.

Terri the Guard Dog is shown here taking a break from work. It's a passable picture, but for publication you would need to make it smaller and cut out most of the background. You open the photo the same way you open any other file with OOo—by selecting File > Open and highlighting the desired file.

Terri on the futon.

You'll see that the photo opens as part of a slide or text page, not on its own.

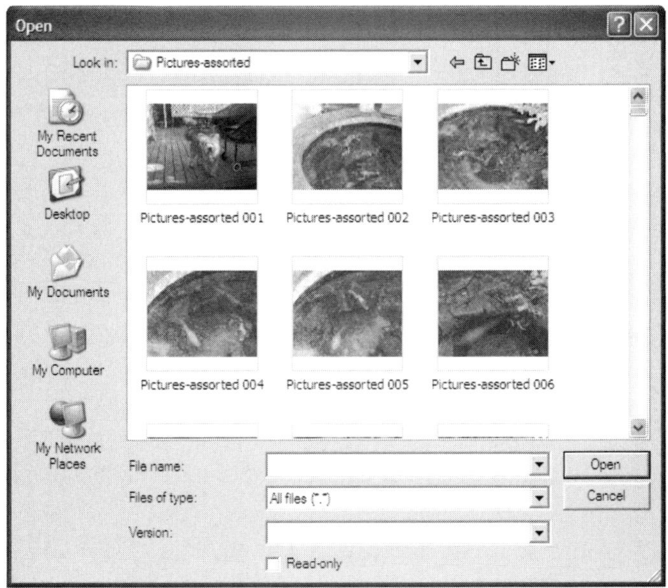

The Open dialog box.

OOo displays pictures as part of something else, not all by themselves. To isolate the image so that you can work with it, click it so that it grows little "handles" at its edges.

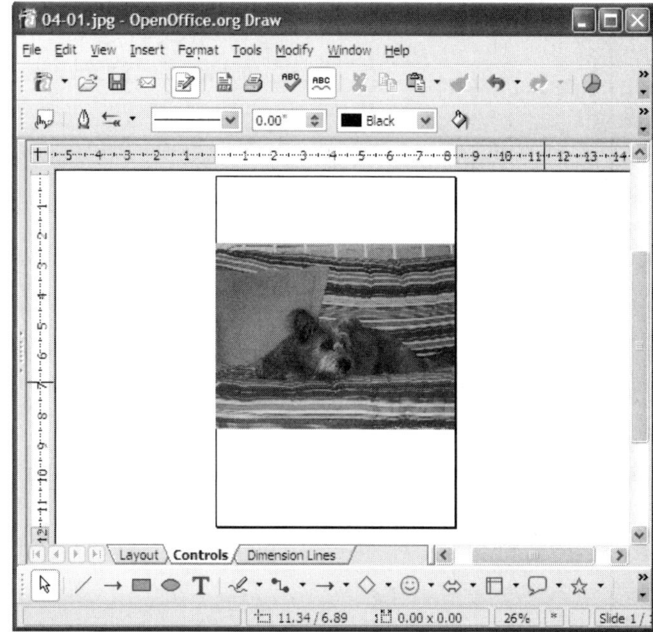

The picture opened.

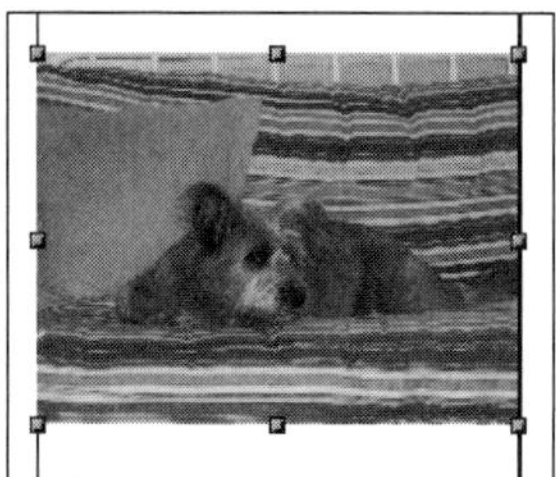

The picture with handles.

As long as you see those handles, you are working only on the material inside them. In this case, you will make the photo smaller so that it takes up less space on the printed page.

There are several ways you can do this. The most obvious is to put the cursor on one of the corner handles and move it toward the opposite corner while holding down the left mouse button. The only problem with this method is that it can distort the photo if you aren't careful.

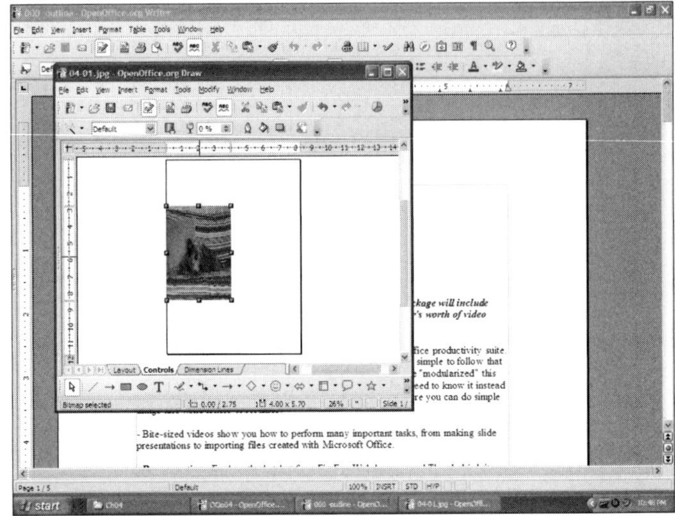

A squashed Terri.

This can be a fun "effect" if you do it on purpose, but this time you'll press Ctrl-Z or select Edit > Undo to take you back to where you were. Now you'll resize the photo correctly by right-clicking it and choosing Position and Size (the third menu choice from the top). You see the Position and Size dialog box.

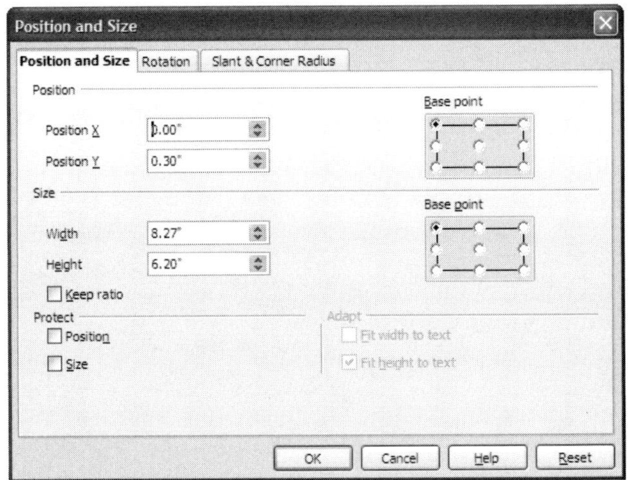

The Position and Size dialog box.

We can do a number of things in this dialog box, but first you'll make the photo smaller. You can decide what size you want, in inches or pixels. If you check the Keep Ratio box, the program automatically keeps the photo the right shape if you change either its horizontal or vertical dimension.

You can also flip or rotate photos with OOo Draw. There are several ways to do this. One is to use the Rotation tab in the Position and Size dialog box. Either click one of the preset sideways, upside-down, or 45-degree angle choices, or use the little window to the left of the "big" choices there to select your rotation angle in 15-degree increments. If that isn't enough choices, you can go to the menu at the top of the OOo window, choose Modify > Rotate, and use the corner handles on the picture to turn it. You can try various angles until you find one you like.

Terri tilted.

You may think this looks silly. No problem; you can undo the change by pressing Ctrl-Z or by selecting Edit > Undo. You can place your dog at any angle you want.

Making (or Altering) Pictures with OOo Draw Drawing Tools

To create your own art, start with a blank drawing slate, which you get by selecting File > New. Then choose Drawing from the "What kind of new work?" choices that show up to the right of the main menu when the cursor is over (or to the right of) the word New.

This gives you tools along the bottom of the work area in addition to the ones along the top that you got when you opened a Text Document window.

The Draw toolbar.

You see a number of icons, starting with a pointer at the left. Each drawing icon has a little down-pointing arrow next to it. Click the arrow next to the Callout icon—the one that looks like a cartoon speech balloon. You see a menu that gives you several different "cartoon balloon" styles.

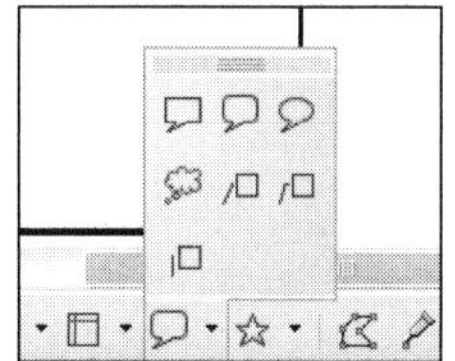

The callout menu.

Select a callout—or any other drawing shape tool—by clicking it. Then choose a point in your picture where you want to insert it, and click and hold down the left mouse button while you move the mouse diagonally until the shape is the size you want it.

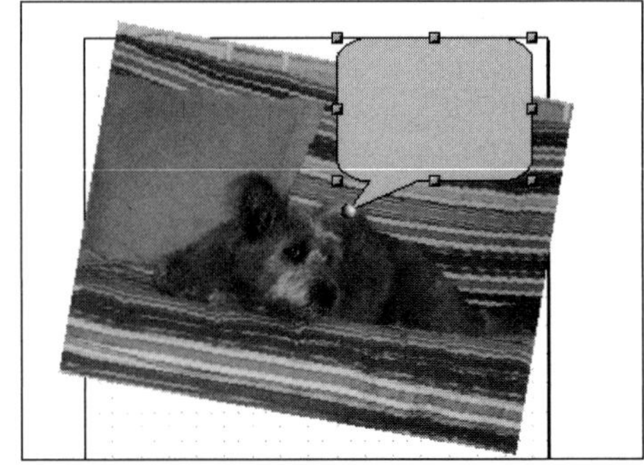

The callout balloon.

Don't worry if you don't get the size or alignment exactly right or if you want to rotate your newly-added bit of art in one direction or the other. You can use the same Size and Position and Rotation tools you used on Terri's picture. You can move it around by clicking it and moving the little cross that this action turns the cursor into. You can even change the shape of your shape with the little handles on the edge of the graphics square that contains it.

Note: This set of actions is much easier to learn from a video than from words and pictures. The "Manipulating Images" video will make all this clear.

The rest of the shape icons work exactly the same as the callout one. You can move the mouse over each one and read the little text box that pops up. It will take you only a few seconds to try each one and see what it does. Mistakes are fine. If you don't save your work after you practice, no one will know you made them. So please experiment freely. All pixels (the little dots that make up pictures on the screen) created with OOo Draw are fully recyclable; no precious resources or landfill space are used by your self-training sessions.

Adding Text to Drawings

The Text Draw icon needs additional explanation but is useful enough for nongraphics people to make its way into this chapter instead of being reserved for Chapter 7, which goes into advanced Draw tricks. To use this icon, click it, and then drag the little cross that the cursor becomes to where you want to type your text. Type it in, alter the font and text size exactly the same way as when you're creating a text document, and you have text.

The Text button.

This example changes the callout size and shape to fit around the text.

Who can resist such a huggable doggie?

Note: This is another set of actions that the videos will help make clear.

Saving Image Files

This is where things get a little tricky. Remember when I said that OOo treats images as part of a page or presentation? That's how it likes to save them, too. If you select File > Save As while you're working with an image file, you'll end up with a file type that works only with OpenOffice.org, not an image file that can be opened by all kinds of picture-editing software. So, being a bit tricky yourself, if you plan to use an image file in anything other than an OOo document or presentation, you export it to the file format you want. Instead of choosing Save As when you want to save your graphics file all by itself instead of as part of something else, select File > Export. This brings up the Export dialog box and a *long* list of graphics file format choices.

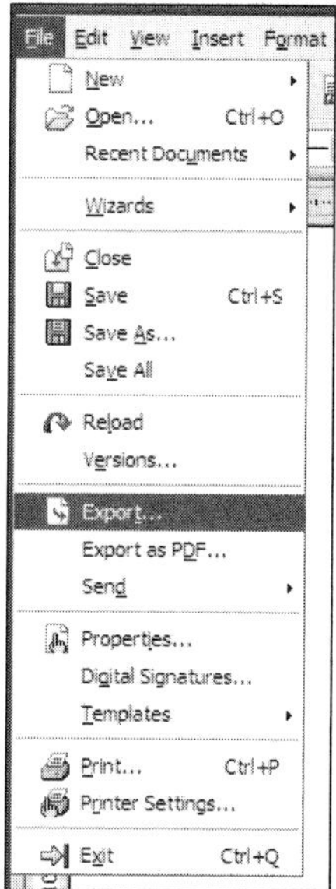

Choosing File > Export.

If you're an experienced artist or Web designer, you'll see most of your favorites here—even Macromedia Flash. If you don't know one graphics file format from another, the safest choice is JPEG. This is the format used by most digital cameras. Virtually all known graphics programs and Web browsers, for all operating systems, can read JPEG pictures.

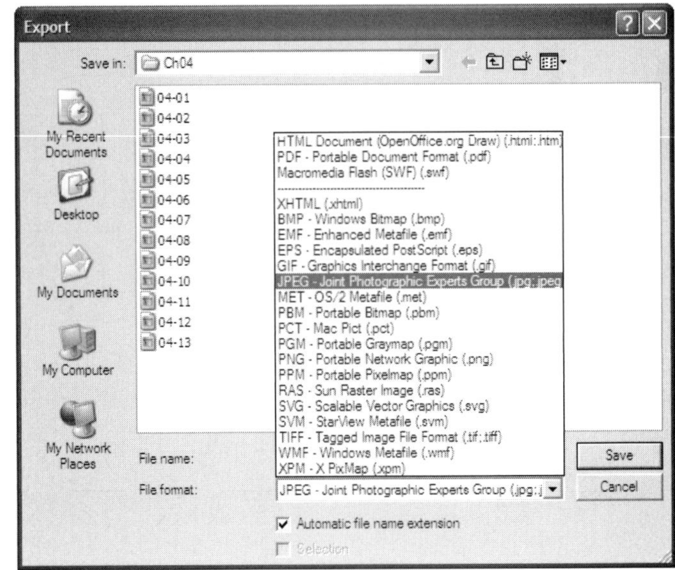

Exporting a graphic.

You need to select only two more options if you decide to save your image in JPEG format: Quality and Color Resolution. The default quality is 75%, which is good enough for Web publishing, but unless you're sure this is all you'll do with this graphic, it's probably better to choose 100%. You can always *lower* the quality later, but after you've lowered the quality, you cannot *raise* it.

In the Grayscale versus True Colors choice, it's better to choose True Colors for much the same reason: You can always turn a color image into a black-and-white one later, but you can't add color into an image you've saved in black and white.

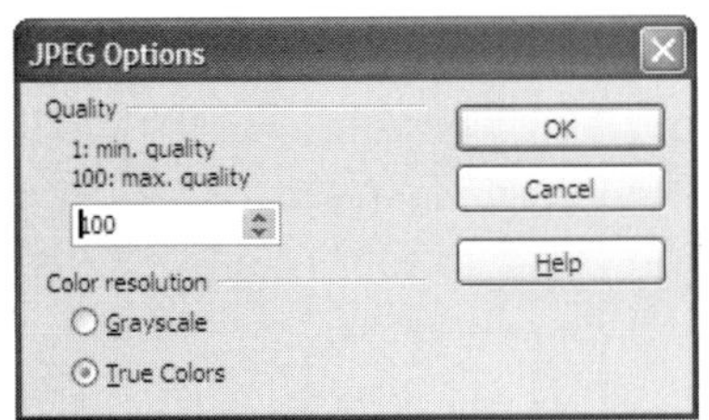

The JPEG options dialog box.

All you need to do now is pick a name for your file, decide which directory and folder are the best place to put it, and click Save. Your picture is now ready to liven up your next text document, slide presentation, spreadsheet, or Web page.

Chapter 5

OOo Calc: Spreadsheets and More

By Lalaine "Lizza" Capucion

With OOo Calc you can create and edit basic spreadsheets. You can also produce colorful, good-looking graphs and charts based on your spreadsheets. You can insert Calc-created graphics in text documents and slide shows or use them on their own. Calc can open and edit spreadsheets created with Microsoft Excel. After you're done creating or editing a spreadsheet with Calc, you can save it in a variety of file formats, including the one used by Excel.

Starting Simply

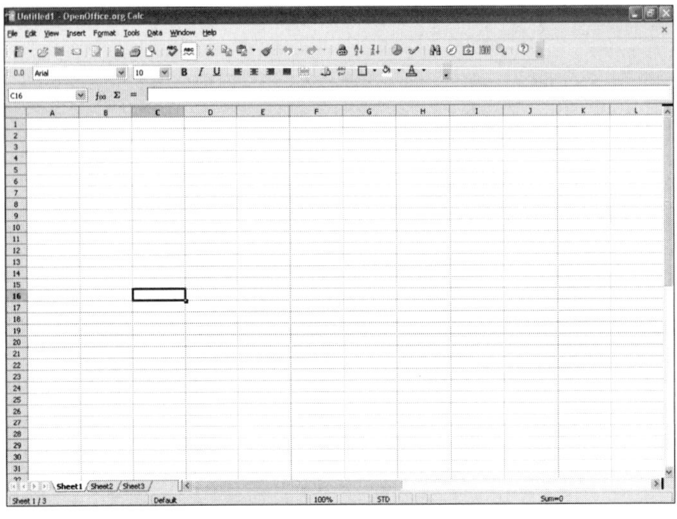

An OOo Calc blank spreadsheet.

In Calc, you can type your information in any column or row. You can navigate through the spreadsheet using either the arrow keys or the mouse. Each box on the raw spreadsheet is called a cell. Each cell is in both a row and a column.

In OOo 2.0, the maximum number of rows in a Calc spreadsheet is 65,536, so whether you need to make a simple record of daily household expenses or track an inventory that includes thousands of products, Calc should be able to handle it.

Let's start our Calc exploration by creating a simple table that tracks sales and salespeople's incentives.

	A	B	C	D	E	F
1	Sales and Incentives					
2						
3	First	Last	Address	Sales	Incentive	Remarks
4	John	Smith	Alabama	6000		
5	Jane	Doe	Kentucky	5000		
6	Jack	Frost	California	7700		
7	George	Bates	Miami	8000		
8	Bob	Patrick	Texas	4500		
9	Eugene	Krabs	Ohio	3000		
10	Bill	Johnson	Mississippi	3300		
11	Connie	Scott	Ohio	5500		
12	Camilla	Wall	Washington	6000		
13	Charlie	Wales	Wisconsin	4500		

A sample table.

Let's say you want to compute the incentive for every salesperson on your list. To do this, you need a mathematical formula. Your salespeople receive a 30% commission for each sale, so the formula is sales multiplied by .3 (30%). (In formulas, you use the usual + and − signs for addition and subtraction, respectively. For multiplication, you use*, and for division, you use /.)

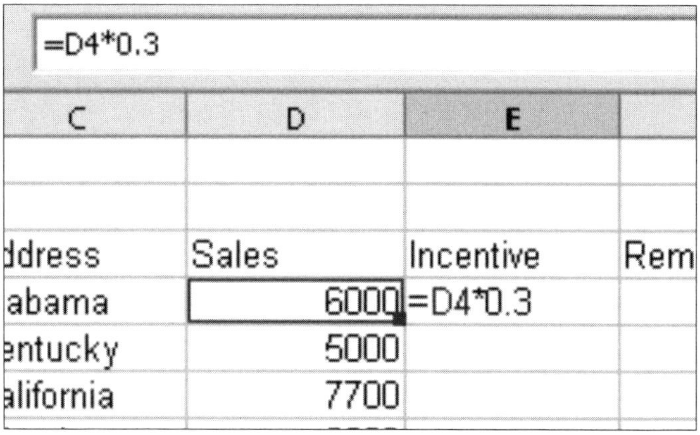

The mathematical formula.

Type =D4*.3 in the designated cell (to get the incentive amount for salesman John Smith by multiplying his sales by a given figure—in this case, 30%, or .30) and press Enter. You see the result of the automatic computation of his incentive. The = signifies the start of a mathematical formula, which is often used in Calc.

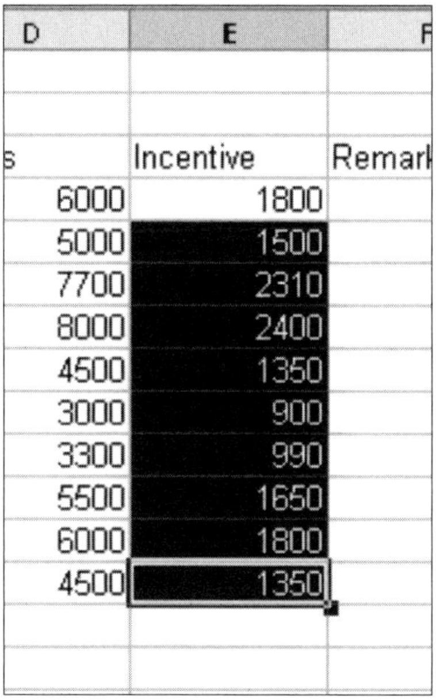

Copying and pasting formulas.

Copy and paste the formula in E4 into the rest of the cells in the Incentive column to get the same results for all your salespeople. You've just created a simple spreadsheet with a few clicks and keystrokes. (We'll cover creating user-defined or custom formulas in greater depth in Chapter 9, "Make Calc Spreadsheets Dance for You.")

Formatting for Fun

Frost	California	7700
Bates	Miami	8000
Patrick	Texas	4500
Krabs	Ohio	3000
Johnson	Mississippi	3300
Scott	Ohio	5500

Highlighting selected information by pressing Ctrl-A.

Calc shares formatting functions with other OOo programs. For instance, the standard keystroke combination Ctrl-A selects all information on the page. You can choose a typeface and size for the entire document, for a group of cells, or for just a single cell. To highlight a single cell or a group of cells, either press Ctrl plus the arrow keys or click and drag over the data you want.

Toolbar/text format buttons.

You can customize your spreadsheets and make them easier on the eye by selecting interesting font types and sizes instead of sticking with the defaults. You can use text alterations (including bold, italics, underline) and alignments (such as left, right, center, and justified). You can also increase or decrease decimal places, add borders and cell backgrounds, and change font colors. Any or all of these changes can make your spreadsheets look interesting instead of boring.

Sometimes when you type long numeric values in a cell, instead of the value, ####### appears. This means you need to make that column wider so that you can see all the data in cells that fall under it. To adjust the width and height of a column or row, drag the divider beside the column header.

Sales and Incentives

First	Last	Address	Sales	Incentive	Remarks
John	Smith	Alabama	$6,000.00	$1,800.00	
Jane	Doe	Kentucky	5,000.00	1,500.00	
Jack	Frost	California	7,700.00	2,310.00	
George	Bates	Miami	8,000.00	2,400.00	
Bob	Patrick	Texas	4,500.00	1,350.00	
Eugene	Krabs	Ohio	3,000.00	900.00	
Bill	Johnson	Mississippi	3,300.00	990.00	
Connie	Scott	Ohio	5,500.00	1,650.00	
Camilla	Wall	Washington	6,000.00	1,800.00	
Charlie	Wales	Wisconsin	4,500.00	1,350.00	

Adjusting column width.

Now let's do some formatting work in OOo Calc. Using the Format menu, try the following settings.

Select cells A1 to F13. Choose the Garamond font, 13 points.

Text formatting options.

Select cells A3 to F3. Click the B button and the center alignment button. The selected text then becomes bold and is centered in the selected cells.

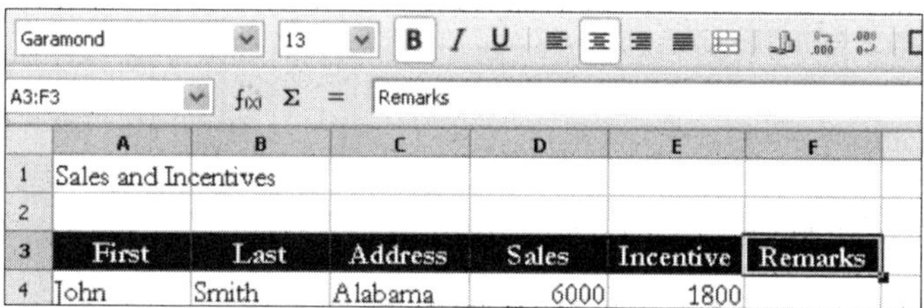

Aligning text and making it bold.

Suppose you want all dollar figures in the document to be separated by thousands (such as 1,350 instead of 1350). To standardize numerical separators, follow the next steps.

ress	Sales	Incentive	Remar
ma	$6,000.00	$1,800.00	
cky	5,000.00	1,500.00	
rnia	7,700.00	2,310.00	
	8,000.00	2,400.00	
	4,500.00	1,350.00	
	3,000.00	900.00	
sippi	3,300.00	990.00	
	5,500.00	1,650.00	
ngton	6,000.00	1,800.00	
nsin	4,500.00	1,350.00	

Numerical separators.

Select D4 to E4 and click the Currency Number Format button.

Select D5 to E14 and click the Comma and Decimal Number Format button to the right of the Currency Number Format button.

Before clicking the Merge Cells button, you must highlight the cells you want to merge. In this case, select A1 to E1, and then click the Merge Cells button. The lines separating the cells in Row 1 disappear.

Merging cells.

Now you have a nice, neat table.

You can still add borders and background colors.

Highlight A1 to F13, click the Border button, and choose the last border. Now a border appears all around the document. Let's also add some background color by highlighting cell A1. Click the Background Color button and select a color—say, light blue. To change the typeface color, highlight A3 to F3, click the Font Color button, and choose orange (or any other color you prefer).

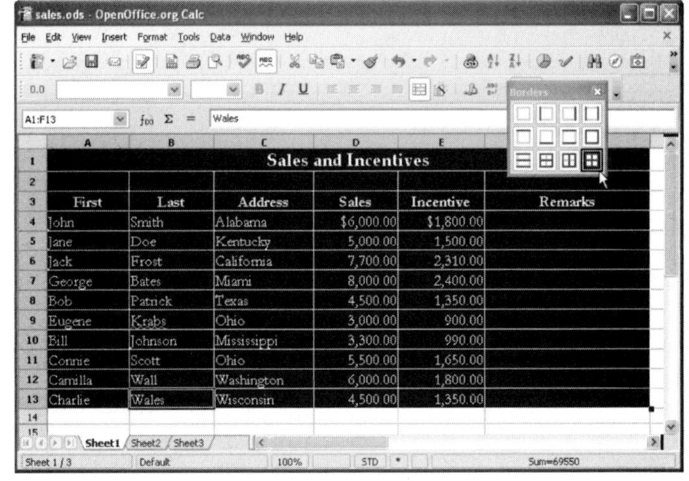

Borders.

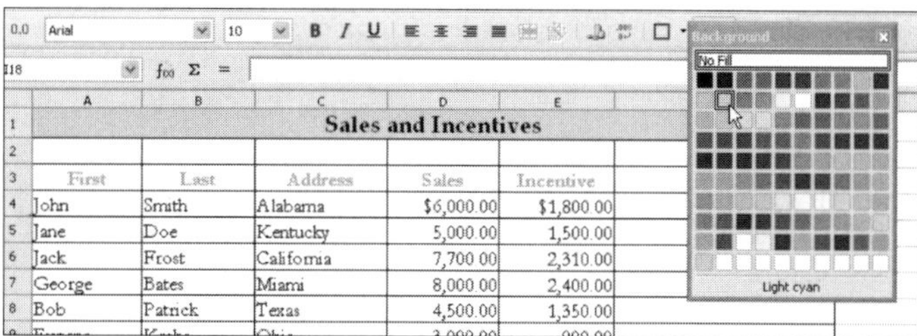

	A	B	C	D	E
1	Sales and Incentives				
2					
3	First	Last	Address	Sales	Incentive
4	John	Smith	Alabama	$6,000.00	$1,800.00
5	Jane	Doe	Kentucky	5,000.00	1,500.00
6	Jack	Frost	California	7,700.00	2,310.00
7	George	Bates	Miami	8,000.00	2,400.00
8	Bob	Patrick	Texas	4,500.00	1,350.00

Background and text colors.

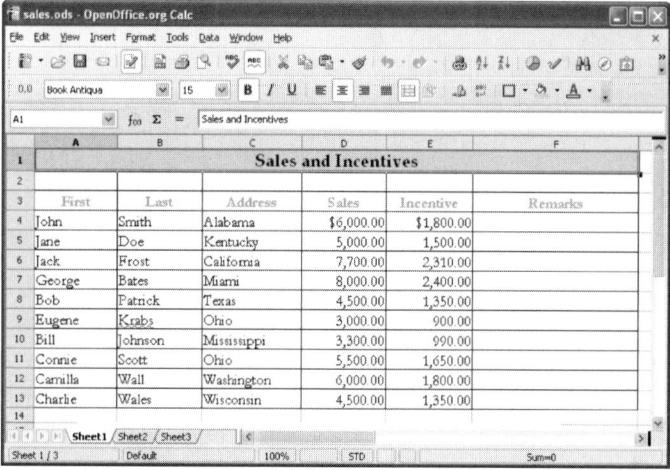

	A	B	C	D	E	F
1	Sales and Incentives					
2						
3	First	Last	Address	Sales	Incentive	Remarks
4	John	Smith	Alabama	$6,000.00	$1,800.00	
5	Jane	Doe	Kentucky	5,000.00	1,500.00	
6	Jack	Frost	California	7,700.00	2,310.00	
7	George	Bates	Miami	8,000.00	2,400.00	
8	Bob	Patrick	Texas	4,500.00	1,350.00	
9	Eugene	Krabs	Ohio	3,000.00	900.00	
10	Bill	Johnson	Mississippi	3,300.00	990.00	
11	Connie	Scott	Ohio	5,500.00	1,650.00	
12	Camilla	Wall	Washington	6,000.00	1,800.00	
13	Charlie	Wales	Wisconsin	4,500.00	1,350.00	
14						

A stylized spreadsheet.

Saving and Doing More

Now save your document. After that, you can add charts or graphs before you print it. (Saving your work frequently is always a good idea, no matter what software you Use.)

Save saves the current document.

Save this file as SALES.ODS. This is the best format if you'll only work on this file yourself or share it with other OOo users. If you need to share it with people who use other spreadsheet programs, you save it—or resave it as a second file with the same data—in the format their program uses by selecting that file format from the dropdown list.

Using the SALES.ODS file, you'll now make a chart based on the data you have.

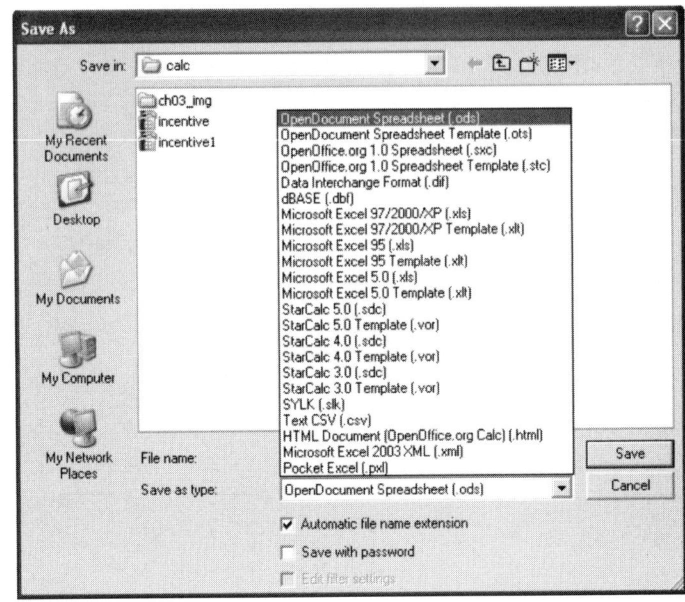

Saving a document.

 **Insert Chart** makes a chart based on the current data.

When you click the Insert Chart button, the icon changes to the chart icon. Click and drag to the area where you want to place the chart; the AutoFormat Chart menu appears. Highlight A3 to D13 for the range, and click Next. Choose the type of chart you want from the selection offered, and click Next. Choose the variant. Enter SALES as the title and click Create. A chart appears below your table. Save your file again.

Sales and Incentives

First	Last	Address	Sales	Incentive	Remarks
John	Smith	Alabama	$6,000.00	$1,800.00	
Jane	Doe	Kentucky	5,000.00	1,500.00	
Jack	Frost	California	7,700.00	2,310.00	
George	Bates	Miami	8,000.00	2,400.00	
Bob	Patrick	Texas	4,500.00	1,350.00	
Eugene	Krabs	Ohio	3,000.00	900.00	
Bill	Johnson	Mississippi	3,300.00	990.00	
Connie	Scott	Ohio	5,500.00	1,650.00	
Camilla	Wall	Washington	6,000.00	1,800.00	
Charlie	Wales	Wisconsin	4,500.00	1,350.00	

Inserting a chart.

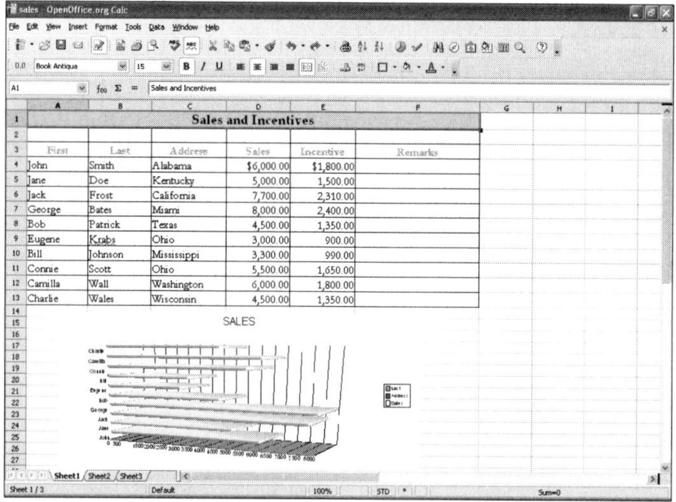

Sales and Incentives

First	Last	Address	Sales	Incentive	Remarks
John	Smith	Alabama	$6,000.00	$1,800.00	
Jane	Doe	Kentucky	5,000.00	1,500.00	
Jack	Frost	California	7,700.00	2,310.00	
George	Bates	Miami	8,000.00	2,400.00	
Bob	Patrick	Texas	4,500.00	1,350.00	
Eugene	Krabs	Ohio	3,000.00	900.00	
Bill	Johnson	Mississippi	3,300.00	990.00	
Connie	Scott	Ohio	5,500.00	1,650.00	
Camilla	Wall	Washington	6,000.00	1,800.00	
Charlie	Wales	Wisconsin	4,500.00	1,350.00	

The finished document.

Finally, you'll print the file.

Print File Directly prints the file to the specified printer.

Or you can highlight only the pages you want to print, select File > Print, and enable the Selection button in the Print Range section.

And that's it. You're done with this job.

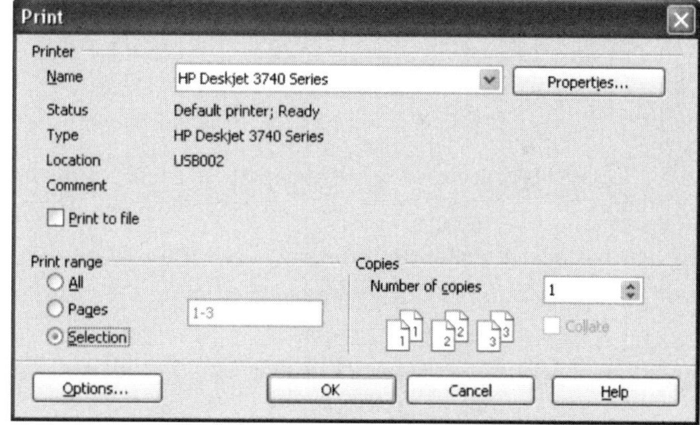

The Print dialog box.

Let's spend a moment looking at some of the buttons (icons) you're most likely to use in Calc. You learned about most of them in Chapter 1, "First Things First," but a little review never hurts.

Reviewing Useful Buttons

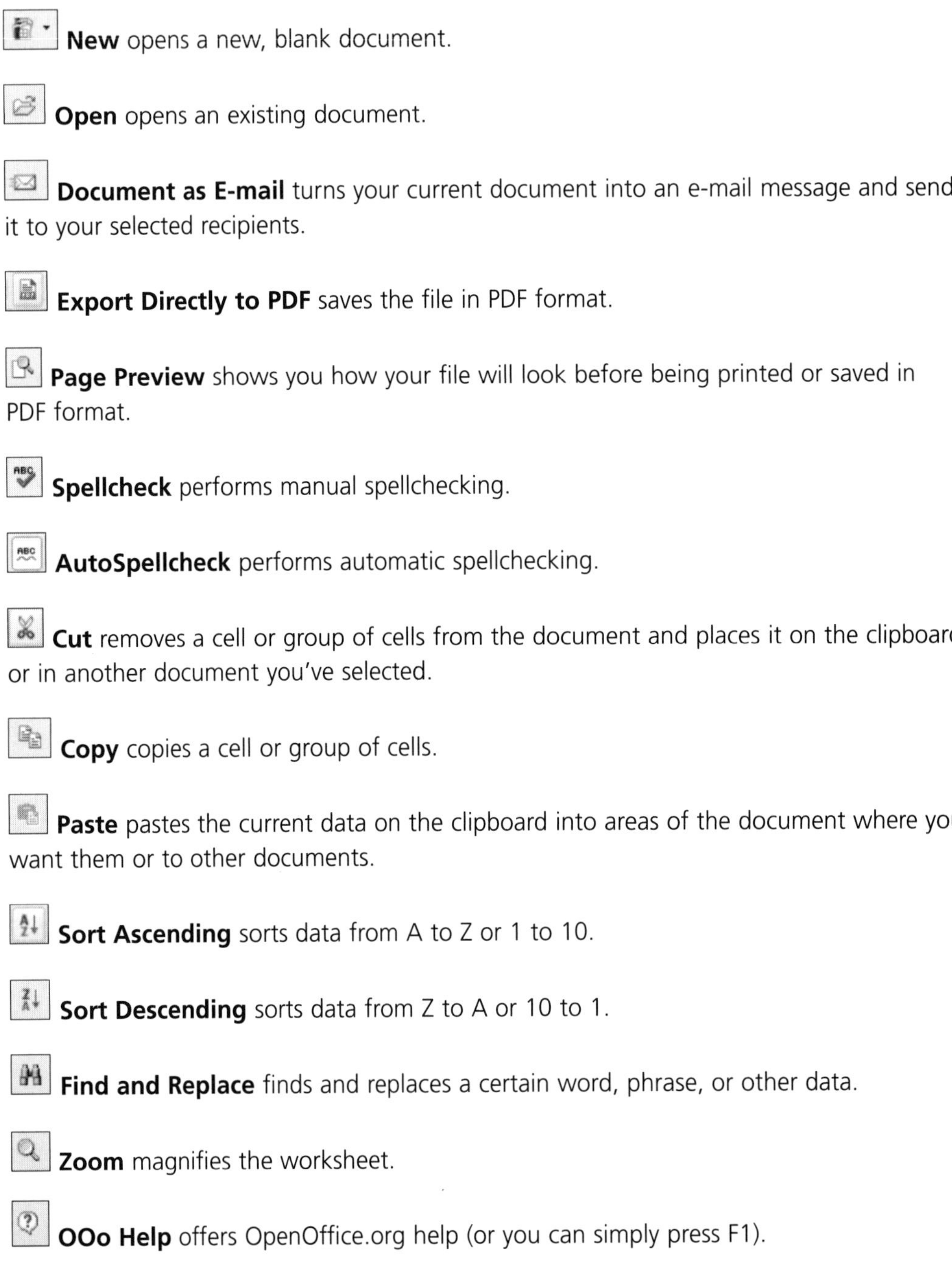

New opens a new, blank document.

Open opens an existing document.

Document as E-mail turns your current document into an e-mail message and sends it to your selected recipients.

Export Directly to PDF saves the file in PDF format.

Page Preview shows you how your file will look before being printed or saved in PDF format.

Spellcheck performs manual spellchecking.

AutoSpellcheck performs automatic spellchecking.

Cut removes a cell or group of cells from the document and places it on the clipboard or in another document you've selected.

Copy copies a cell or group of cells.

Paste pastes the current data on the clipboard into areas of the document where you want them or to other documents.

Sort Ascending sorts data from A to Z or 1 to 10.

Sort Descending sorts data from Z to A or 10 to 1.

Find and Replace finds and replaces a certain word, phrase, or other data.

Zoom magnifies the worksheet.

OOo Help offers OpenOffice.org help (or you can simply press F1).

Recognizing OOo Calc's Limitations

While there are things OOo Calc can do that Microsoft Excel can't, such as producing PDF files directly from your work, there are a few limitations to what Calc can do and a few ways in which Excel is not completely compatible with Calc:

- Like Microsoft Excel, Calc supports array formulas—but it doesn't support array formulas with two ranges.
- Array constants are unavailable in OOo. To deal with this problem, you must have constant values in cells on a sheet and refer to them.
- Excel provides some chart types that Calc does not.
- Calc is slower to update than Excel, and it has fewer axis options.
- Some menu settings are different in Calc from what you may be accustomed to in Excel (for example, the printing menu).

However, with a little practice, you will soon learn how to handle these differences, and you will find that they do not lessen Calc's usefulness and functionality as your primary tool for 99% of the spreadsheet work you're likely to do at home or at work.

Section II

Advanced OpenOffice.org

Chapter 6

Slick OpenOffice.org Writer Tricks

By Daniel Carrera

Whether you are creating a newsletter with a complex layout or you want to make a change to every paragraph in a book manuscript, OpenOffice.org can make the task easy. This chapter introduces some of the features that make OpenOffice.org invaluable for complex jobs.

Wizards: Create a Layout Once; Use It a Million Times

Wizards can automate letters and presentations, install fonts from the Web, and more. Select File > Wizards to see a list of available wizards.

We will use the Letter Wizard as an example. Go to File > Wizards > Letter. Along with the wizard, you see a preview of the letter.

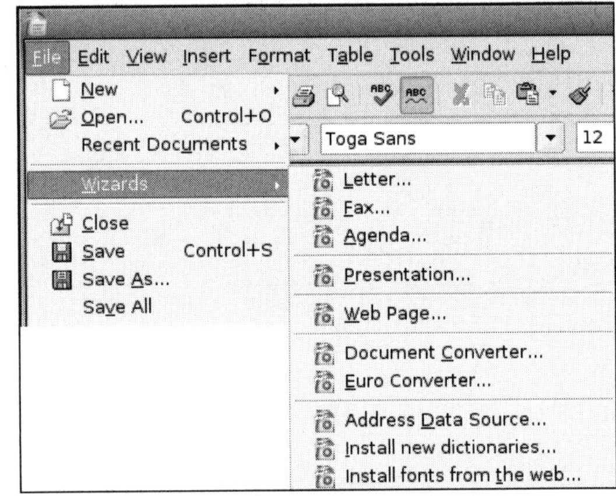

OpenOffice.org wizards.

In step 1 you select the page design (business, formal, or personal letter). When you make changes, the preview updates automatically. If you select Business Letter, you can also have a letterhead. You configure it in step 2. If you don't want a letterhead, step 2 is unavailable.

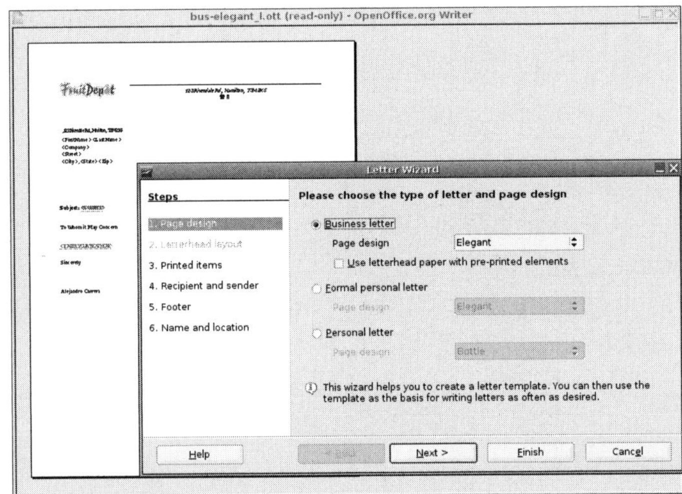

Step 1: Page design.

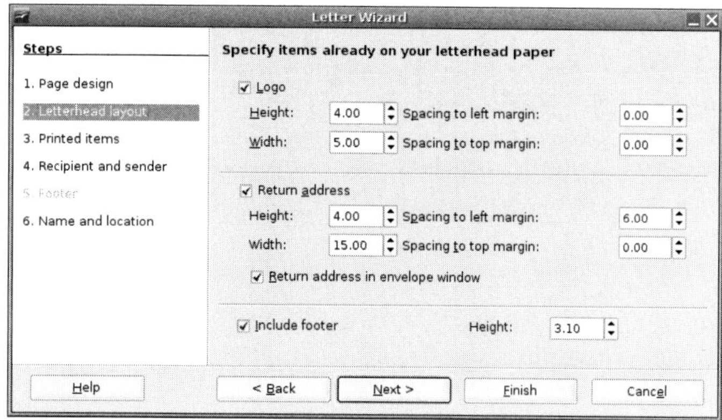

Step 2: Letterhead layout.

In step 3 (not shown), you choose whether you want a logo, footer, and other visual items. You don't actually select the logo here. That is done in step 6. Here you simply decide whether to have one. Next, in step 4, you set the address of the sender and recipient.

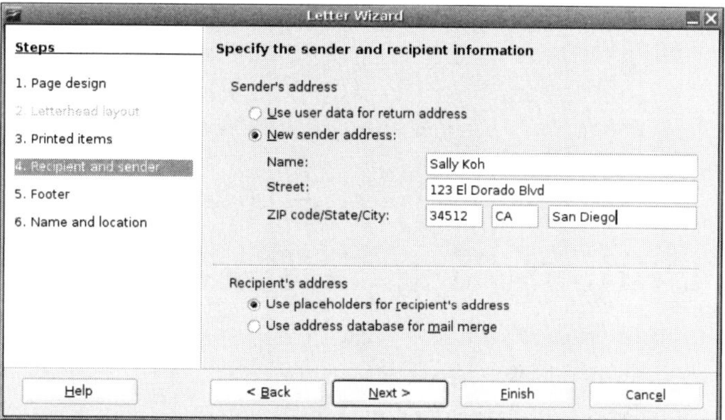

Step 4: Recipient and sender address.

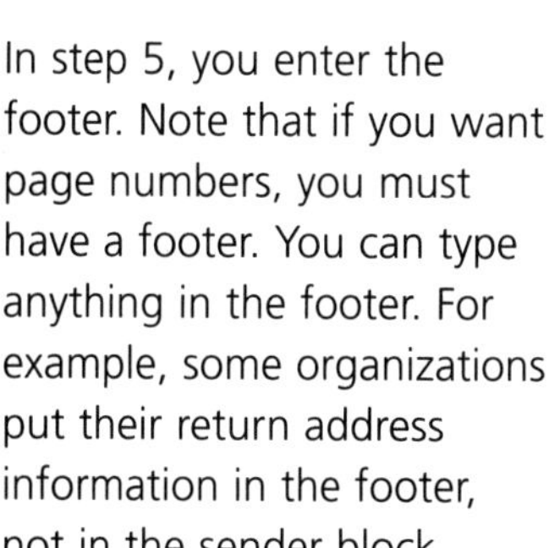

In step 5, you enter the footer. Note that if you want page numbers, you must have a footer. You can type anything in the footer. For example, some organizations put their return address information in the footer, not in the sender block.

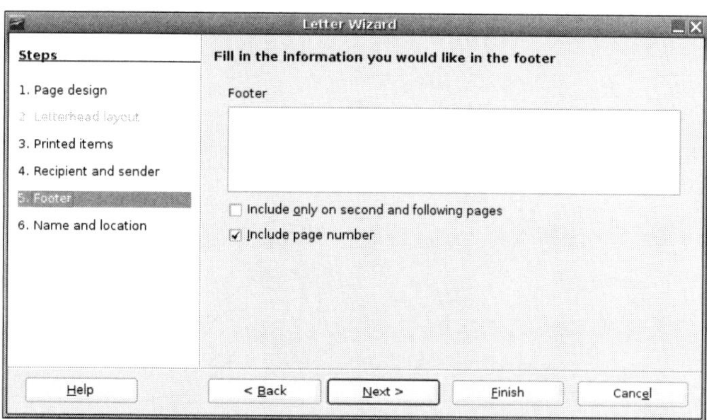

Step 5: Footer. To have a page number, you must have a footer.

In the last step, you can optionally name the template. In this example I call it "letter." When you are done, click Finish.

OpenOffice.org remembers the settings you choose, so next the time you run the wizard, you won't have to design the letter from scratch.

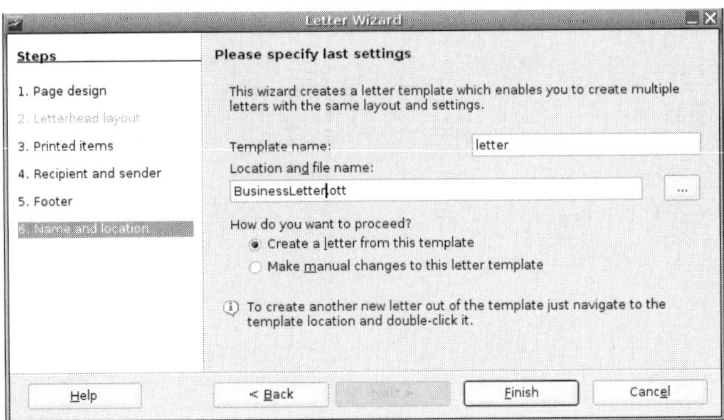

The last step.

Often you will want to make edits beyond what's provided by the wizard (for example, changing the logo). To do this, click "Make manual changes to this letter template" in step 6 of the Letter Wizard dialog box, and then click OK. You can edit the template manually. When you're finished, select File > Save.

Creating a Sample Document

What are styles? Before this question is answered, you need an example. Start a new document and select Format > Styles and Formatting (or press F11).

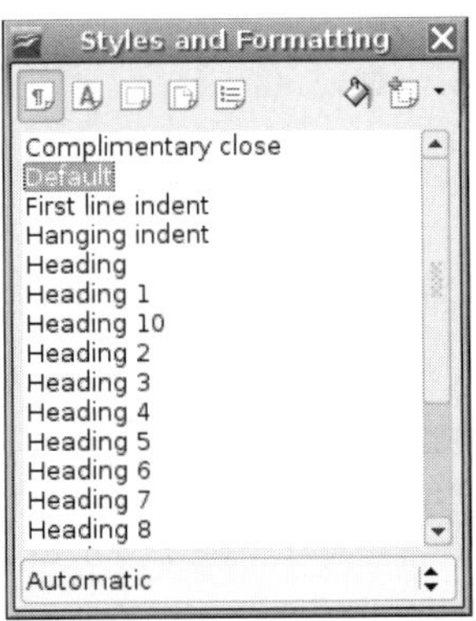

The Styles and Formatting window.

By default, this window displays Paragraph styles. The other types of styles are Character, Frame, Page, and Numbering styles. This section covers Paragraph styles only. For this example, type three lines of text that say Section 1, Subsection 1.1, and Subsection 1.2.

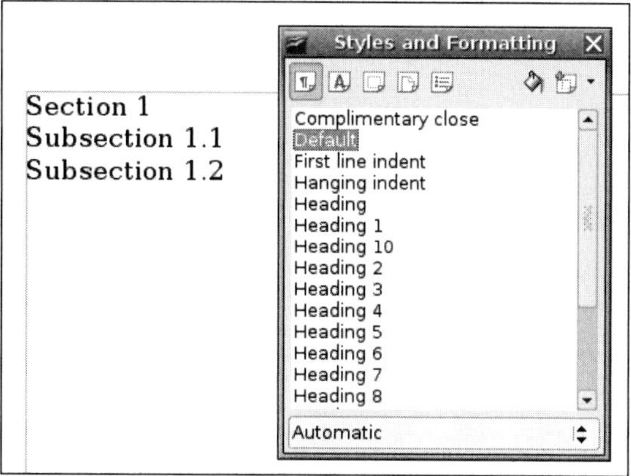

Type three lines of text, as shown.

Put the cursor on the first line (Section 1). In the Styles and Formatting window, double-click Heading 1. You should see the font change. You just applied the Heading 1 style to the first paragraph. Similarly, apply the Heading 2 style to the second and third lines.

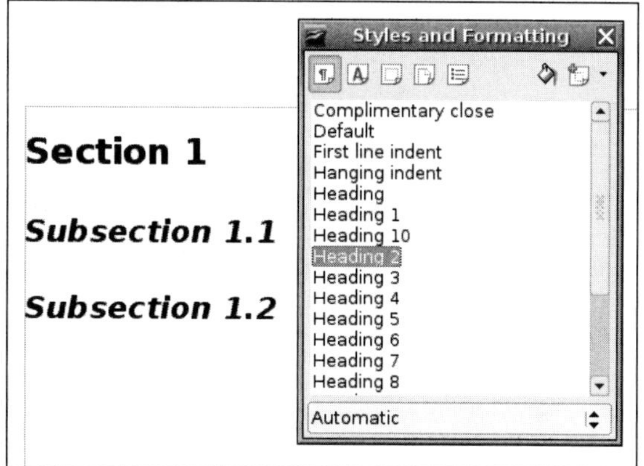

Section 1 has the Heading 1 paragraph style, and the subheadings have the Heading 2 paragraph style.

So, what are styles? Styles are a *logical* description for the document. Styles mean that you stop saying "bold, 14 points, centered" and start saying "title."

Modifying Styles

The power of styles lies in your ability to modify them to suit your needs. Suppose you want to make sections centered and subtitles indented. In the Styles and Formatting window, right-click Heading 1 and choose Modify.

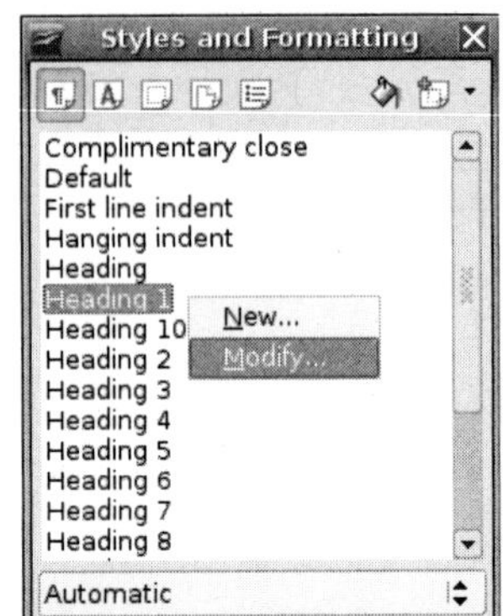

Right-click and choose Modify to edit a style.

In the Paragraph Style window, choose the Alignment tab, enable the Center button, and click OK.

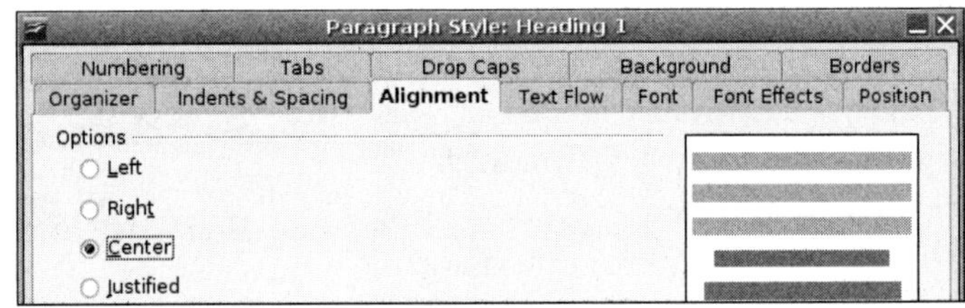

Setting the Heading 1 style to be centered.

Now everything marked as Heading 1 will be centered.

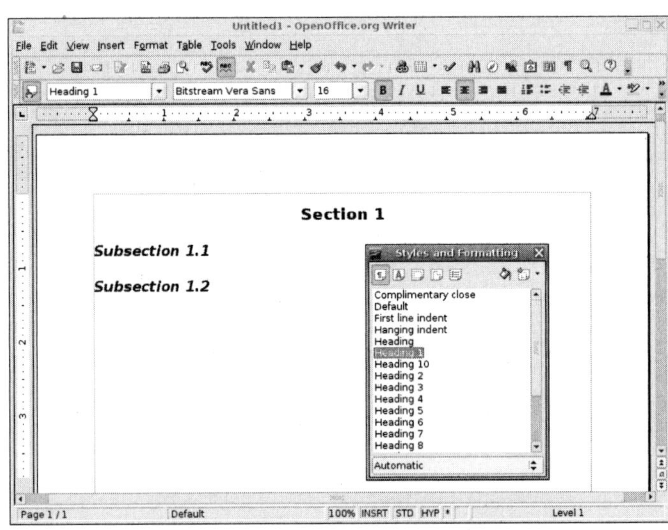

Section 1 is centered because it has the Heading 1 page style.

Next, indent Heading 2. Right-click Heading 2 and choose Modify (as before). Click the Indents & Spacing tab, set the indentation before the text to 0.50 inches, and click OK.

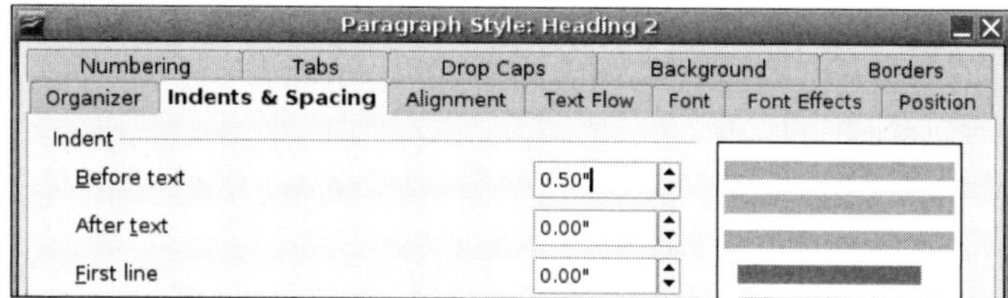

Indenting the Heading 2 page style.

At this point, the paragraphs that have the Heading 2 style are indented.

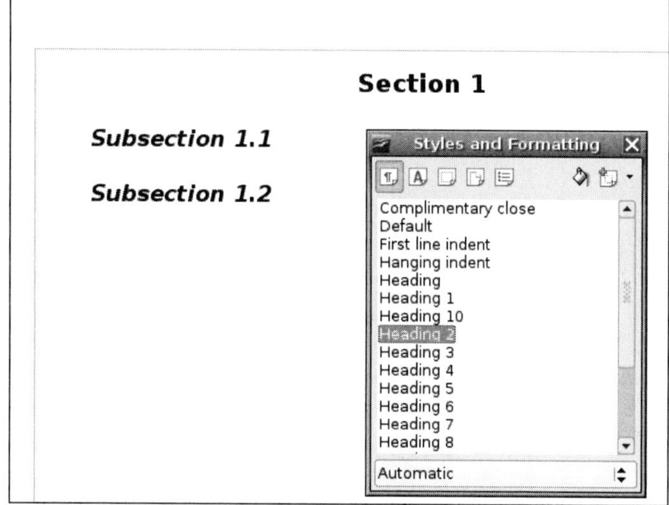

The subsections are indented because they have the Heading 2 paragraph style.

The styles currently in use are available from a menu on the top bar.

You can use this menu to change the style of the current paragraph (that is, where the cursor is located). This is often easier than using the Styles and Formatting window.

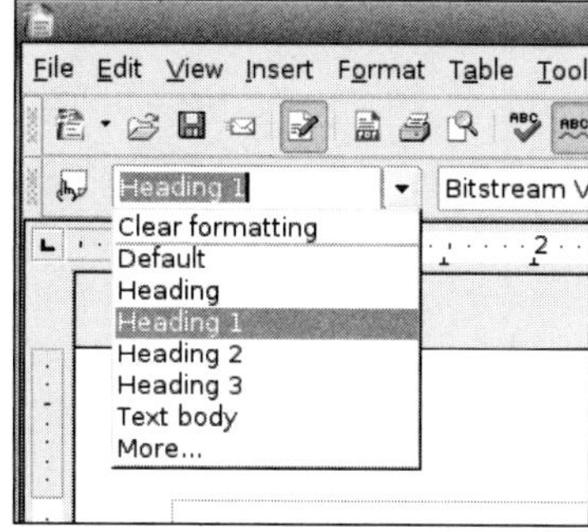

All paragraph styles currently in use are on a menu.

Working Faster with AutoCorrect

Suppose that you often use the word "internationalization." You can define a short form of the word, such as "itn," and have OpenOffice.org replace it for you.

Select Tools > AutoCorrect, and click the Replace tab. Under Replace, type "itn"; under With, type "internationalization."

Inserting an AutoCorrect shortcut.

Click New and then OK. Now, if you type "itn" in any document and press the spacebar, OpenOffice.org replaces it with "internationalization."

This feature has a myriad of uses. It can correct common typos (such as changing "teh" to "the") and insert special characters (such as "(c)" for the copyright symbol ©).

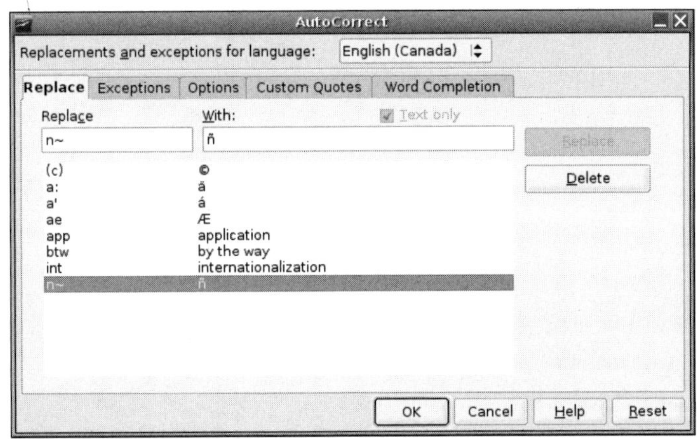

Sample shortcuts.

Use Word Completion (or Not)

AutoCorrect can be used for more than shortcuts. OpenOffice.org "learns" from the current document to guess which words you are likely to type. For example, if you type "international" often, the next time you type "int," OpenOffice.org suggests the rest of the word.

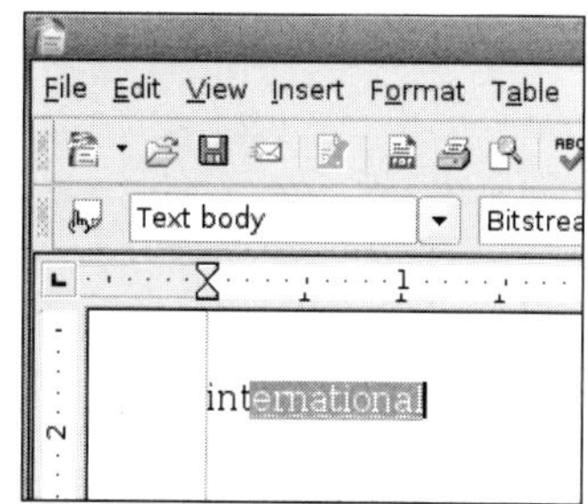

OpenOffice.org suggests words based on what you have already typed in the document.

To accept the suggested word, press Enter. This feature is called word completion. To configure this feature (for example, to disable it), open the AutoCorrect dialog box and click the Word Completion tab.

Configure Other Autocorrect Options

AutoCorrect has other configuration options. By using the Options tab, you can enable and disable some standard options such as replacing 1st with 1st and capitalizing the first letter of every sentence. On the Exceptions tab you can add exceptions to the rules, such as terms with two initial capitals (such as OOo for OpenOffice.org).

Automating Footers and Page Numbers

Earlier we talked about Paragraph styles. OpenOffice.org also has Page styles, where you can assign page properties such as margins, headers, footers, and page numbers. The status bar shows the page style of the current page.

The status bar shows the current page style (Default in this case).

Here, the page has the Default page style. To add a footer, select Insert > Footer > Default. When the footer appears, you can click it and type text, insert images, and so on.

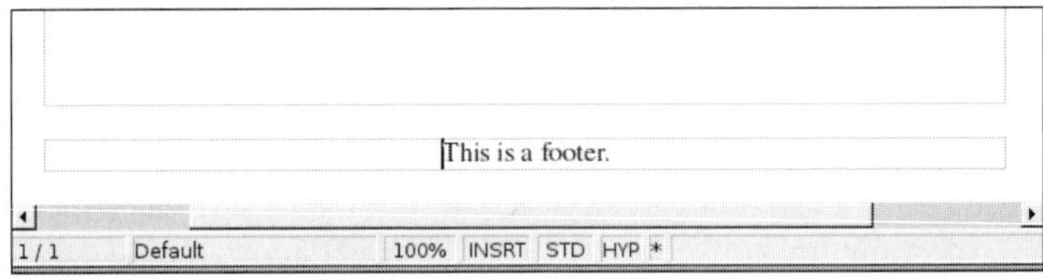

A page with a footer.

The footer appears on every page with the same page style (in this case, Default). To insert a page number, select Insert > Fields > Page Number.

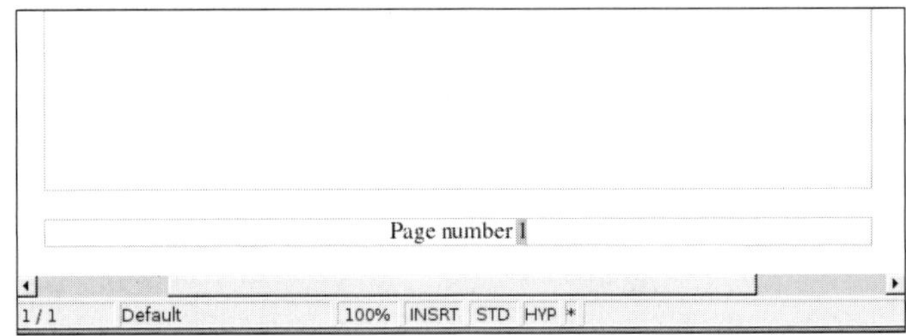

The page number field.

The page number updates automatically and appears on every page with this page style. The gray background means that it is a *field* and not regular text. When you print the document, the background is the same as the rest of the document. You can turn the gray background on and off with View > Field Shadings.

Adding Footnotes However and Wherever You Want Them

First, put the cursor where you want the footnote number. Then select Insert > Footnote.

Most people choose Automatic numbering, but if you prefer to number the footnotes by hand (or you don't want to use numbers), select Character and type the name of the footnote in the space provided.

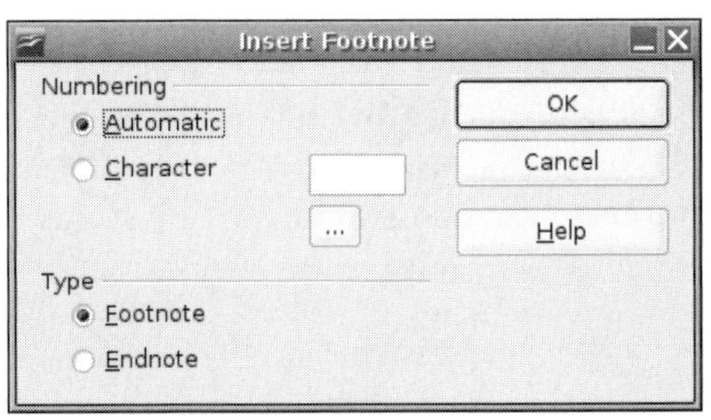

The Insert Footnote dialog box.

Under Type are two options, Footnote and Endnote. Footnotes appear at the bottom of the page where they are referenced. Endnotes appear together at the end of the document (similar to a bibliography). Make your selection and click OK.

Windows users: unzip the .zip file on the CD by clicking on it, same as any other "zipped" Windows program you have installed.

Linux users: Follow the instructions in the "Linux Notes" appendix – or use the binary version supplied for your Linux distribution, and install OOo the same way you install any other program.

1 Once installed, OpenOffice.org works exactly the same in either operating system.

A sample footnote.

Simplifying Complexity in Special-Purpose Documents

Frames are boxes that can contain text and images. With frames you can easily make complex documents such as newsletters. To insert a frame, select Insert > Frame. The Frame dialog box appears.

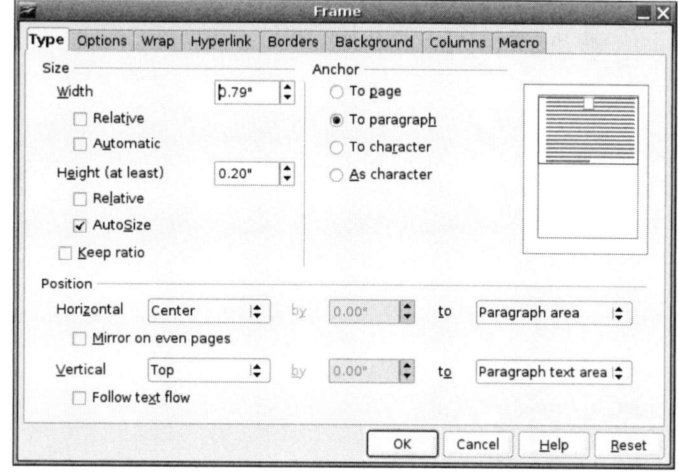

The Frame dialog box.

Here you can configure the frame's size, background, and so on. After you click OK, you see a box with green handles.

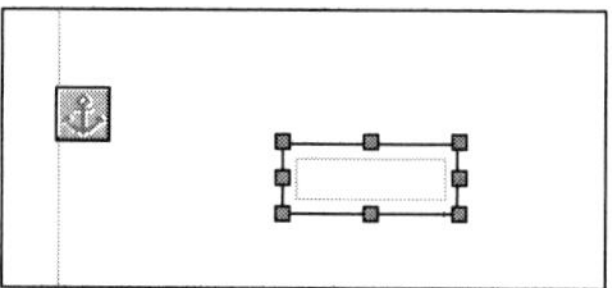

When a frame is selected, it has green handles.

You can move the frame with the mouse and resize it using the green handles. To enter text, first deselect the frame (click the document

My first text frame

You can type text and insert images in a frame.

background), and then click inside the frame to put the cursor inside the frame. Then type your text.

If you want to change frame properties (background color, border, and so on), select the frame (click the frame border) and select Format > Frame.

You can link frames so that text flows from one to another. This is useful for complex documents. For example, a newsletter might start a story on the front page and continue it on page 3. First, make two frames and select one of them.

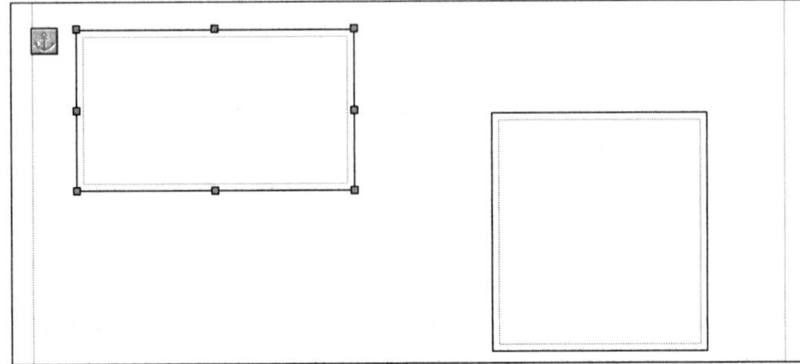

Make two frames and select one of them (click the frame border).

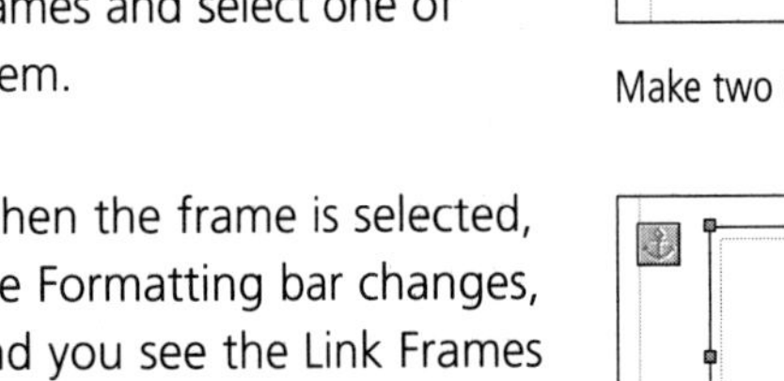

When the frame is selected, the Formatting bar changes, and you see the Link Frames icon. Click it and select the second frame.

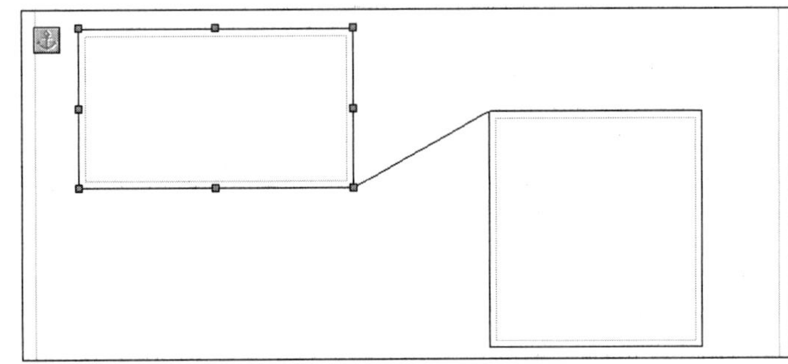

Click the second frame to finish the link.

The line going from the first frame to the second denotes the link. Now, if you type text in the first frame, after the space in that frame is used up, the text flows to the second. You can resize the frames and move them around without affecting the link.

Text flows from the first frame to the second.

Similarly, you can link the second frame to a third frame, and so on. To remove the link, select the first frame (not the second) and click the Unlink icon.

Generating a Table of Contents and Index

If you use Heading styles as shown in this chapter, OpenOffice.org can use that information to make a table of contents for you. Consider the document shown here.

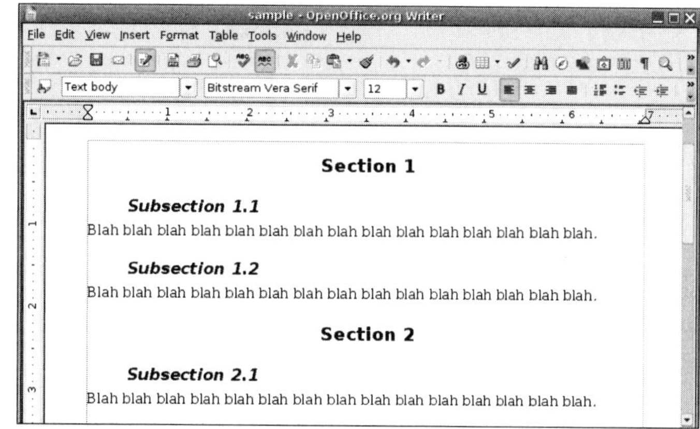

A sample document using the Heading styles.

In this example, the sections have the Heading 1 style and the subtitles the Heading 2 style. This is important. If you don't use Heading styles, the table of contents feature won't work correctly.

Put the cursor where you want the table of contents. In this example I'll put it before Section 1. Select Insert > Indexes and Tables > Indexes and Tables. A new window appears.

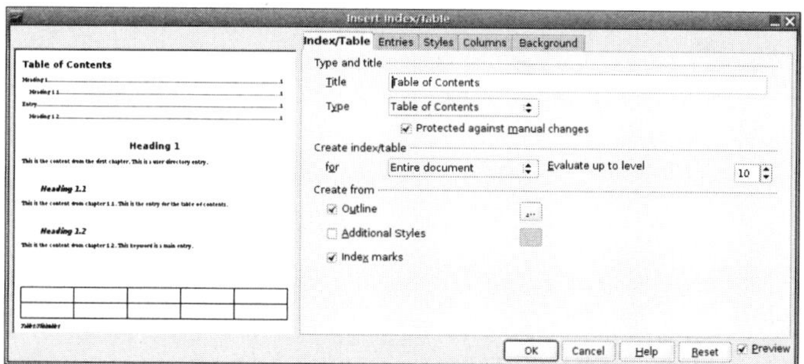

The Insert Index/Table window.

Under Type, select Table of Contents and click OK. OpenOffice.org then inserts a table of contents, including all sections and page numbers.

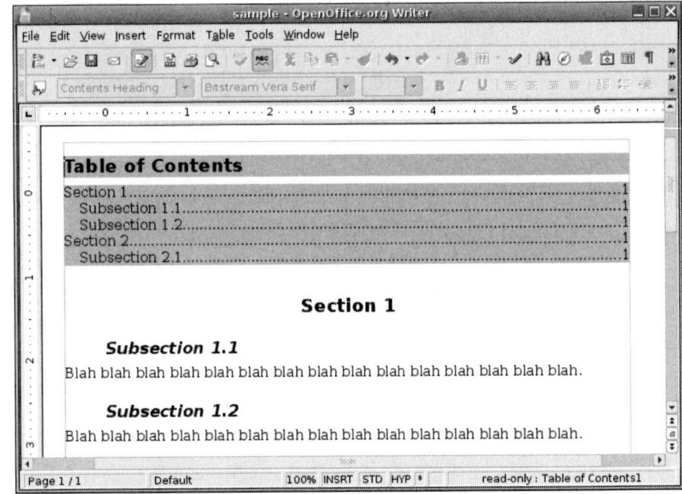

The table of contents is made from the Heading styles.

As you work on your document, you will naturally move sections around, change titles, and so on. To update the table of contents to include any changes in your document since you first created it, put the cursor anywhere on it, right-click, and select Update Index/Table.

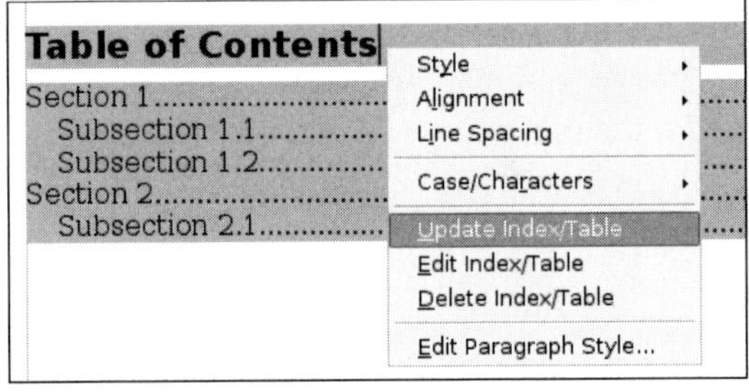

Updating a table of contents.

The Indexes and Tables window can also give you an alphabetical index. Under Type, choose Alphabetical Index and click OK.

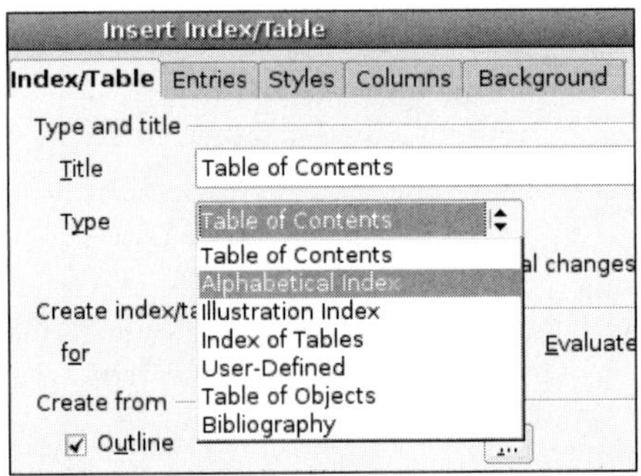

Inserting an index.

When you first create it, the index is empty.

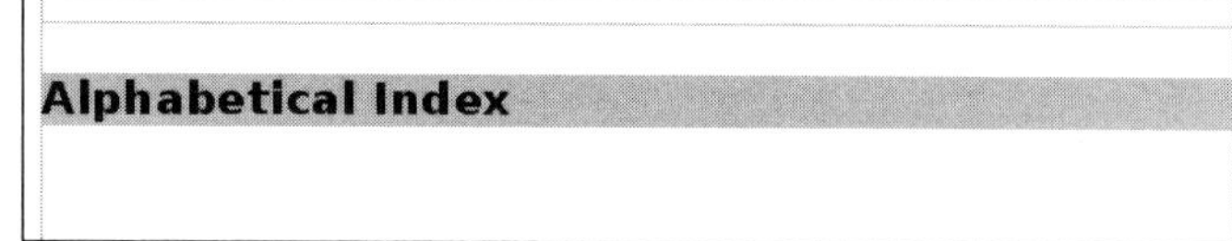

When you first create an index, it is empty.

You need entries for the index. Highlight a word (such as "hybrid," as shown here) and select Insert > Indexes and Tables > Entry.

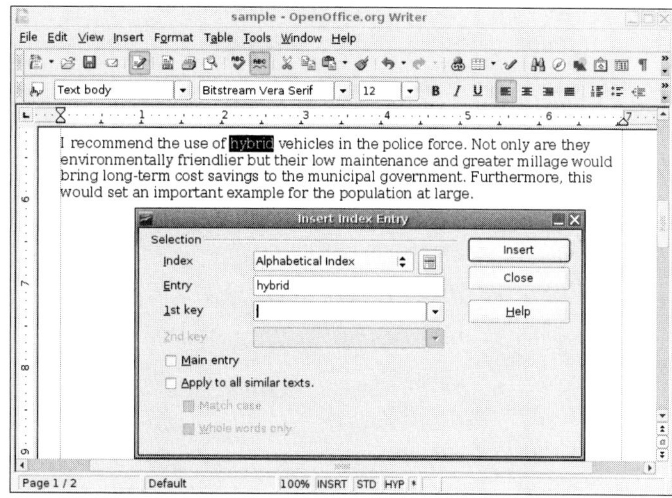

Inserting an index entry.

For a top-level entry, leave "1st key" blank. Click Insert. The word "hybrid" now has a gray background to denote that it is an index entry. (Don't delete this word unless you want to delete the entry from the index.)

I recommend the use of hybrid vehicles in the police force. Not only are they environmentally friendlier but their low maintenance and greater millage would bring long-term cost savings to the municipal government. Furthermore, this would set an important example for the population at large.

The index entry has a gray background.

You update an index the same way you update a table of contents. Put the cursor on the index, right-click, and choose Update.

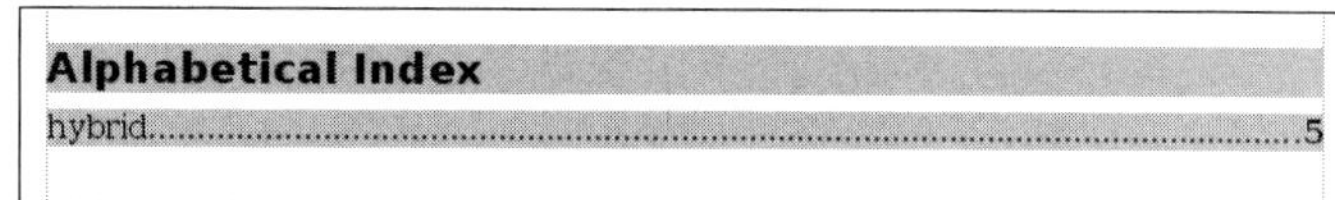

An updated index.

OpenOffice.org can use your email client to send a document as an email attachment. There is a slight difference between platforms.

In Windows, select File > Send > Document as Email (or click on the Document as E-mail icon). OOo opens your default email client, with the current document as an attachment.

In Linux, you need to tell OpenOffice.org what email client you are using. Select Tools > Options and choose Internet > E-mail.

Under E-mail program, select your email client, and then click OK. Now you can select File > Send > Document as Email (or click the Document as E-mail icon) to send the current document as an attachment.

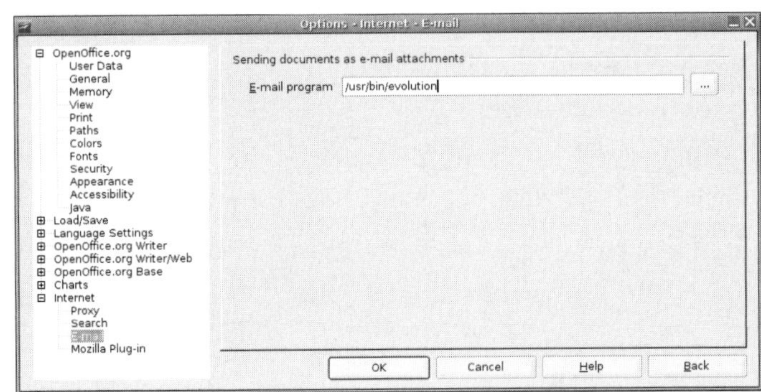

Select your email client (Linux).

Downloading and Using Templates Made by Others

OpenOffice.org has a large community of volunteers who provide templates you can use. You can download templates from http://ooextras.sourceforge.net/ and http://documentation.openoffice.org/Samples_Templates/. These sites have dozens of templates, including invoices, newsletters, and brochures. Suppose you want to use the template resume.ott.

Installing a Template

Open the template and select File > Templates > Save.

Type a name for the template (such as "resume"). Under Categories, most people would choose My Templates. Click OK.

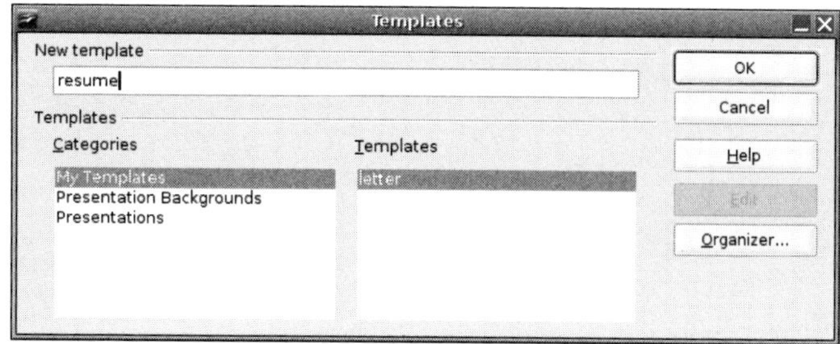

Installing a template.

Using the Template in a New Document

Select File > New > Templates and Documents. Go to My Templates and double-click the template.

OpenOffice.org creates a new document using this template.

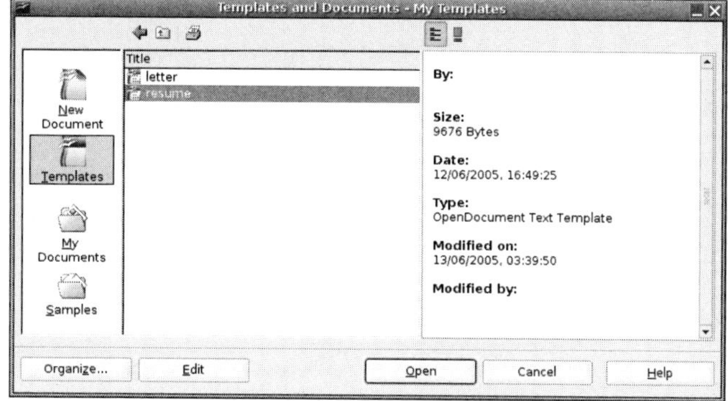

Opening an installed template.

Chapter 7

Draw: Not Your Father's Drawing Board

By Linda Worthington

Draw is a vector graphics drawing tool. You learned a bit about it in Chapter 4, "OOo Draw: Documents with Imagination." Now it's time to see what you can do with Draw beyond basic photo alteration and making simple line drawings.

Because Draw is integrated into the OpenOffice.org suite, it's easy to exchange graphics with all the components of OOo. For example, if you are creating a newsletter in Writer and you need to spice up the boss's photo, you can use images and shapes in Draw to create some neat effects.

Grouping Objects

Grouping objects can be temporary or assigned. Objects are grouped on a temporary basis when you select each object while holding down the Shift key. To assign group objects, hold down the Shift key while clicking each object you want to group, and then select Modify > Group or press Ctrl-Shift-G. To ungroup the objects, click to activate the group, and then select Modify > Ungroup. All group functions can be found on the Modify menu. To edit grouped objects, click the group and choose Modify > Enter Group or press F3. This allows you to edit each object separately.

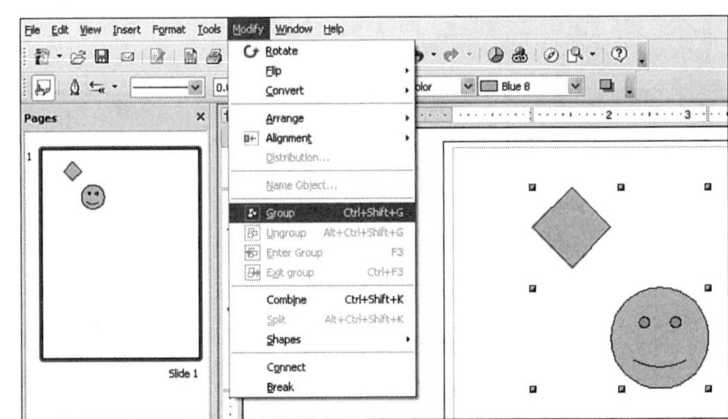

The Group command.

Any changes made to a group affect all objects in that group. You can move or rotate grouped objects.

Creating Flowcharts and Organizational Charts

To create a flowchart or organizational chart, choose a shape from the Flowchart toolbar, located on the Drawing toolbar in OOo Draw. The most common flowchart symbols are provided.

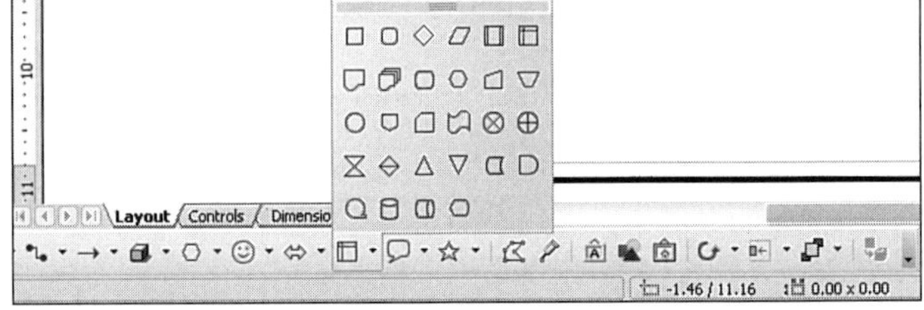

The Flowchart toolbar.

Click the shape you want, and drag it to create the shape. You can draw your own shapes as well, and you can put multiple shapes in one illustration.

After you've created the shapes, you need to add the necessary connectors from the Connectors toolbar, located on the Drawing toolbar.

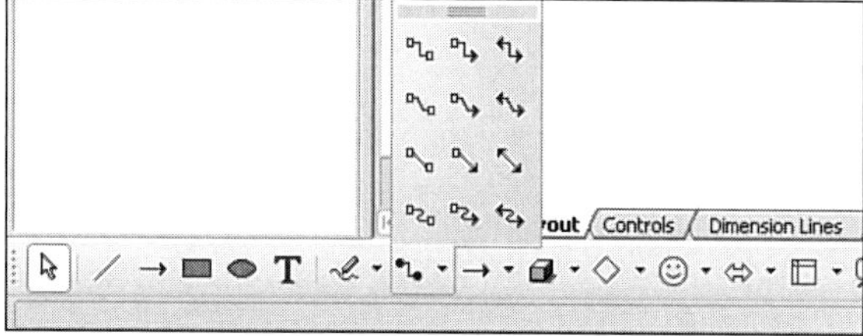

The Connectors toolbar.

To use the connector, move the mouse pointer over the edge of the flowchart shape. You see the connector sites. Click a connector site, and then click another connector site. When the flowchart or organizational shapes are moved, the connectors move with the shapes.

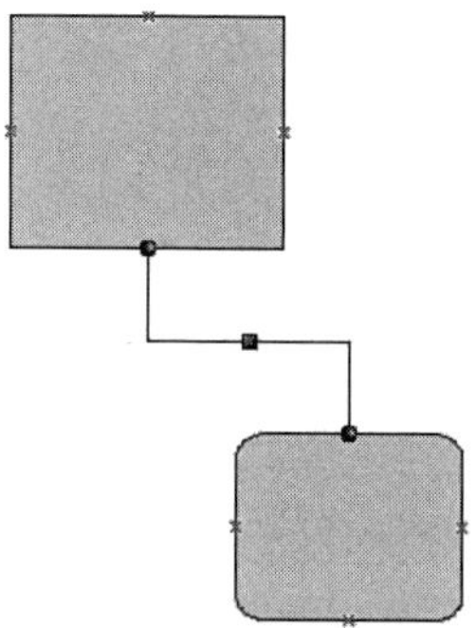

A Connector site.

To add text to a shape, double-click the shape and either type your text or paste in text from another file. You can type vertical text as well. This button is available on the Drawing toolbar.

To change your shape's color background, click the shape and select Format > Area or click the Area icon on the Line and Filling toolbar.

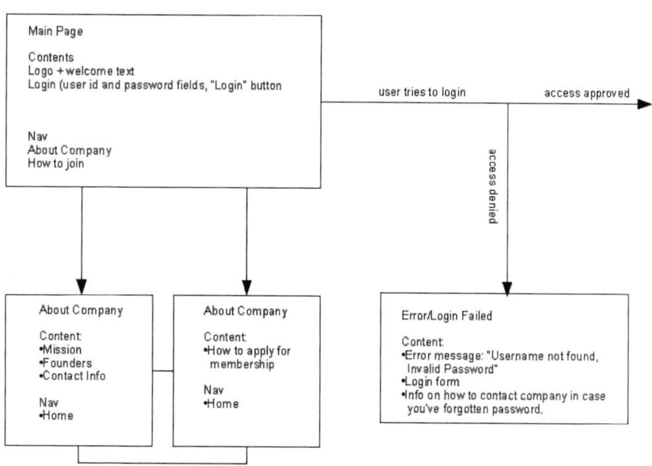

A flowchart example.

Shaping Cool Effects

You can create cool effects with bitmap images and shapes. Open a bitmap image. Draw a shape or shapes on the bitmap image, and then Shift-click all the shapes.

Shapes bitmap example 1.

Right-click and choose Shapes > Intersect.

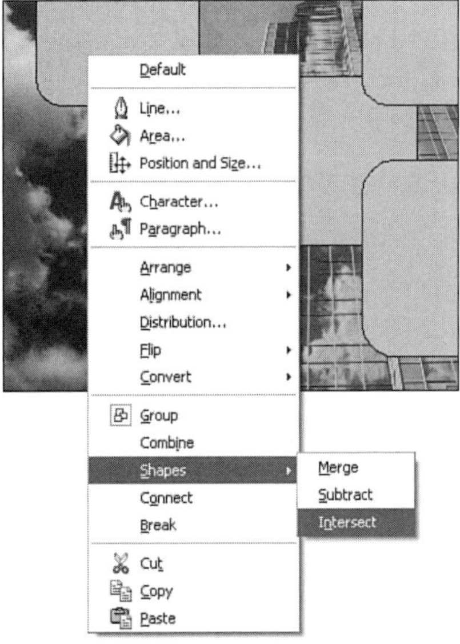

Shapes bitmap example 2.

This trims the bitmap image to the shape of the objects.

Shapes bitmap example 3.

Converting a Shape to 3D

You can select a shape, right-click it, and select Convert > 3D. This makes a three-dimensional object.

A 3D example.

Creating a 3D Logo from Font Characters

Open an empty Draw document. Create a text box containing a single capital letter. Highlight the letter. Right-click the letter and choose Character, or select Format > Character. You see the Character dialog box.

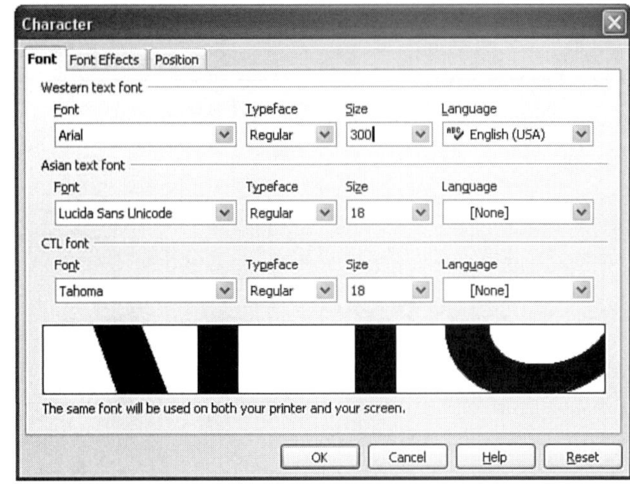

The Character dialog box.

Choose a character set for formatting, set the font size to 300 points, and click OK. Select Modify > Convert > 3D. You can modify the color by changing the settings in the Area Style of the Line and Filling toolbar. Right-click the letter and choose 3D Effects. Here you can apply different settings to achieve many different looks and shapes. Add text to the logo. Add an object for the background. Right-click and select Arrange > Send to Back.

A logo example.

Casting Shadows

You can apply shadows to objects by using the 3D Effects dialog box. Right-click the object and choose 3D Effects. Click the Shading button and then Shadow, and set the shadow's surface angle.

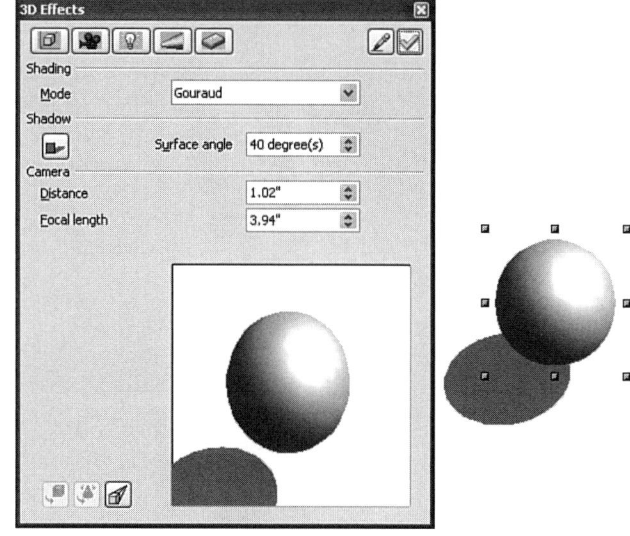

A shadow example.

Modifying Transparency

To modify transparency, right-click the object and choose Area and Transparency. Adjust the transparency amount settings under this tab.

Advancing to Specific Needs

Draw contains several advanced functions that are useful in certain specific instances, especially Web images and data exchange.

Duplicating a Shape

This function allows you to duplicate a selected shape while changing the options applied to the duplicates.

Right-click an object (or a group of selected objects), and then select Edit > Duplicate. You see the Duplicate dialog box.

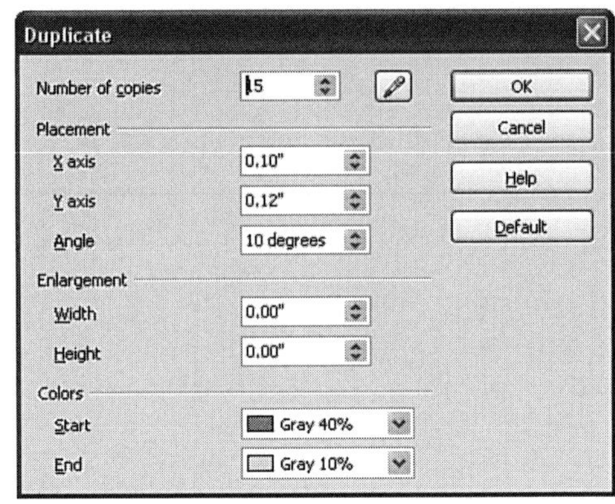

The Duplicate dialog box.

You can choose the following:

- The number of copies
- The placement along the X and Y axes between two copies
- The angle of rotation between two copies
- The change in size between each copy
- The colors of the start and end copies

These options applied to a rectangle produce the following result.

The end result of duplication is a new group.

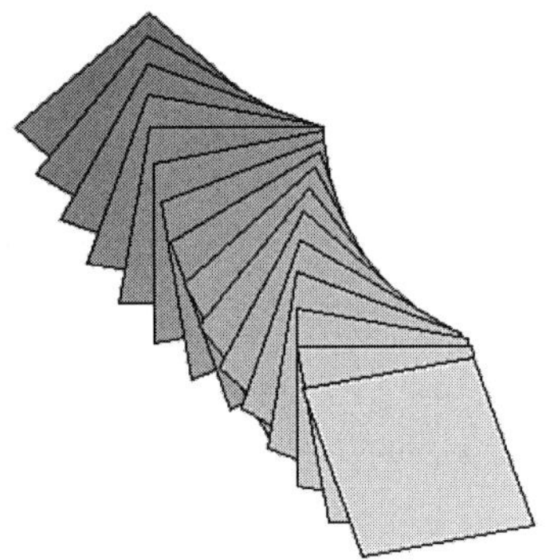

A duplicate example.

Cross-Fading Objects in a Transition

Cross-fading transforms a shape from one form to another. This option is available only in OOo Draw. You can copy the objects into Impress and, by using the animation editor available with Impress, animate the objects and use your animations as transitions between slides.

To carry out a cross-fade, hold down the Shift key while selecting each object. Then select Edit > Cross-fading. You see the Cross-fading dialog box.

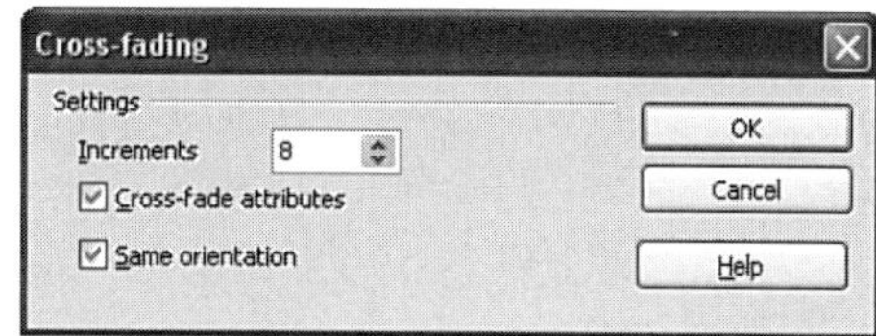

The Cross-fading dialog box.

Set the desired increments, attributes, and orientation. In this example you start with two shapes.

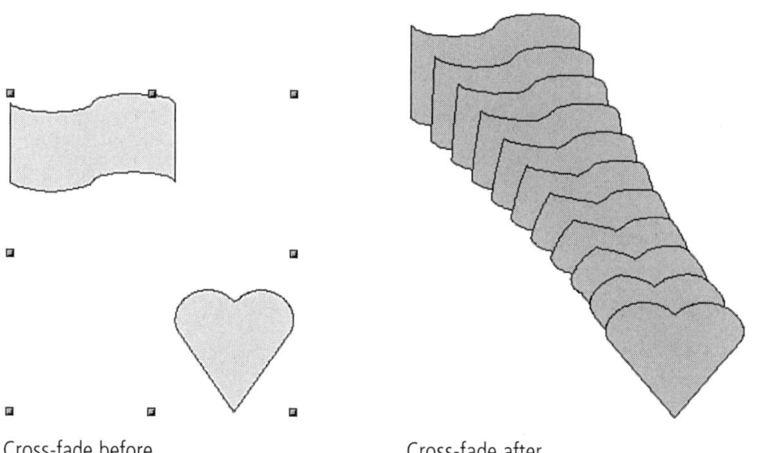

Cross-fade before.

Cross-fade after.

Increments is set to 8, which means that there are eight shapes between the original two shapes. OOo Draw makes eight transitions that gradually change the shape of a banner into a heart, so you see a total of nine images including the original.

Exchanging Objects with Other Programs

To save a Draw image in a foreign format, select File > Export. You can choose from many different format options.

Depending on the file type, you are prompted with other menu options after you name the file and click Save. For example, if you choose to save the file in HTML format, you see the Conversion Wizard. This wizard creates a Web page for each page in your Draw document. You can choose to create the Web page at any time by clicking the Create button.

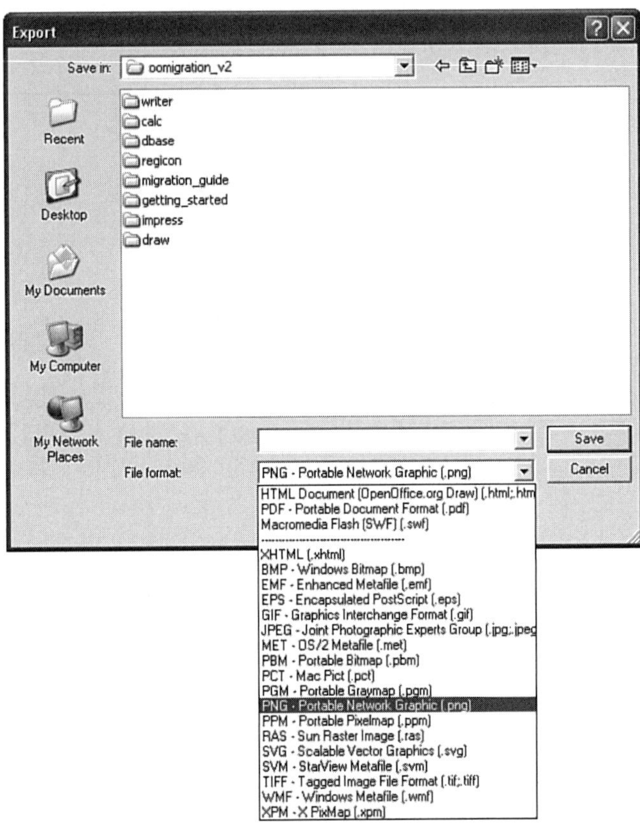

Export options.

The first screen of the wizard allows you to choose the design for all the pages, either from an existing design or by creating a new one.

Export step 1.

Next you choose how you want to publish your Web document: Standard HTML Format, Standard HTML with Frames, Automatic, or Webcast (using ASP or Perl; unfortunately, OOo has no direct support for PHP yet). You can also create a title page.

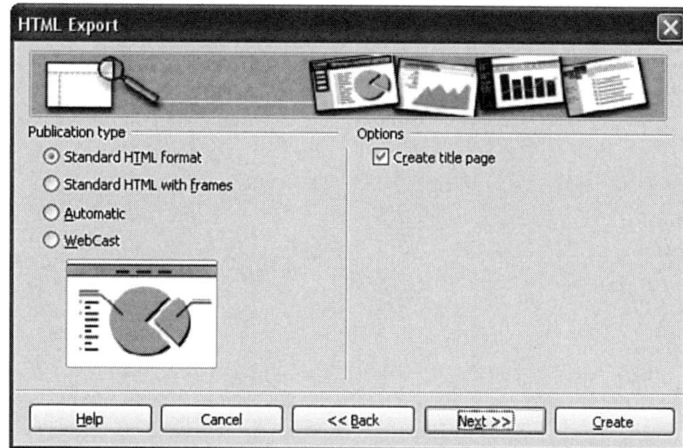

Export step 2.

Decide how the images will be saved (GIF or JPG). Choose Monitor resolution and Effects if needed.

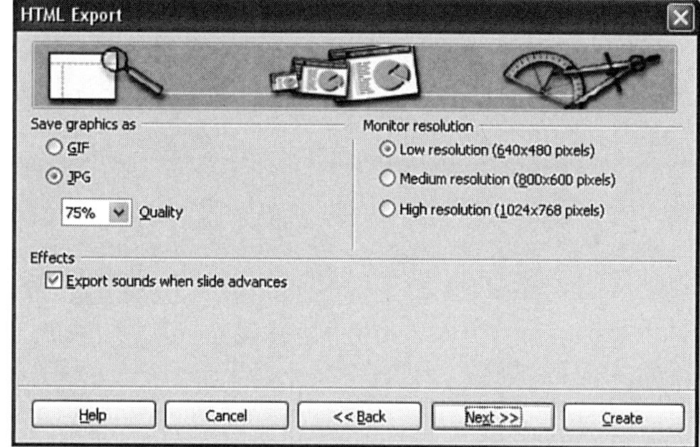

Export step 3.

Enter details about the author if you like; this is optional.

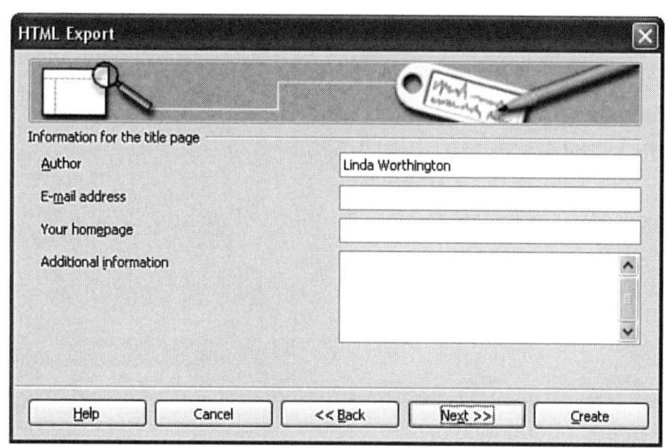

Export step 4.

Choose the navigation button style that will be used to move from one page to another.

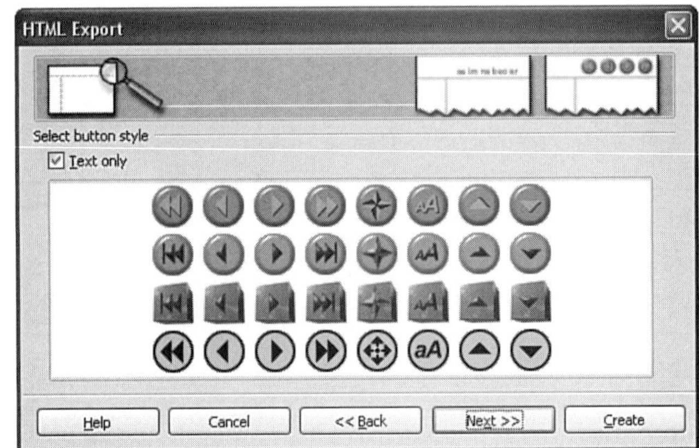

Export step 5.

Define the color scheme for the created pages. If you want to change the default colors, click the Text, Hyperlink, Active Link, Visited Link, or Background buttons. You see the color palette.

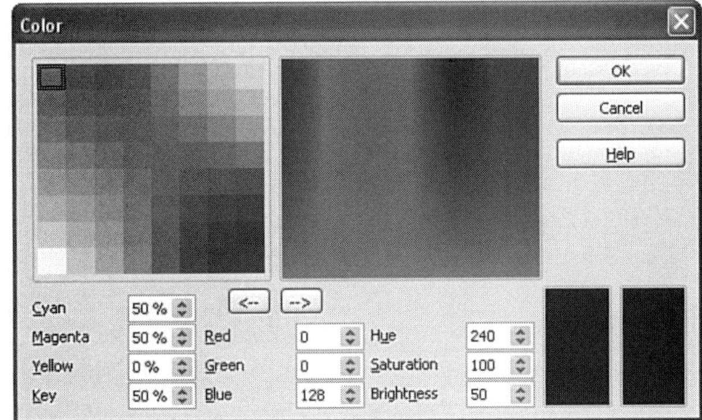

The color palette.

Here is where you can change the color to reflect the desired CMYK, RGB, Hue, Saturation, and Brightness.

You can save your color scheme so that it will appear on the first page of the HTML Export Wizard.

When your color scheme is complete, click the Create button.

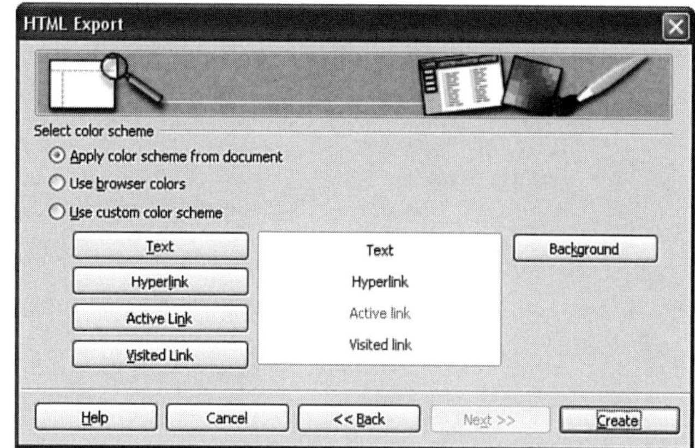

Export step 6.

Going with The Gimp

Although OOo Draw is a wonderful tool, it has its limits. If you want to create graphics for a Web site; do extensive photo retouching, image composition, or image authoring; or perform most other truly advanced image functions, you should try The Gimp (http://gimp.org). This program is free and runs on many different operating systems, including Linux, UNIX, Windows, and Mac OS X.

The Gimp offers many features, plug-ins, and capabilities:

- A full suite of painting tools: brushes, pencil, airbrush, and cloning
- Memory management
- High-quality anti-aliasing
- Alpha channel support
- Multiple undo/redo
- Supports the GIF, JPEG, PNG, XPM, TIFF, TGA, MPEG, PS, PDF, PCX, and BMP file formats and many others

This is only a small list of the features and capabilities that The Gimp has to offer.

But if your graphic needs are simple, OOo Draw will probably do everything you need to liven up your text documents, slide shows, and spreadsheets.

Chapter 8

OOo Impress: Smooth, Sophisticated Slide Shows

By Rob Reilly

Chapter 3, "OOo Impress: Slide Shows That Will Impress Almost Anyone," covered the basics of using OpenOffice.org Impress. Now we'll take it a step further and explore more advanced features such as slide transitions, object animations, and using different view modes. We'll also look at interesting ways to customize text and graphic objects. We'll wrap up the chapter with a few productivity tips to help you streamline your show production.

Getting from Slide to Slide with Transitions

To move from slide to slide in Impress, click to advance to the next slide and right-click to go backwards. If you don't want to use the mouse, you can use the Page Up/Page Down keys.

But to add a little more excitement, you might want to have one slide fade into another or have the current slide checkerboard into the next one. Impress has many different slide transition effects you can use. Use the Tasks pane to choose which ones you want.

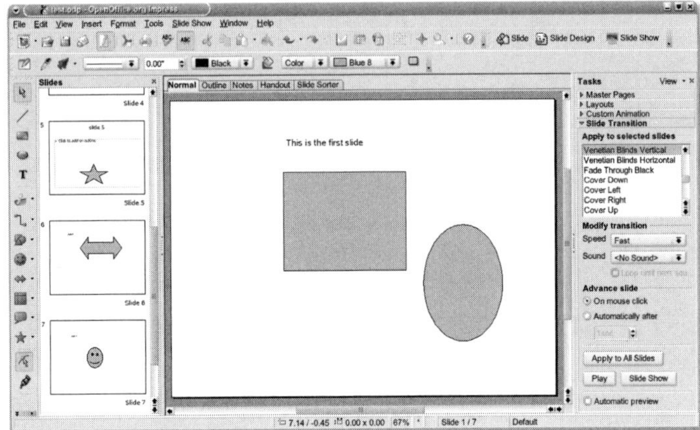

Viewing the Tasks pane in the main window.

You can turn the Tasks pane on or off by selecting View > Task Pane from the main Impress toolbar.

Choose the slide you want to transition from, and then select the transition effect from the Tasks pane and the Slide Transition menu.

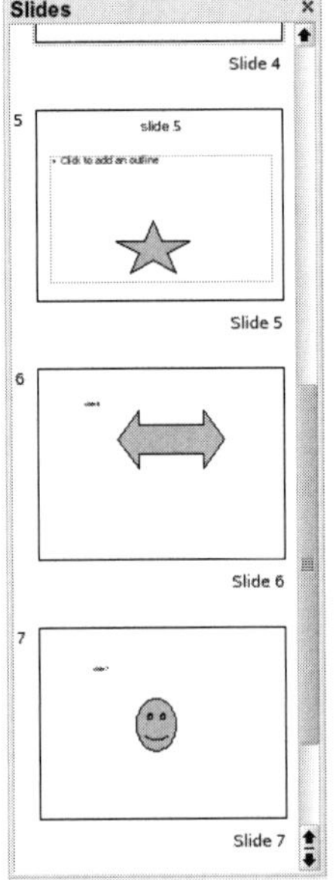

Choosing a slide to transition.

You can apply the same transition to all slides by clicking the Apply to All Slides button at the bottom of the Slide Transition menu. You can also apply a transition to certain slides by holding down the Ctrl key while clicking the ones you want.

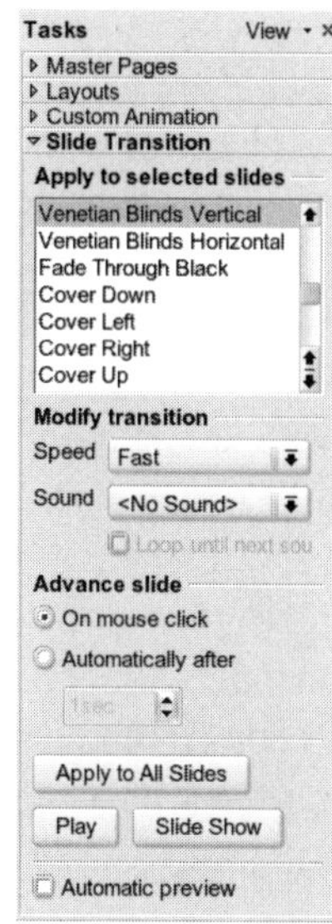

Choosing the transition type.

Bringing Life to Your Show with Object Animations

Object animations are used to make things move in your slide show.

You can add an animation effect to an object (such as text, a box, or a picture) by clicking the object and then clicking the Add button in the Custom Animation pane.

A new window appears. This is where you select the animation effect you want to apply.

Select an effect. Then click the Play button to see how the object moves with your chosen effect. You can use the Slide Show button to see the animation full-screen.

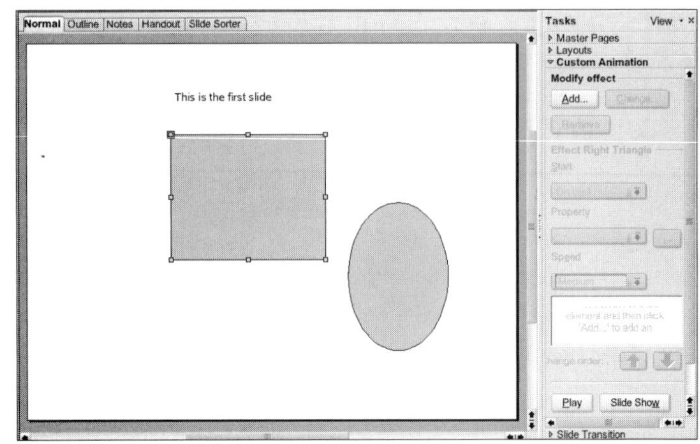

Choosing an animation effect.

You can animate more than one object on your slide. Select a different object, click the Add button, and add a new animation effect. The second object's name appears in a little window above the Play and Slide Show buttons. To change the order of animation, select the object's name and use the adjacent arrow buttons to change the sequence.

Animation effects are organized in the menus as Entrance, Emphasis, Exit, and Motion Paths. The Entrance and Exit effects refer to how an object enters or exits a slide. Emphasis brings attention to an object. An example is the Flash Bulb animation, where the original object starts growing and eventually pops like a flashbulb. Motion paths make an object follow a predetermined path. An example is the Star motion path, where an object appears and traces an invisible star pattern on the screen.

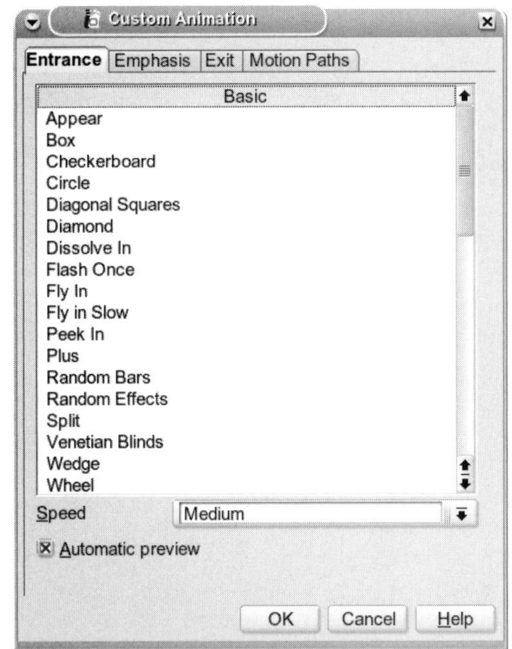

Selecting a specialized animation effect.

The degree of an animation effect also has a range. These include Basic, Exciting, Moderate, and Special. They're grouped under the Entrance, Emphasis, Exit, and Motion Paths menus and can be seen by scrolling up and down through the selections. A basic effect is a simple animation, such as when an object appears on the screen. More dramatic effects are found in the "exciting" group, such as making an object bounce or boomerang. You can explore the other two and see if they meet any of your needs.

You can change animation effects by double-clicking the object's name in the little window. For example, the Effect Option window lets you set the direction in which an object flies into the slide. You can add sounds from this window, too. Of course, the options that appear in the window vary depending on the effect.

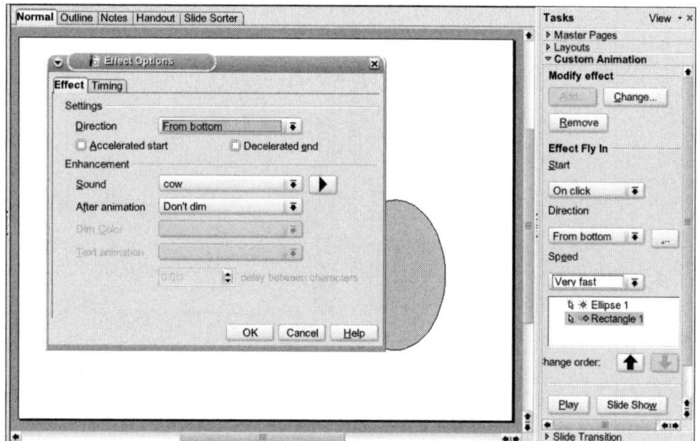

Changing the effect object direction.

Using Normal Mode for Most Work

OpenOffice Impress has several different ways for you to view your slides. You can change the view mode by clicking one of the tabs at the top of the main Impress edit screen area or by selecting a mode on the View tab on the main toolbar.

Normal Mode

Most of your time will be spent in Normal view mode as you work on slides. Normal mode is for adding graphics, moving objects, aligning things, and generally editing what is on the slide.

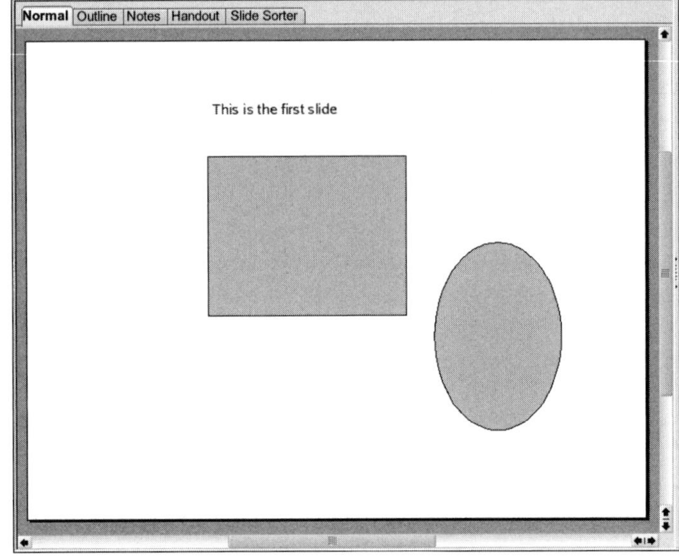

Viewing in Normal mode.

Outline Mode

Outline mode is a great way to organize your slide show in the beginning. It lets you create an outline of your main points, one per slide. You can also use subtopics, which show up as bullet points. Notice in the figure that the main points and subtopics show up on the slide-sorter thumbnails as you add text to the outline.

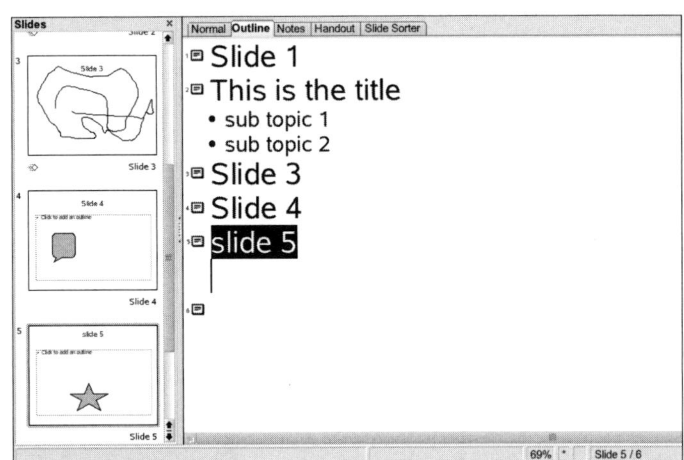

Viewing in Outline mode.

Handout Mode

Another useful view is Handout mode. Handouts let you group slides in book form, with six slides per page by default. The slide books can then be stapled together and given to audience members as take-home material. Some presenters like to distribute handouts at the beginning of a slide show so that the audience members can take notes on their printed slides.

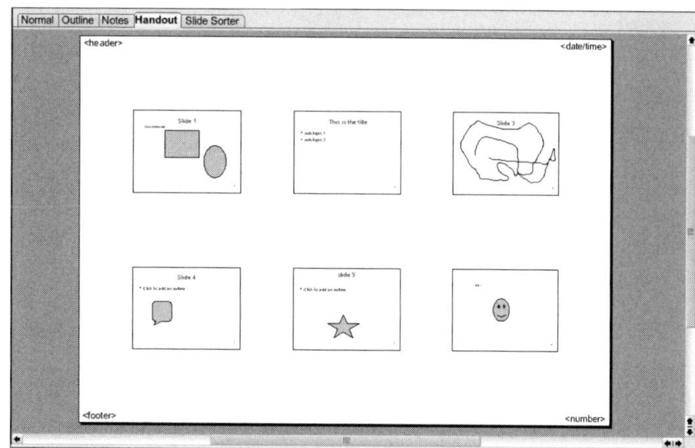

Viewing in Handout mode.

If you look closely at the Handout screen, you'll see a small field in each corner. On the default screen these are <header>, <time/date>, <footer>, and <number>. These are nothing more than text boxes with standard fields inserted in them. If you want to customize these fields instead of using the defaults, click the text in the field. An outline box appears. Go to the Insert tab on the main Impress toolbar and choose Fields to see a list of available standard fields that you can use. Click a field name to insert it in the text field.

To print your handouts, select File > Print, and then click OK. The whole slide show goes to the printer, with six slides per page. You can then run off as many copies as needed using a copier.

Notes Mode

The Presentation Notes function lets you add information (notes) to pictures of your slides that can be printed and used as handouts. The notes themselves don't show up on the slides during your presentation. You might print a copy of the notes for yourself if you have a big presentation and need some additional prompting beyond the slides' content. This is a great way to create a "speaker's outline" that keys directly to your slide show so that you don't lose your place.

To add a note to a slide, click the Notes tab at the top of the edit window. Select the "Click to add notes" section at the bottom of the edit window, and enter any text you like. The slide is displayed in the top part of the view. To get back to regular slide editing, minus the notes, click the Slide Sorter tab. The notes are still there; you just can't see them in Slide Sorter mode.

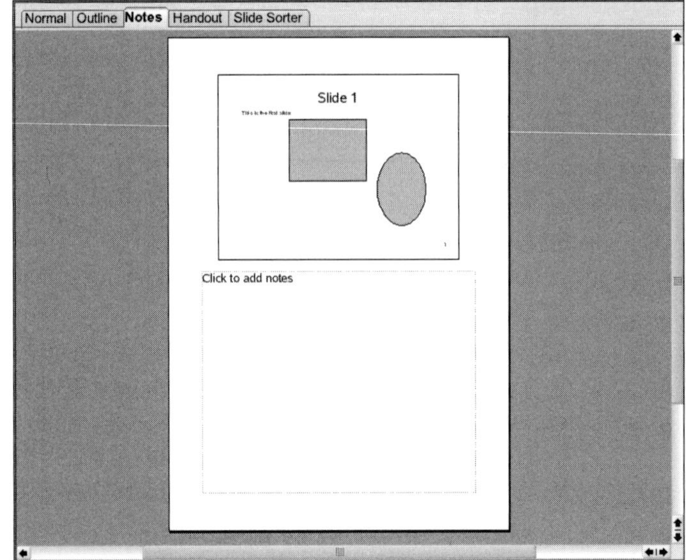

Viewing in Notes mode.

Jazzing up Your Text

OpenOffice.org Impress has some nice text tools that help you look like a presentation pro, including a wide range of fonts, colors, alignments, and other options.

You add basic text to a slide by using the text button on the left side of the main Impress slide edit screen. It's marked with a T. Click the button, move the cursor to the slide, and start typing. When you finish typing your text (or pasting text from another file), click the arrow button to get back to object selection mode.

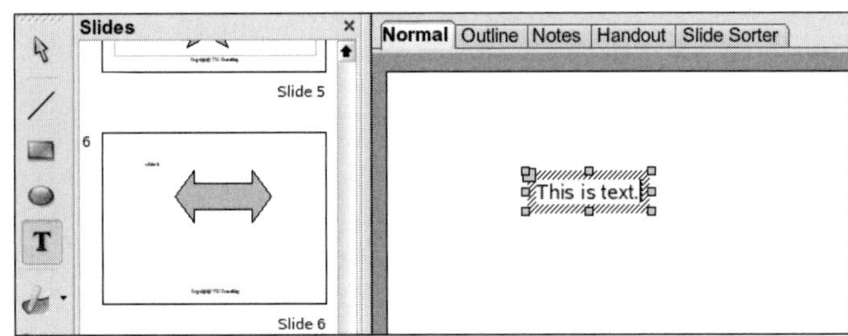

Adding text to a slide.

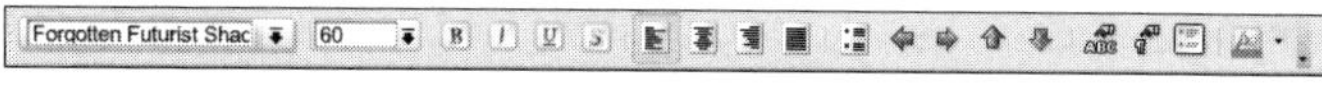

Using the text toolbar.

Every operation that can be done to text in OOo Writer or Calc can also be applied to text in Impress. Common changes such as fonts, text size, color, and boldfacing are done by highlighting the text you want to change and then choosing the attribute to change from the main Impress toolbar. There are literally hundreds of fonts from which to choose. (The text toolbar shows up when you are active within a text box.)

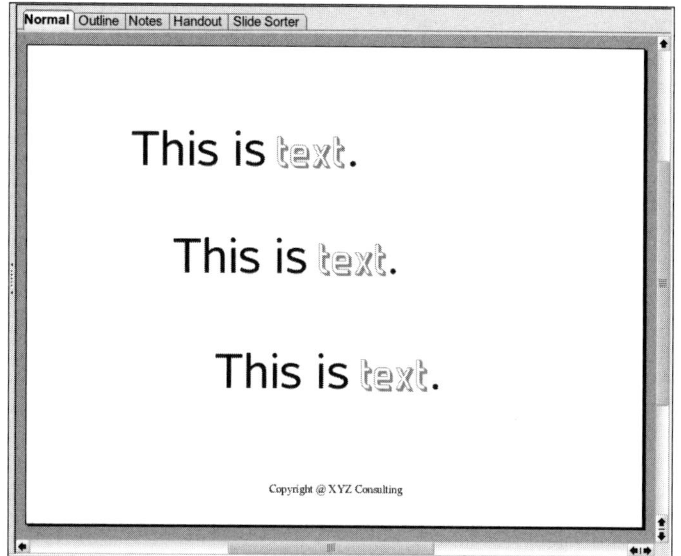

Using the alignment tool.

As you brainstorm your slide show, you might add text very quickly as ideas stream out without worrying about where they are placed on the slide. Later, you can use the alignment tools to help get everything arranged in nice, neat rows or columns. Click and hold to draw a box around the text you want to align. Next, roll the cursor over the edge of the text box to get the four-sided arrow. Right-click and choose the Alignment and Left menu items. The selected text becomes left-aligned. You can also cut, copy, paste, and arrange from the same text menu. Explore the menu and experiment with some of the other effects.

Another worthwhile text tool is called Fontwork. Click the tiny arrow at the bottom of the left-side toolbar.

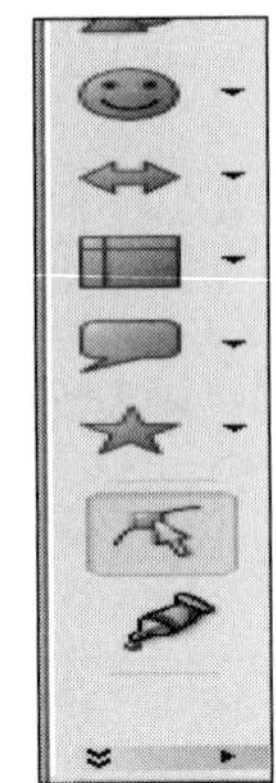

Selecting the Fontwork icon.

At the top of the menu this brings up, you can click the Fontwork item to get the Gallery screen. Select a style by highlighting it. A text box shows up in your slide. Click the text box and start typing to add your own text. If you click the text box, the Fontwork options screen appears. This is where you change your text's shape, height, alignment, and character spacing.

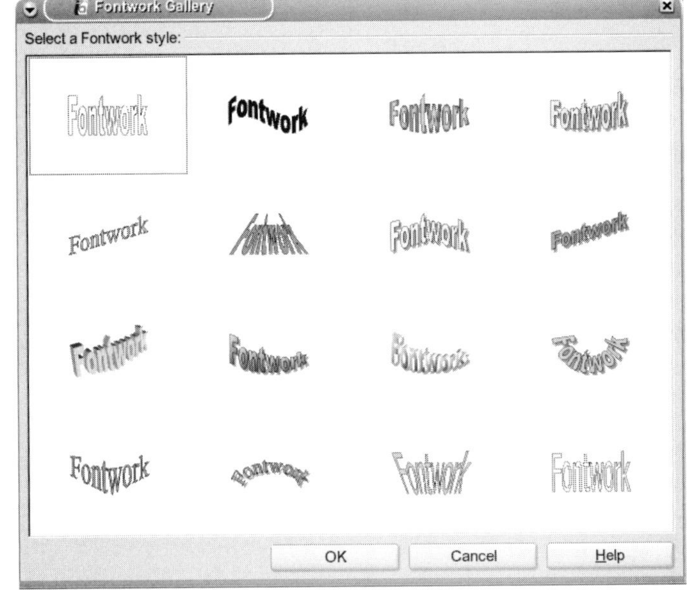

Various Fontwork styles.

Customizing Graphics

OOo Impress has a lot of interesting shapes that you can drag from the toolbar on the left side of the main edit screen into your slide. Choices include circles, ellipses, squares, faces, stars, and various other geometric shapes. Some of the buttons also have dropdown menus of specialized shapes.

There are buttons for freehand and connector lines as well. Use a connector line when you want to "connect" one shape to another. This type of line is great for charts where you want to show a process flow. A nice feature of the connector line is that even if you move the shapes, your lines stay connected and reroute themselves automatically. (Impress uses vector graphics, which means that shapes are objects, not collections of pixels.)

You can also add images to your slides by selecting Insert > Picture > From File.

You can then resize the image by grabbing the outline handles and dragging the image to its new size. Click the graphic to get the four-sided arrow, and then move the graphic around on your slide.

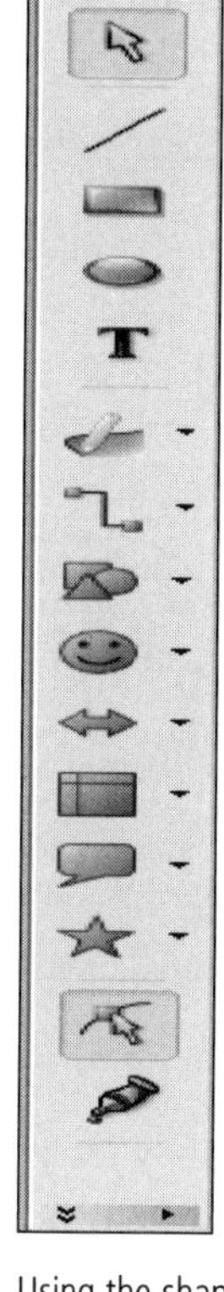

Using the shapes toolbar.

Stepping up Your Productivity

No discussion of advanced features would be complete without a few helpful parting productivity tips. These will help you save some time and effort.

Create a Master Slide

Master slides help set the overall look and feel of your presentation. They can also save time by putting commonly repeated objects on a "master" slide that functions as a basic slide template for the whole presentation. All slides display what is on the master slide. Common information on a master slide might be a company name, a corporate logo, or a copyright notice.

Make changes to the master slide by clicking the View tab on the main Impress toolbar, followed by the Master menu item, and finally Slide Master. You can then insert text, graphics, and so on into the slide using the various tools and insert menus. Remember that whatever you put on the master slide shows up on all the other slides, so it may take a little jockeying to get everything in the right spot.

Add a Background Image

Using a background color, pattern, or image on your slides can make them more appealing and professional. It can also help set the theme for your entire slide show. While you can set a background for just one slide, you also have the choice of applying a selected background to the whole presentation.

To do this, select Format > Page on the main toolbar. You can then click the Background tab to make changes. Your choices include filling a background with a color, a gradient, a crosshatch, or a bitmap image. Try a few of the backgrounds to get a feel for what they look like in your slides. To undo a background, select Edit > Undo on the main toolbar.

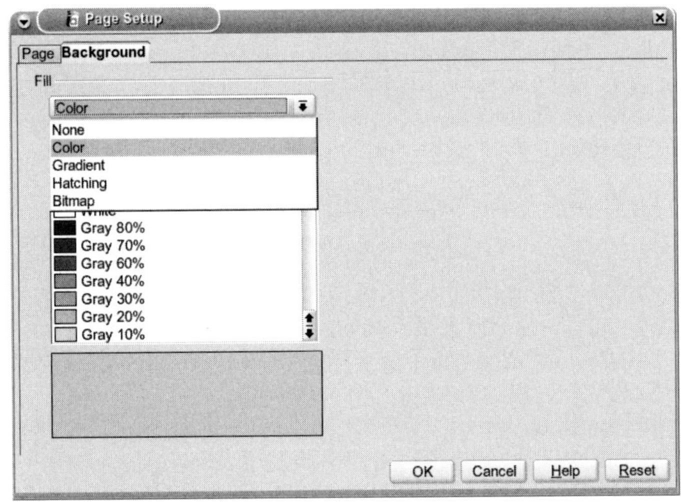

Choosing a background color.

If you'd like to add a custom background, such as a picture or graphical image, insert the image on your master slide. Select View > Master > Master Slide to get to the edit screen. Select Insert > Picture > From File to get a list of pictures. Use the arrow keys to move to the folder that contains your desired image.

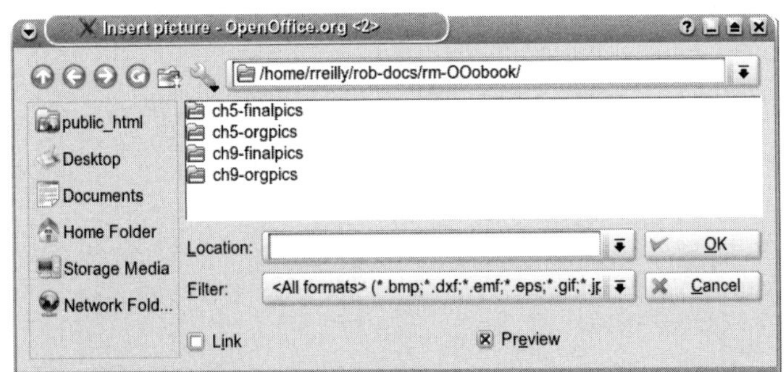

The menu for choosing a background image.

Double-click the image to insert it into your slide. Highlight the image and drag its edge to the desired size. Keep in mind that a vivid, complicated scene may make reading the text on the slide difficult. You might want to use images that are very light or have been "washed out" so that you can see the information contained on your slides.

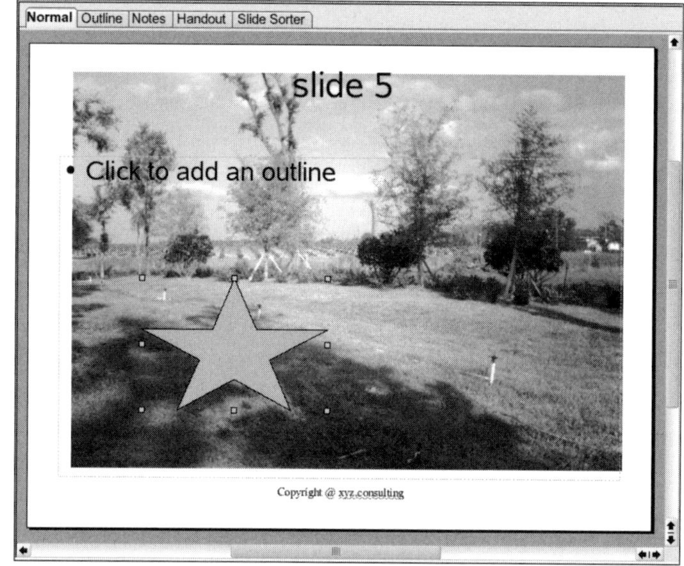

Hard-to-read text.

Back up Your Slides with Transparencies

Sometimes, bad things happen to laptops, projectors, and slide show presentations. A good way to be prepared in case of disaster is to print your entire slide show on transparent film for use with an overhead projector. Just load transparent film into your color printer and use the Print button under the File tab on the main toolbar.

Slide Shows Are Only Part of Public Speaking

Most slide shows are used to make speeches more interesting. While a good slide show can help hold an audience's attention, you also need to speak clearly and coordinate what you say with your slides. Practice is the key to becoming a good speaker. Practicing making slides helps you make better slides. But the most important thing of all is to practice giving your presentation while running your slide show so that your words and your slides work together to give your audience the information they need instead of working at cross-purposes and leaving them confused.

Chapter 9

Make Calc Spreadsheets Dance for You

By Lalaine "Lizza" Capucion

"Advanced" doesn't necessarily mean "complicated." With a little practice, OOo Calc's advanced features will help you make elegant spreadsheets for almost any home or office need.

Creating "Natural-Language" Formulas

OOo Calc can compute any formula as long as the syntax is right. With Microsoft Excel, you have to know the coordinates of the values you want to compute. But OOo Calc has a "natural language," meaning you can create formulas using column and/or row labels.

Using the file Sales.ods, you will make a "natural-language" formula.

Our original formula in cell E4 was =D4*0.3. Instead of using that formula, let's change the coordinate D4 to the word *Sales,* because we are computing sales multiplied by 0.3, or 30 percent. The results are the same.

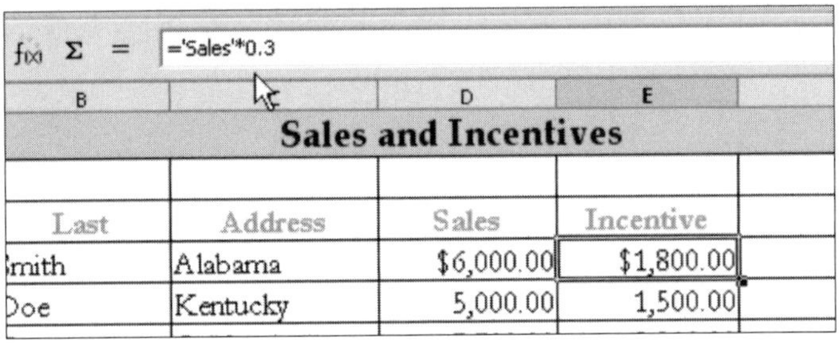

A "natural-language" formula.

Using the "Intelligent Sum" Button

Making a "natural-language" formula is fine, especially when you're working with only one cell, but the Intelligent Sum or Sum button can change a formula for a number of cells at the same time.

For example, if you want to know the total amount of the figures in the Sales column, type "Total Sales" in C15 and change the font to bold 15-point Garamond. Then place the cell pointer on the cell where you want to put the total sales amount. (Changing the font is optional, but it helps your calculation stand out.)

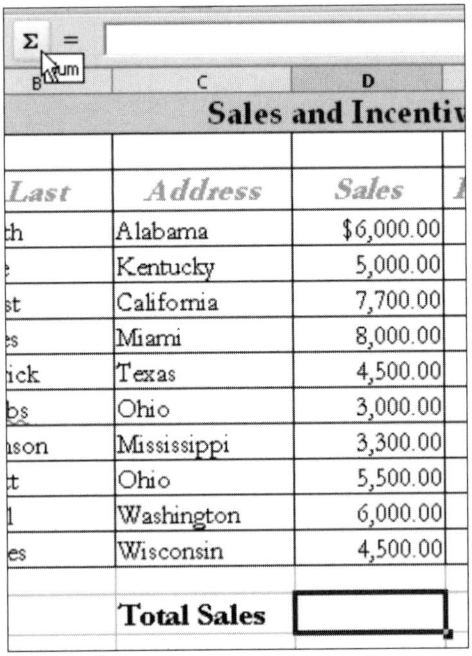

The Intelligent Sum button.

Click the Intelligent Sum button. It shows a blue border around the column with the sales values. You can adjust the cell range by using the arrow key. Press Enter.

=SUM(D4:D14)

C	D
Sales and Incentiv	
Address	Sales
Alabama	$6,000.00
Kentucky	5,000.00
California	7,700.00
Miami	8,000.00
Texas	4,500.00
Ohio	3,000.00
Mississippi	3,300.00
Ohio	5,500.00
Washington	6,000.00
Wisconsin	4,500.00
Total Sales	=SUM(D4:D14)

How the Intelligent Sum button works.

You see the Total Sales amount.

Wisconsin	4,500.00
Total Sales	**$53,500.00**

Total Sales.

Working with Stylist and Autoformat in Calc

Next you will work with styles and formatting using the Autoformat function in OOo Calc. In other words, you will design (style) your table to make it more presentable. There are two ways to do this.

One way is to put in styles manually. Highlight the cell range you want to format, and then select Format > Styles and Formatting or press F11.

First	Last	Address	Sales	Incentive	Remarks
John	Smith	Alabama	$6,000.00	$1,800.00	

Choosing a range to format.

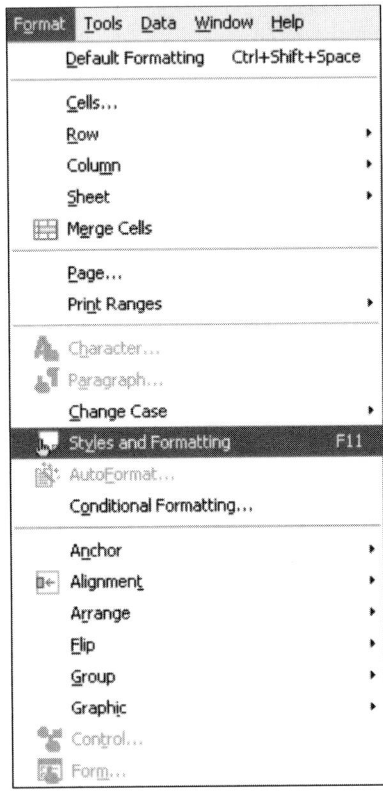

The Styles and Formatting option.

You see the Styles and Formatting box. Click Heading. All the headings in your table automatically change.

	First	Last	Address	Sales	Incentive	Remarks
4	John	Smith	Alabama	$6,000.00	$1,800.00	
5	Jane	Doe	Kentucky	5,000.00	1,800.00	
6	Jack	Frost	California	7,700.00	1,500.00	
7	George	Bates	Miami	8,000.00	2,310.00	
8	Bob	Patrick	Texas	4,500.00	2,400.00	
9	Eugene	Krabs	Ohio	3,000.00	1,350.00	

Styles and Formatting
Default
Heading
Heading1
Result
Result2

The Styles and Formatting box.

First	Last	Address	Sales	Incentive	Remarks
John	Smith	Alabama	$6,000.00	$1,800.00	

Styles output.

Another way to format styles is by using the AutoFormat button. Unlike Styles and Formatting, AutoFormat has its own templates for the whole worksheet. Let's see how it works.

Highlight the main worksheet. In this case, this is all the cells from A3 to F15.

First	Last	Address	Sales	Incentive	Remarks
John	Smith	Alabama	$6,000.00	$1,800.00	
Jane	Doe	Kentucky	5,000.00	1,800.00	
Jack	Frost	California	7,700.00	1,500.00	
George	Bates	Miami	8,000.00	2,310.00	
Bob	Patrick	Texas	4,500.00	2,400.00	
Eugene	Krabs	Ohio	3,000.00	1,350.00	
Bill	Johnson	Mississippi	3,300.00	0.00	
Connie	Scott	Ohio	5,500.00	0.00	
Camilla	Wall	Washington	6,000.00	1,650.00	
Charlie	Wales	Wisconsin	4,500.00	1,800.00	
		Total Sales	**$53,500.00**		

The highlighted worksheet.

Select Format > AutoFormat or click the AutoFormat button.

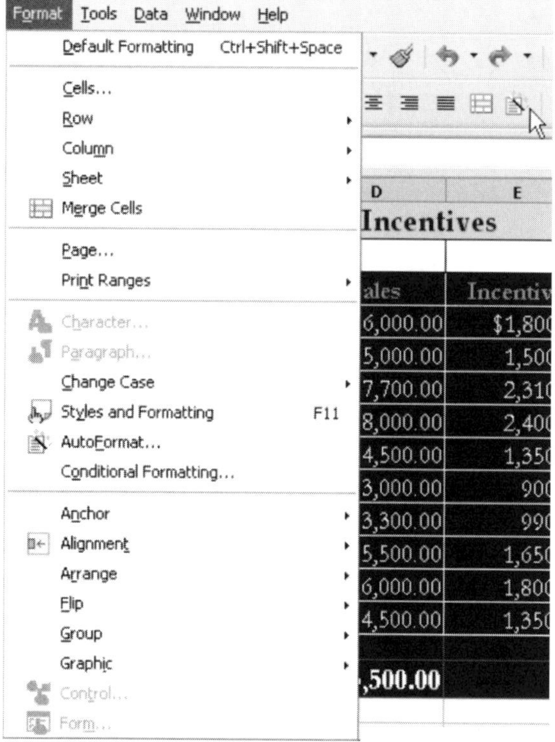

The AutoFormat menu option and button.

This displays the AutoFormat box. Here you can choose from several formats. It has a preview feature so that you can easily visualize the output. You can also add custom formats and formatting options, such as the Number Format, Borders, Font, Pattern, Alignment, and AutoFit Width and Height. Choose the Default format and uncheck the AutoFit Width and Height, because you want to retain the original dimensions. Click OK.

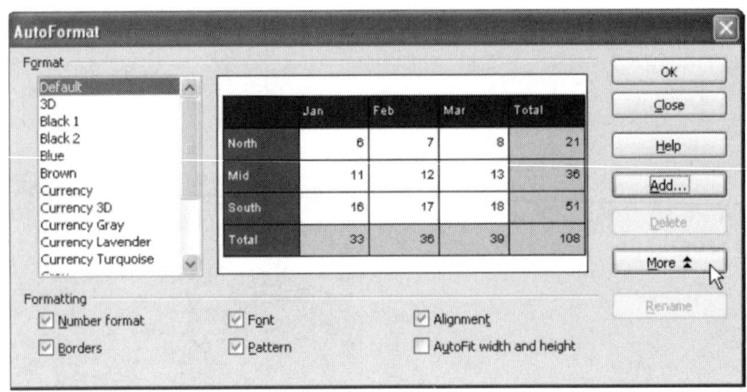

The AutoFormat box.

The spreadsheet now has a new look.

Sales and Incentives

First	Last	Address	Sales	Incentive	Remarks
John	Smith	Alabama	6000	$1,800.00	
Jane	Doe	Kentucky	5000	$1,800.00	
Jack	Frost	California	7700	1500	
George	Bates	Miami	8000	2310	
Bob	Patrick	Texas	4500	2400	
Eugene	Krabs	Ohio	3000	1350	
Bill	Johnson	Mississippi	3300	0	
Connie	Scott	Ohio	5500	0	
Camilla	Wall	Washington	6000	1650	
Charlie	Wales	Wisconsin	4500	1800	
		Total Sales	$53,500.00		

AutoFormat output.

Letting Scenario Manager Help with What-If Projections

The Scenario Manager is another useful OOo Calc tool. It is used to make in-depth calculations or to create formulas that include a what-if situation.

Let's look at our table. Let's say the Incentive formula needs to be changed because you want to give a 30% incentive for every salesperson who makes sales of $4,000 and more. You also want to note that those with sales of $3,999 or less are not eligible for the incentive.

First, I put the incentive multiplier—0.3 percent, or 30% of a salesperson's production—under the Total Sales figure.

Total Sales	$53,500.00	
Incentive Multiplier	0.3	

The incentive multiplier.

Next, you change the formula in cell E4. Type =IF(D4>4000;D4*D17;0). The incentive is now automatically computed if Sales is greater than $4,000, and 0 if it's less than. Remember to use a ; (semicolon) as the formula separator. You should also put a $ (dollar sign) before and after the D in D17 in the formula to make it an absolute value. You can now copy the formula from cells E5 to E13 to automatically get the incentives for the other salespeople.

IF =IF(D4>4000;D4*D17;0)

	A	B	C	D	E	F
1	Sales and Incentives					
2						
3	First	Last	Address	Sales	Incentive	Remarks
4	John	Smith	Alabama	$6,000.00	=IF(D4>4000;D4*D17;0)	
5	Jane	Doe	Kentucky	5,000.00	1,800.00	
6	Jack	Frost	California	7,700.00	1,500.00	
7	George	Bates	Miami	8,000.00	2,310.00	
8	Bob	Patrick	Texas	4,500.00	2,400.00	
9	Eugene	Krabs	Ohio	3,000.00	1,350.00	
10	Bill	Johnson	Mississippi	3,300.00	0.00	
11	Connie	Scott	Ohio	5,500.00	0.00	
12	Camilla	Wall	Washington	6,000.00	1,650.00	
13	Charlie	Wales	Wisconsin	4,500.00	1,800.00	
14						
15			Total Sales	$53,500.00		
16						
17			Incentive Multiplier	0.3		
18						

The what-if projection.

In other words, the formula says the following: If a certain salesperson achieves sales of $4,000 or greater, his or her incentive is the result of Sales multiplied by 0.3. If his or her sales are less than $4,000, no incentive is given.

Sales and Incentives					
First	Last	Address	Sales	Incentive	Remarks
John	Smith	Alabama		=IF(E4=0;"Amateur";"Outstanding")	
Jane	Doe	Kentucky	5,000.00	1,800.00	Outstanding
Jack	Frost	California	7,700.00	1,500.00	Outstanding
George	Bates	Miami	8,000.00	2,310.00	Outstanding
Bob	Patrick	Texas	4,500.00	2,400.00	Outstanding
Eugene	Krabs	Ohio	3,000.00	1,350.00	Outstanding
Bill	Johnson	Mississippi	3,300.00	0.00	Amateur
Connie	Scott	Ohio	5,500.00	0.00	Amateur
Camilla	Wall	Washington	6,000.00	1,650.00	Outstanding
Charlie	Wales	Wisconsin	4,500.00	1,800.00	Outstanding
		Total Sales	$53,500.00		
		Incentive Multiplier	0.3		

Final output.

You also want to know who your outstanding salespeople are, so you will make another formula using the what-if projection. If E4 equals 0, it generates an "Amateur" remark in column F4, and "Outstanding" otherwise. So type =IF(E4=0;"Amateur";"Outstanding").

Using and Creating Spreadsheet Themes

OOo Calc comes with a default set of formatting themes that you can apply to your worksheet. Click the Choose Theme icon; the Theme Selection box appears. Choose from several OOo Calc themes, and then click OK.

The Choose Theme icon.

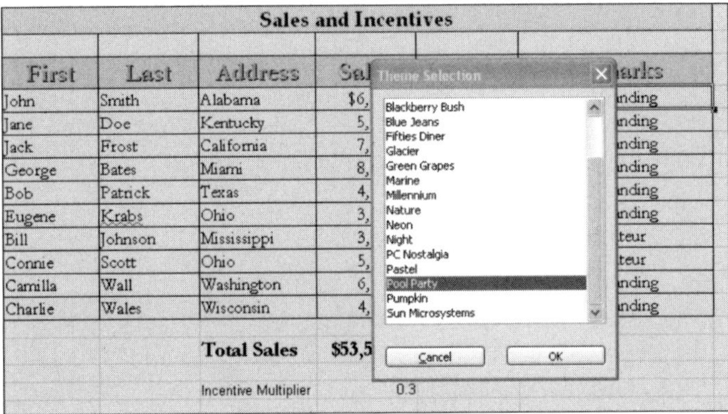

The spreadsheet Theme Selection box.

You can't add spreadsheet themes using OOo Calc, and they cannot be modified. But you can change their styles after you apply them in your spreadsheet, in essence creating your own themes.

Using DataPilot to Import and Manipulate Information from Databases Created with Other Software

Another feature of OOo Calc is the DataPilot. You can summarize your data and then arrange it so that you view only the data you need. It works like Microsoft Excel's Pivot Table. However, DataPilot has limitations. For one thing, it has no PivotChart feature. Also, you cannot have more than eight fields in the data, row, or column areas. However, you can use the data you already have to make a simple summary.

Going back to the sample table, let's make a summary showing only the Last, Sales, Incentive, and Remarks columns.

Select Data > DataPilot > Start. This automatically highlights your data.

The DataPilot menu option.

The Select Source box appears. Choose Current selection and click OK.

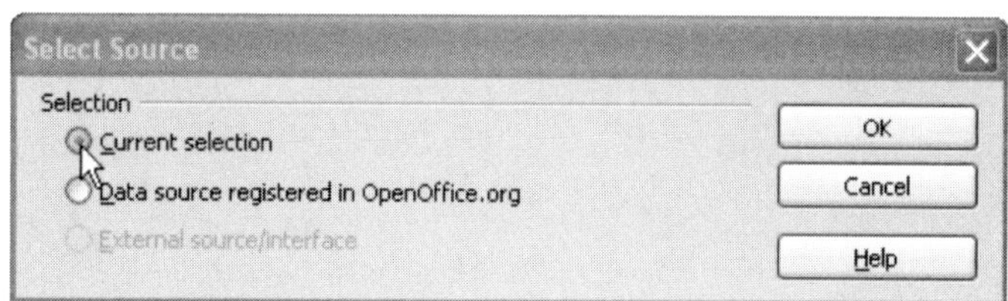

The Select Source box.

You now see the DataPilot options box. Place the fields you want to include in your summary in the desired box. In this case, you want only Last, Sales, Incentive, and Remarks. In the Results to box, choose new sheet and click OK.

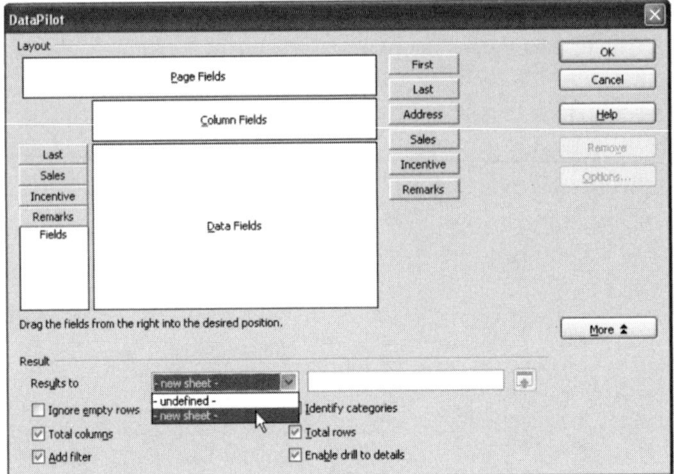

The DataPilot options box.

The summary is placed in a new worksheet. Now you can view only the data you need.

	A	B	C	D	E
1	Last	Sales	Incentive	Remarks	
2	Bates	8000	2310	Outstanding	
3	Doe	5000	$1,800.00	Outstanding	
4	Frost	7700	1500	Outstanding	
5	Johnson	3300	0	Amateur	
6	Krabs	3000	1350	Outstanding	
7	Patrick	4500	2400	Outstanding	
8	Scott	5500	0	Amateur	
9	Smith	$6,000.00	$1,800.00	Outstanding	
10	Wales	4500	$1,800.00	Outstanding	
11	Wall	$6,000.00	1650	Outstanding	
12	**Total Result**				
13					

Sample output from DataPilot.

Mail Merging with OOo Writer Documents and Calc Data

Mail Merge is probably one of OOo Calc's most helpful features. What if you have a letter or email you want to send to all your salespeople? Let's say the body of the letter for each salesperson is essentially the same; the only things you need to change are the names of the recipients and information on their sales performance. Imagine how long it would take you to create all those letters if you did so manually and you had thousands of salespeople. Mail Merge does this tedious task for you.

I made a simple letter, mail.odt, using OOo Writer. Take note of the words that are in bold italic. Those words will be replaced automatically with the data in your sales and incentives table in OOo Calc.

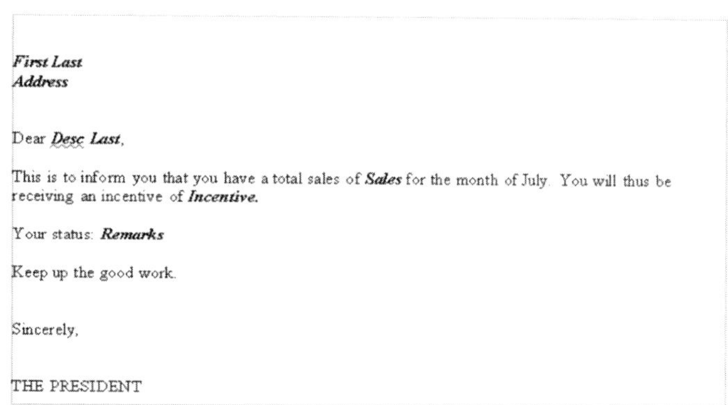

First Last
Address

Dear ***Desc Last,***

This is to inform you that you have a total sales of ***Sales*** for the month of July. You will thus be receiving an incentive of ***Incentive.***

Your status: ***Remarks***

Keep up the good work.

Sincerely,

THE PRESIDENT

A letter using OOo Writer.

I edited the sales and incentive table and took only the needed data and saved it as merge1.ods. You will merge the data from this table to make multiple copies of the letter for multiple recipients.

	A	B	C	D	E	F	G
1	Desc	First	Last	Address	Sales	Incentive	Remarks
2	Mr.	John	Smith	Alabama	$6,000.00	$1,800.00	Outstanding
3	Ms.	Jane	Doe	Kentucky	5,000.00	1,800.00	Outstanding
4	Mr.	Jack	Frost	California	7,700.00	1,500.00	Outstanding
5	Mr.	George	Bates	Miami	8,000.00	2,310.00	Outstanding
6	Mr.	Bob	Patrick	Texas	4,500.00	2,400.00	Outstanding
7	Mr.	Eugene	Krabs	Ohio	3,000.00	1,350.00	Outstanding
8	Mr.	Bill	Johnson	Mississippi	3,300.00	0.00	Amateur
9	Ms.	Connie	Scott	Ohio	5,500.00	0.00	Amateur
10	Ms.	Camilla	Wall	Washington	6,000.00	1,650.00	Outstanding
11	Mr.	Charlie	Wales	Wisconsin	4,500.00	1,800.00	Outstanding
12							

The edited sales and incentive table.

First, you need to tell OOo Writer what data you need for merging. Click the Data Sources button. You see a window containing files for Mail Merge.

The Data Sources button.

Data sources.

Because the file you need is merge1, click the + box next to merge1. You see the categories under merge1. Click the + box next to Tables; it shows Sheet1. When you click Sheet1, the whole table shows on the right side.

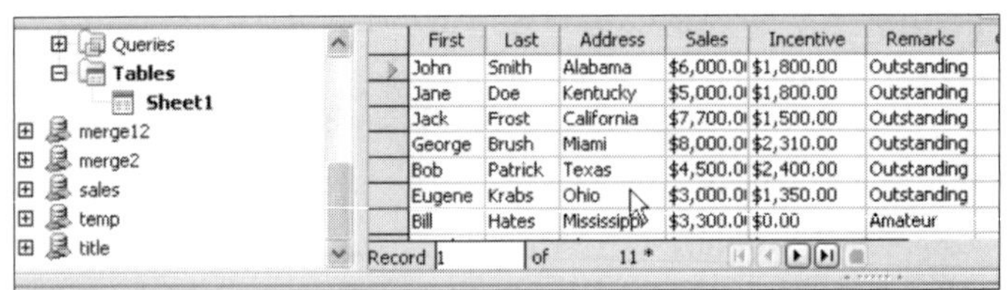

The data sources directory.

Replace all the bold italic words with the corresponding fields by dragging the field name from the OOo Calc table to the letter. It is replaced by the field name enclosed in angle brackets. You are now ready to run the Mail Merge Wizard.

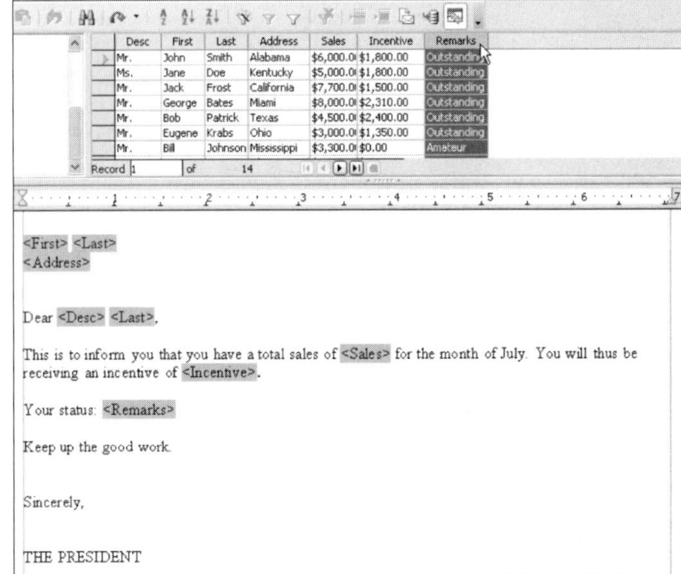

Click-and-drag fields.

Select Tools > Mail Merge Wizard.

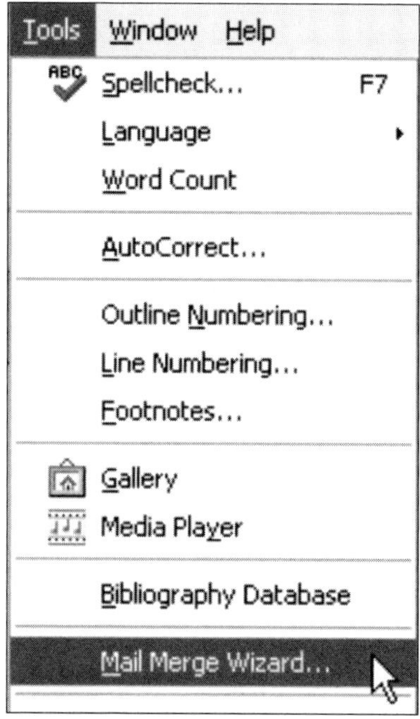

The Mail Merge Wizard.

The Mail Merge Wizard gives you an easy step-by-step process. First, select the starting document. You will use the default, which is "Use the current document." Click Next.

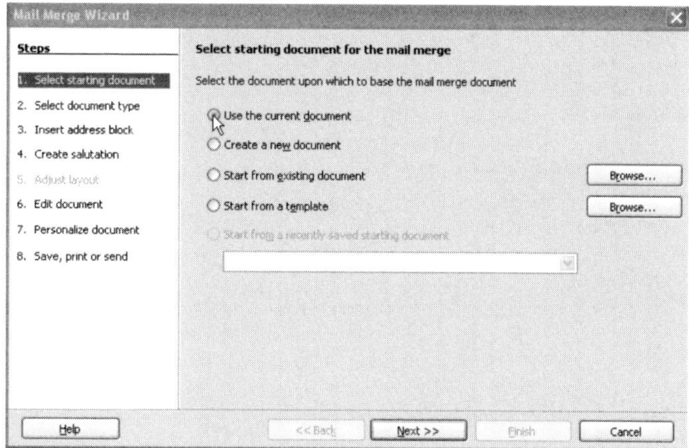

Mail merge step 1.

Now you need to select the document type, which in this case is Letter. Click Next.

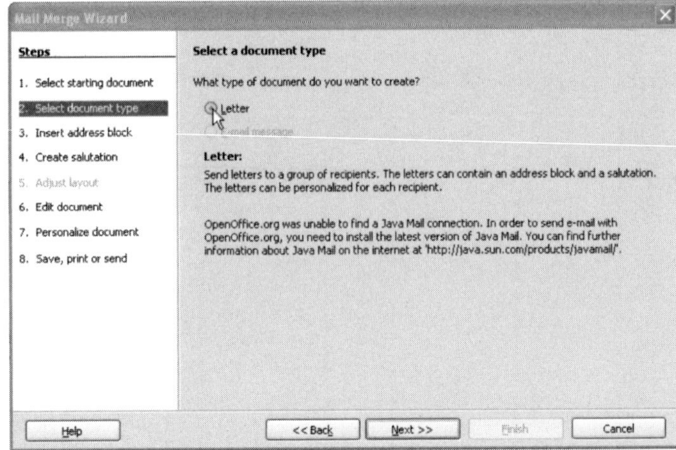

Mail merge step 2.

The wizard asks for the address list. Because you have already defined the OOo Calc file to use, you will skip this. Click Next.

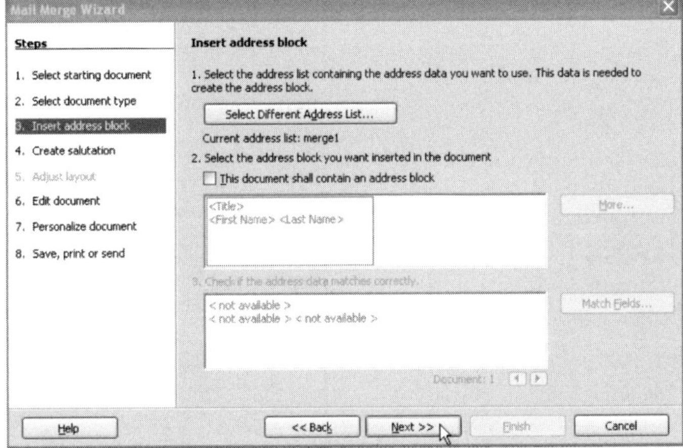

Mail merge step 3.

You don't need to create a salutation for this document, so click Next.

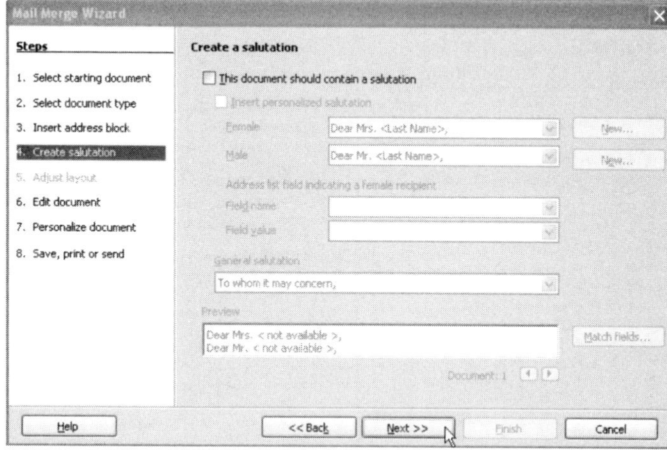

Mail merge step 4.

The wizard skips step 5 because you don't need to adjust the layout. In step 6, you have the option of previewing and editing your document, but because you've already edited the file, just click Next.

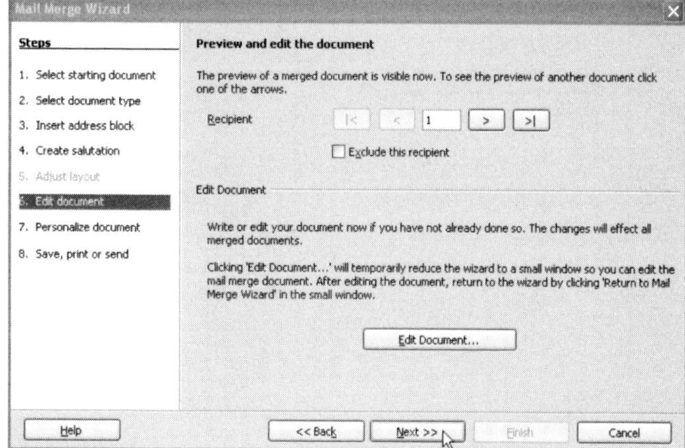

Mail merge step 6.

When you click Next, the Mail Merge process starts.

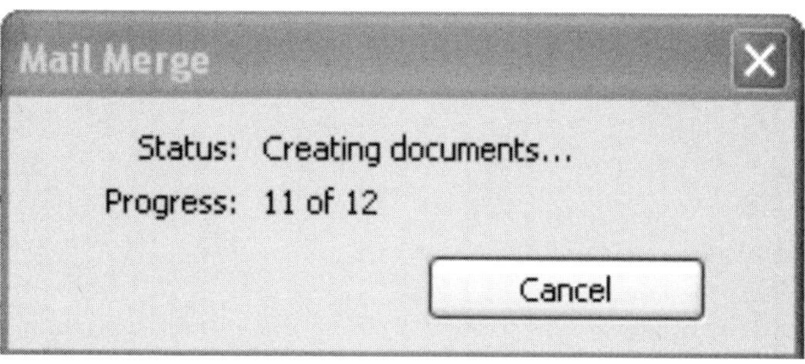

The mail merge process.

In the next step, the wizard asks if you want to personalize the mail merge document. Skip this for now and click Next.

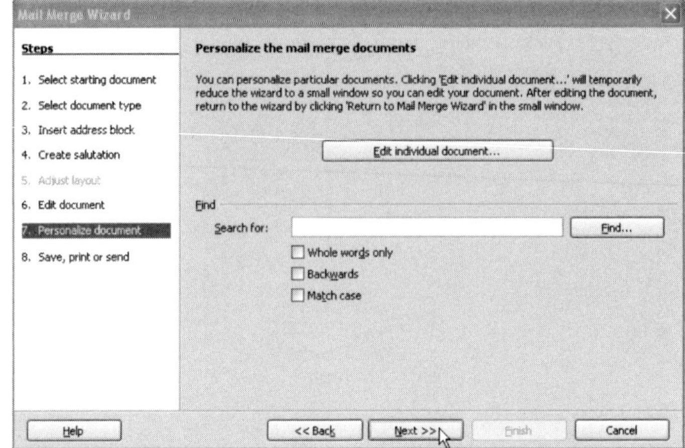

Mail merge step 7.

You will save the merged document as a single file, so enable the "Save merged document" and "Save as single document" options, and click Save Documents.

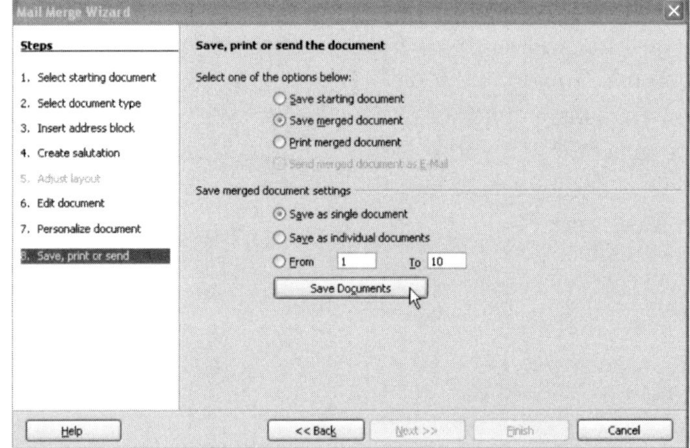

Mail merge final step.

Give the file a name, such as mailmerge.odt, and click Save.

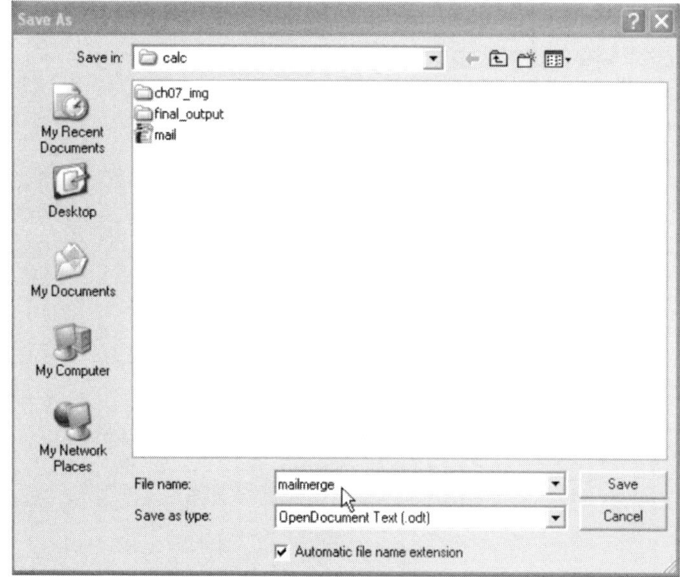

Saving.

You're almost done. Click Finish.

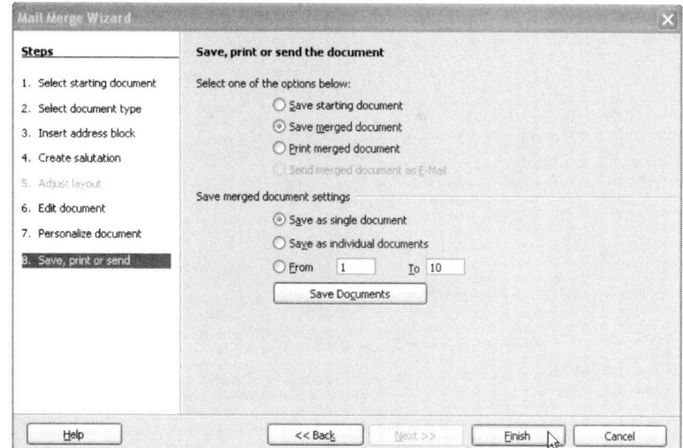

Finish.

Open mailmerge.odt to view the merged file.

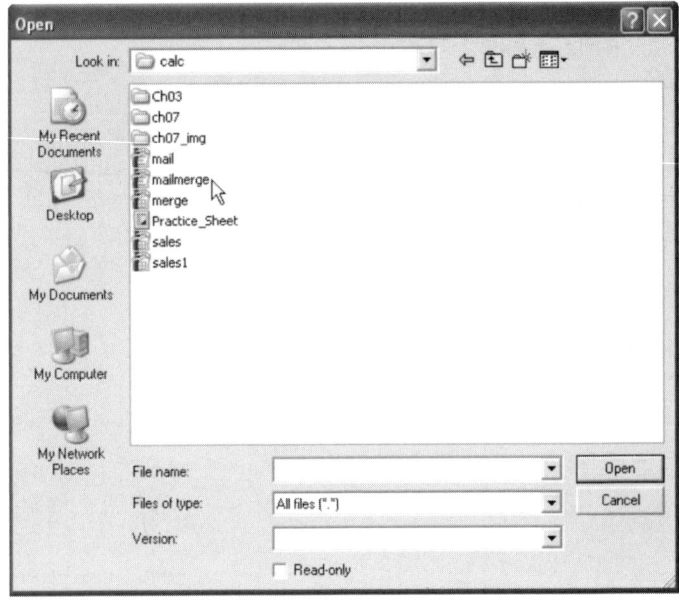

Opening the merged file.

You now have the final merged file. Whether you're dealing with several dozen letters or several thousand, Mail Merge does the work quickly and painlessly.

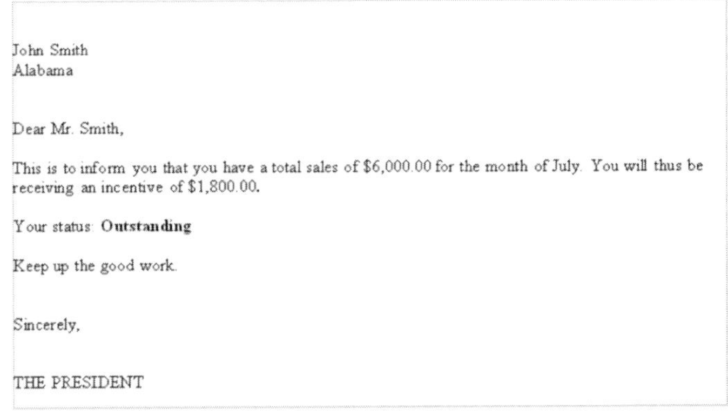

John Smith
Alabama

Dear Mr. Smith,

This is to inform you that you have a total sales of $6,000.00 for the month of July. You will thus be receiving an incentive of $1,800.00.

Your status: **Outstanding**

Keep up the good work.

Sincerely,

THE PRESIDENT

Final mail merge output.

Summing Up

So there you have it. You've seen how useful and practical Calc can be in several common spreadsheet situations. Keep in mind that the more you use Calc, the more you'll appreciate and become familiar with its time-saving features.

Chapter 10

OOo Database "Front End": Your Free Pass

By Rob Reilly

OOo can connect you to many types of databases, including MySQL, PostgreSQL, and others. Using the new Base application that is part of OOo 2, you can display, sort, filter, and even edit the data. You can also connect to your data while in Writer or Calc. You can create business letters or sales sheets using names, address, and other data contained in a database. And Base lets you grab and drop your data right into your Writer or Calc documents.

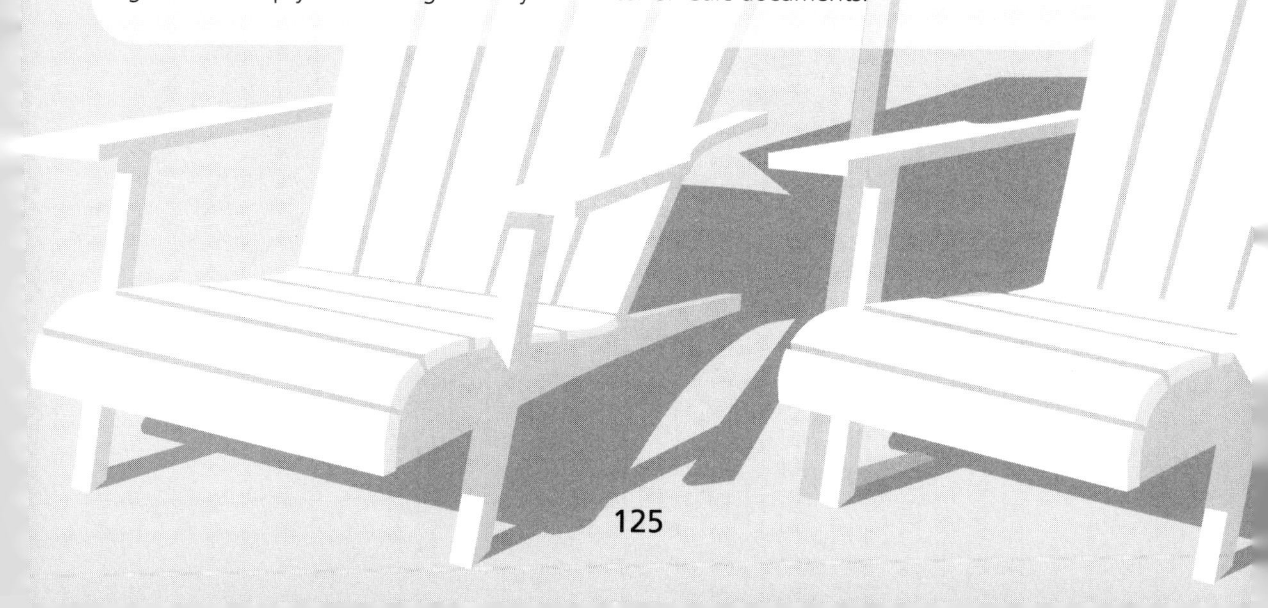

Do you need to build reports or forms? OOo can create those things, too.

The first step is to connect OOo to your data source.

Connecting to OpenOffice.org's Data Sources

MySQL is a common open source database, so we'll use it in our example.

The easiest way to make a connection to a database is to use the built-in OOo Base application to set things up. Then you have the choice of working with your data in Base or linking to the database within Writer or Calc.

Start OOo and select File > New > Database.

On the Database Wizard—Select Database screen, enable Connect to an Existing Database and use the dropdown Database type menu to select MySQL (because you're using MySQL). The Database Wizard descriptions and steps show up on the left. Click Next.

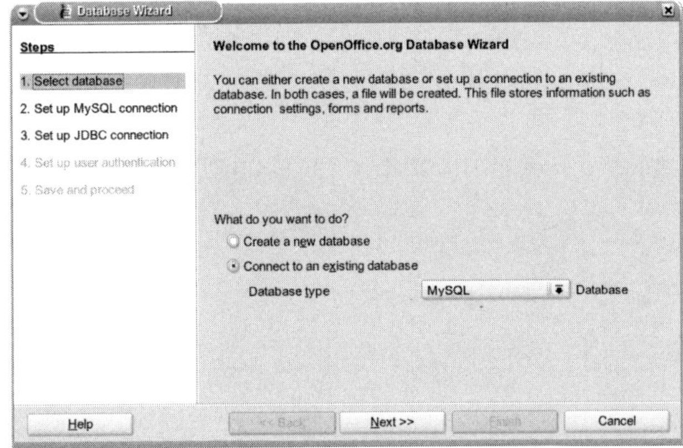

Selecting a database.

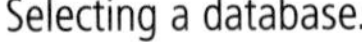

In step 2, enable Connect Using JDBC. This is the easiest driver to configure. Click Next.

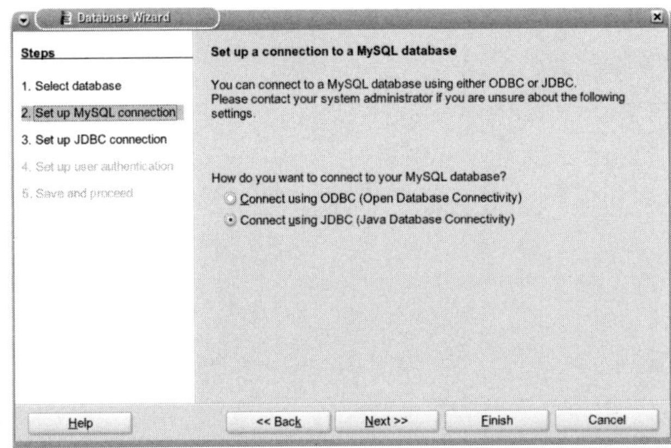

Connecting using JDBC.

In step 3, you can add the database name and server URL. If the MySQL database is running on your machine, you can use "localhost" as the server URL. (Your network or database administrator can help you gain access to a database on another machine. Try to develop a cooperative working relationship with your administrators.) Click Next.

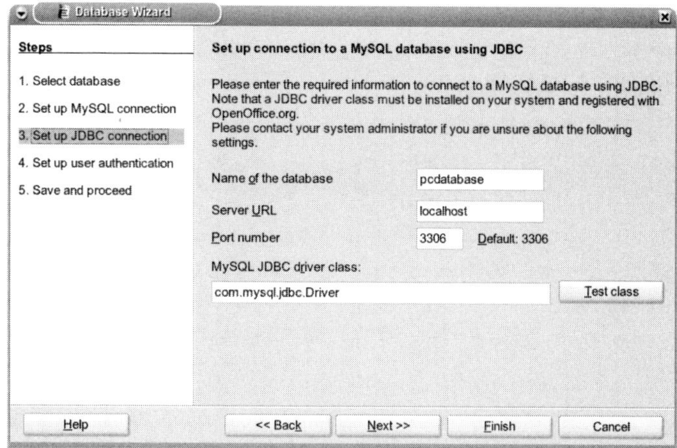

Adding a database name and server URL.

In step 4, you can enter your user name for the database and check the Password Required box. (Talk to your network or database administrators if you need help with this.) Click Next.

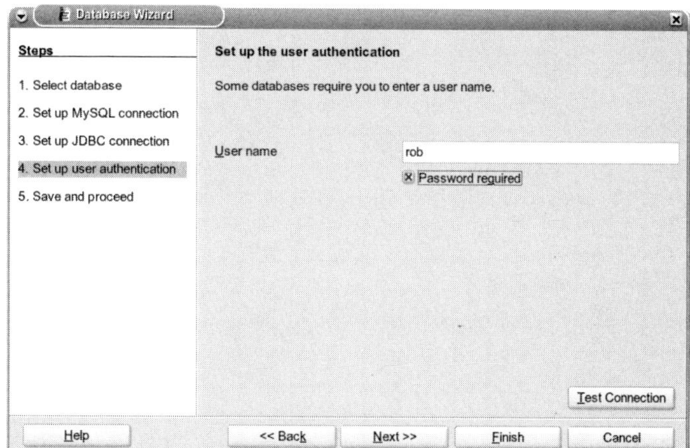

Setting up a database user name.

Step 5 finalizes the settings for the Database Wizard by registering your database (posting your database name to the internal OOo connection listing) within OOo. If you have write access to the MySQL database tables, check the Open the Database for Editing box.

Click Finish.

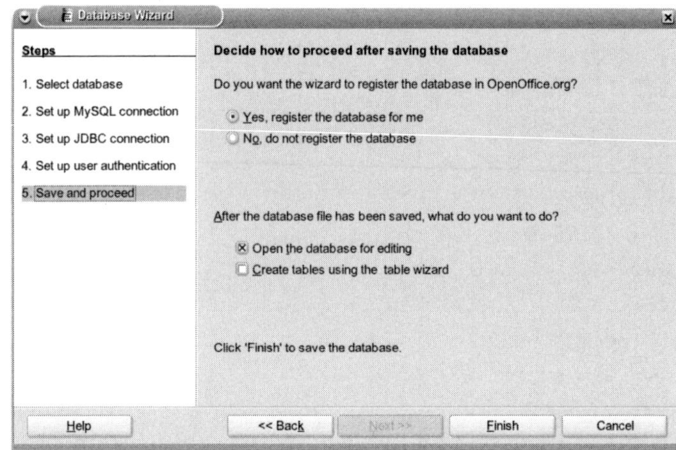

Opening the database for edits.

You can then save the setup to a Base file.

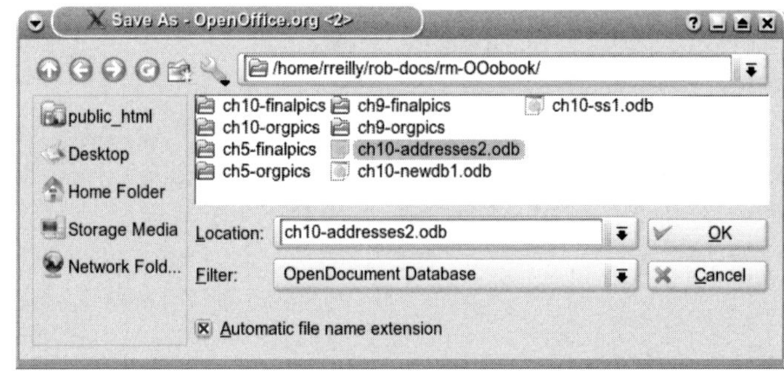

Saving the setup.

After you save the file, the Base application automatically opens, and you can start working with the database records.

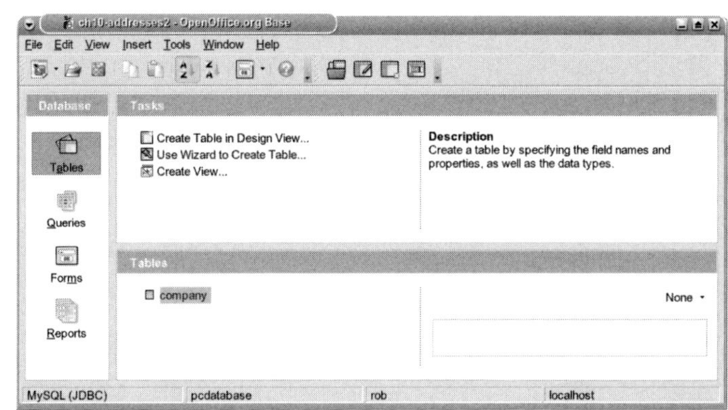

The main Base application screen.

Take a look at the records in your database by clicking the Tables icon (in the Database pane) and then the table name (in the Tables pane).

Your data appears in a tabular format.

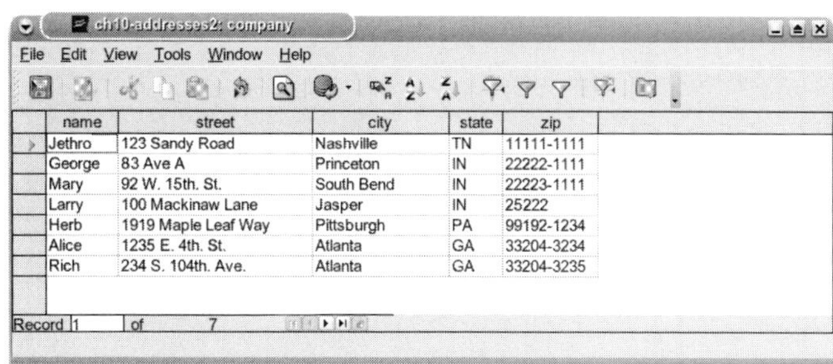

name	street	city	state	zip
Jethro	123 Sandy Road	Nashville	TN	11111-1111
George	83 Ave A	Princeton	IN	22222-1111
Mary	92 W. 15th. St.	South Bend	IN	22223-1111
Larry	100 Mackinaw Lane	Jasper	IN	25222
Herb	1919 Maple Leaf Way	Pittsburgh	PA	99192-1234
Alice	1235 E. 4th. St.	Atlanta	GA	33204-3234
Rich	234 S. 104th. Ave.	Atlanta	GA	33204-3235

Viewing your data in table form.

You are now connected to a MySQL database and can work with the records using the OOo Base application. Connections to other databases are created in a similar way. Some of the screens might be a little different, but they generally work the same as MySQL.

You may also want to connect to a spreadsheet or a delimited text file. Instead of using JDBC as the database connection, choose Spreadsheet or Text. Then select the filename and a few other parameters to complete the connection.

Once you've built a connection to your database, Writer and Calc will know about the connection the next time you start them up.

Leave the Base window open. You'll set up some SQL queries in a little while. Use the Window tab to switch back and forth between Base and Writer or Calc files.

Accessing a Data Source in Writer or Calc

Follow these steps to grab data from your database and insert it into your Writer documents.

Select New > Text Document. The procedures work almost exactly the same way for Calc.

Select Data Sources under the View tab. A new window appears with a listing of all the registered database names. Click Data Sources again to hide the window.

In the data sources window, click the database you set up in Base. Click the + in a box to the left of the Tables icon to show which ones are available. Click the table name to make the records appear. The sample database includes only the name, street, city, state, and zip.

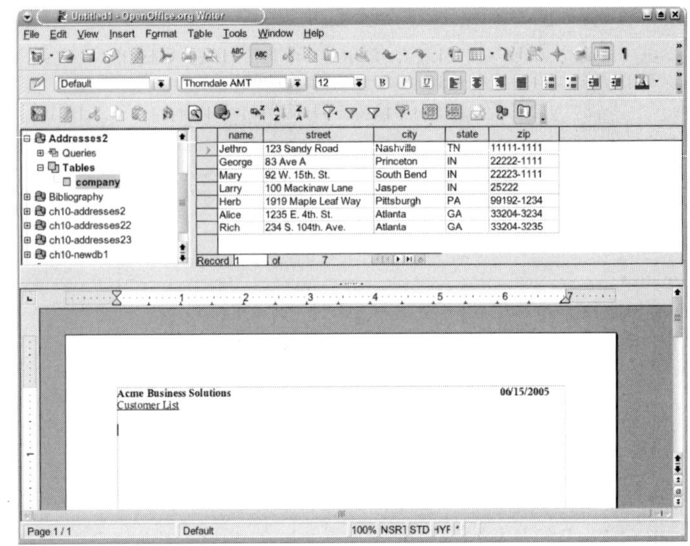

Using the data sources window to insert data into a document.

To paste a field from the database into your document, click the record field and drag it where you want it in the Writer editing window. In this example, the George, Herb, and Rich names are individually pulled down into the customer list.

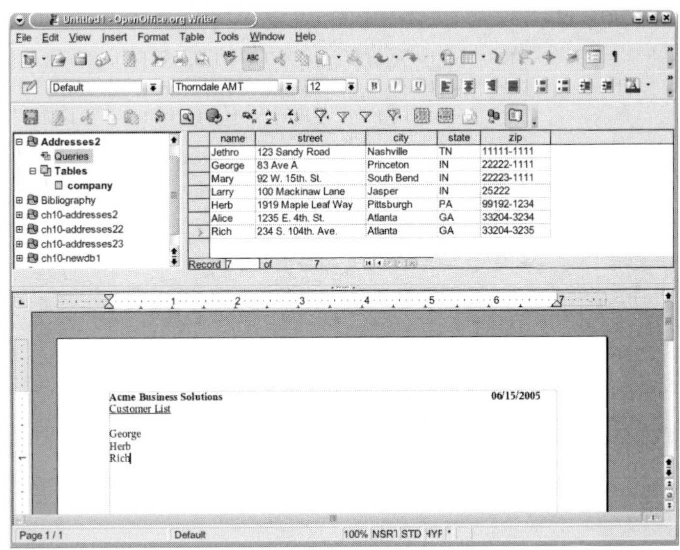

Dragging data into the document.

Click the box in the table's upper-left corner (just left of the names) to highlight all the fields. Then click the Data to Text button (the icon to the right of the funnel icons—text with little right arrow). Use the resulting window to drag down the fields as a table, fields, or text.

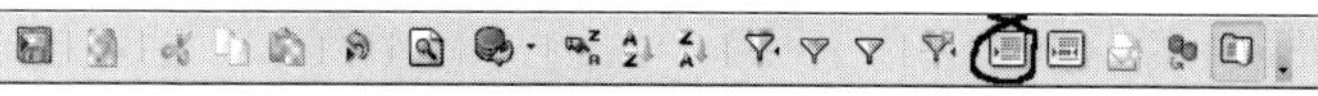

Dragging data as a table, fields, or text.

Enable the Text radio button, and then select and arrange the fields.

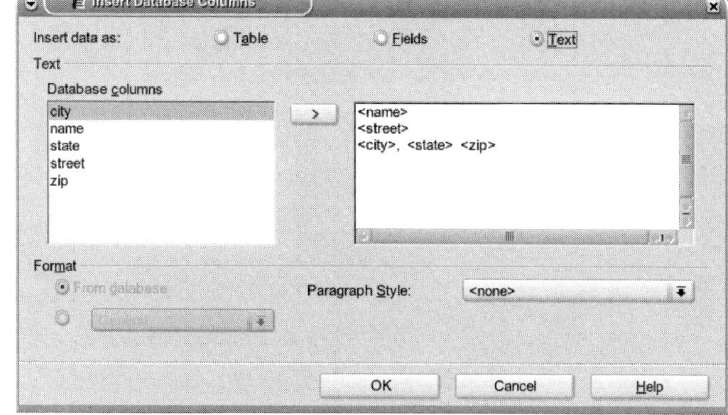

Arranging fields with the Text radio button.

Click OK. The contents of each record are copied into the document. This is a great way to make a list of addresses. Use this technique with other types of data to make basic text-oriented reports. Regular corporate-level reports will be discussed a little later.

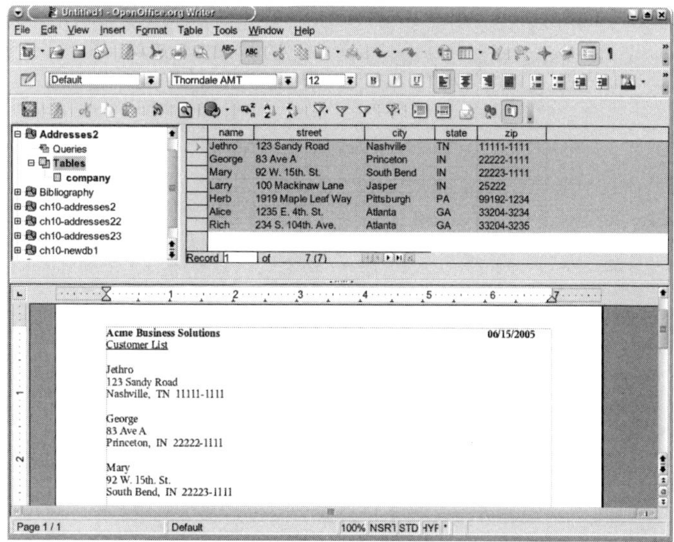

Copying the contents of each record into a document.

Highlighting a row (clicking the box to the left of the first field) and then clicking the Data to Text button copies the contents of that row into your document.

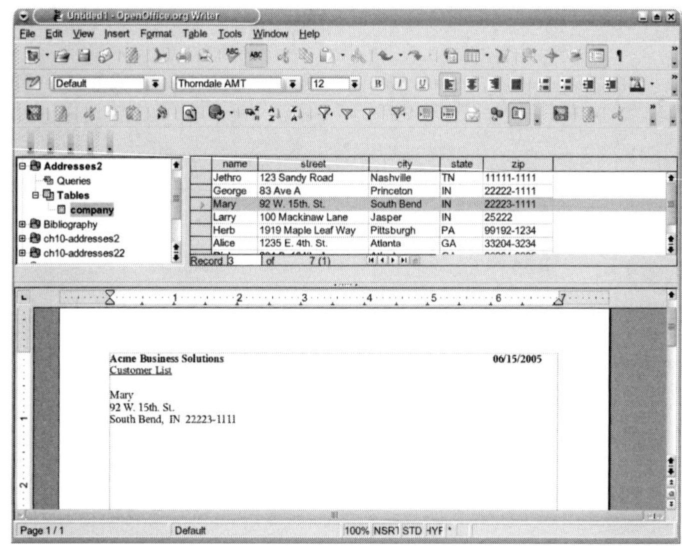

Copying a row of data into your document as text.

To create a table in your document instead of formatted text lists, use the Table radio button under the "data to text" button. This example uses only the name and city fields.

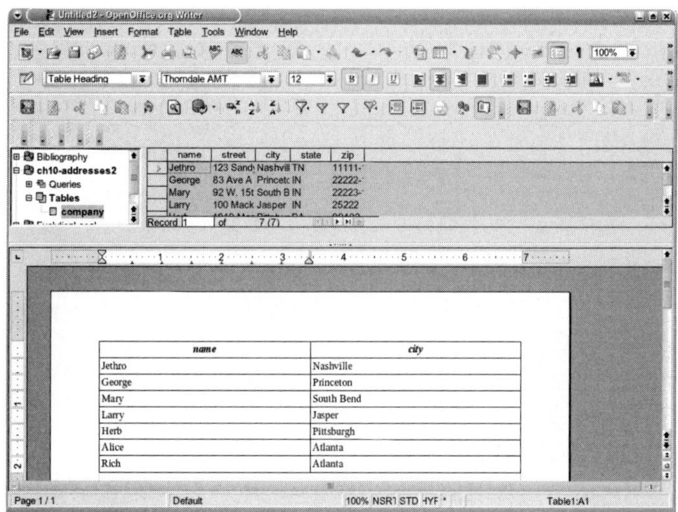

Copying a row of data into your document as a table.

Formulating SQL Queries—Even if You Know Nothing About Databases

A query picks out certain types or groups of data within a database for use in your document (or for any purpose, for that matter). This saves you the trouble of manually looking through all the records to find just what you want. Use the wizard to help set up SQL queries in OOo. Here's how it's done.

Click the Windows tab and select your Base file.

Click the Queries icon in the Database pane at the left. In the Tasks pane, select Use Wizard to Create Query.

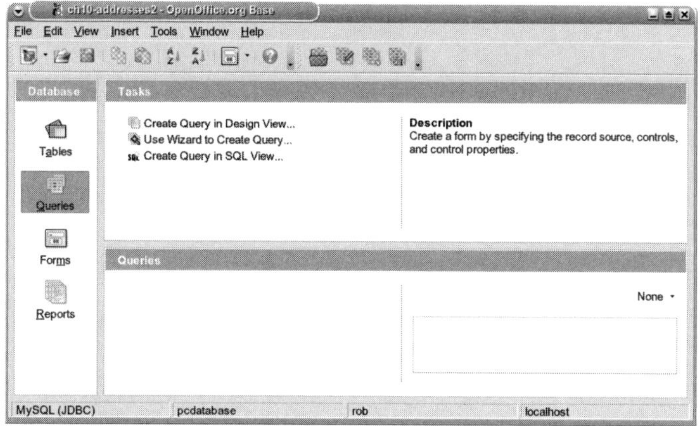

The main Base query screen.

In the field selection screen, choose the desired table from the Tables dropdown menu. Choose your fields by selecting a field and then clicking the right arrow to move the field to the Fields in the Query window. Click Next.

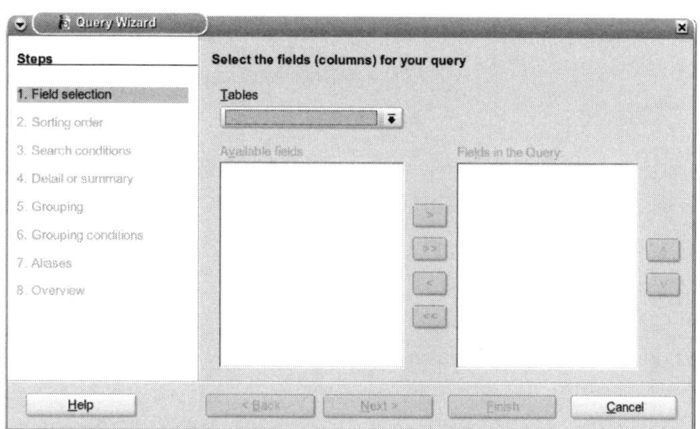

The field selection screen.

Choose the sort order in step 2. Pick a field from the Sort by dropdown menu. Secondary fields are sorted using the Then by dropdown menu. Click Next.

The sorting order screen.

In step 3 you can conditionally select which fields will be displayed. For instance, if you want to show records with a field that is a certain value, you could query for the value here.

Steps 4 through 7 deal with more selection options. In our example, click Next to get to the Overview step.

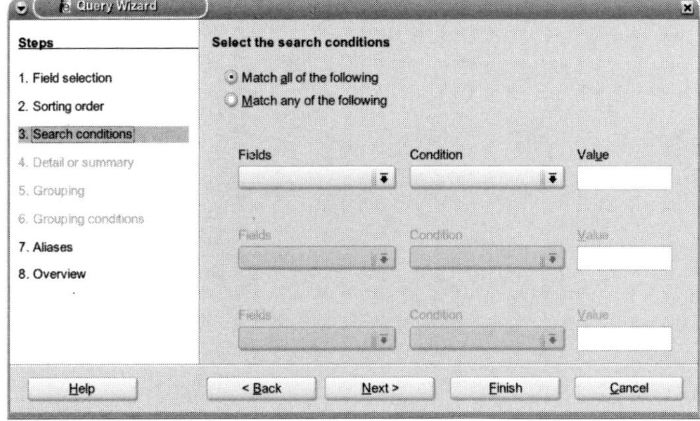

The search conditions screen.

Use the overview screen to name your query, and then click Finish. The query runs and produces the results in a regular spreadsheet-style screen.

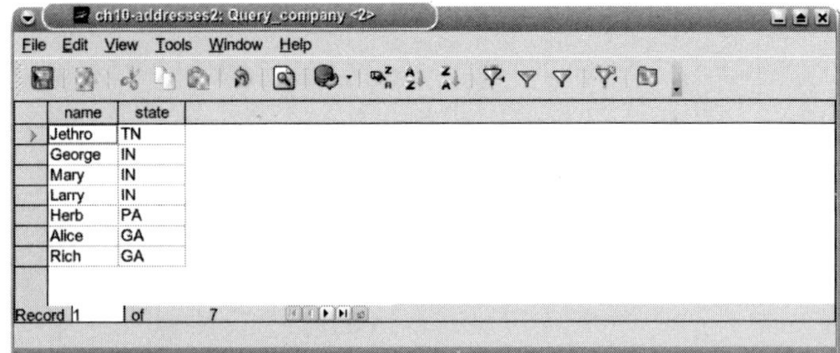

The query produces the results.

An SQL query whittles data into manageable chunks. Switch back to the Writer document via the Window tab. The query results appear when you click the + next to the Query icon. The database itself is visible via the View button and the Datasources menu item.

The next step is to create a printable report.

Making Elegant, Printable Reports from Your Database

Corporate people love pretty reports. To make one from a database, flip back to the OOo Base application and click Reports in the Database pane. Click the Use Wizard to Create Report item in the Tasks pane.

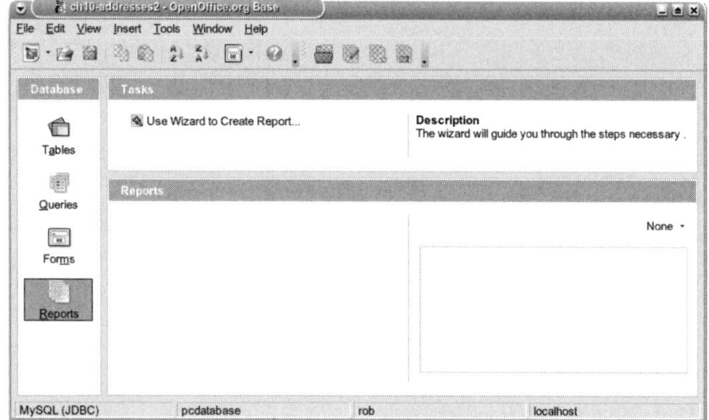

The main Base report screen.

The table and field names are selected from the Report Wizard screen. Click Next. The figures show sample values for the various fields.

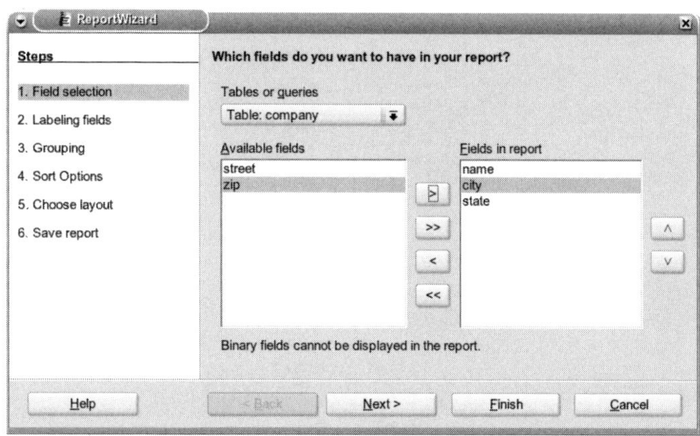

The Report Wizard screen.

Fields are labeled in step 2. Click Next.

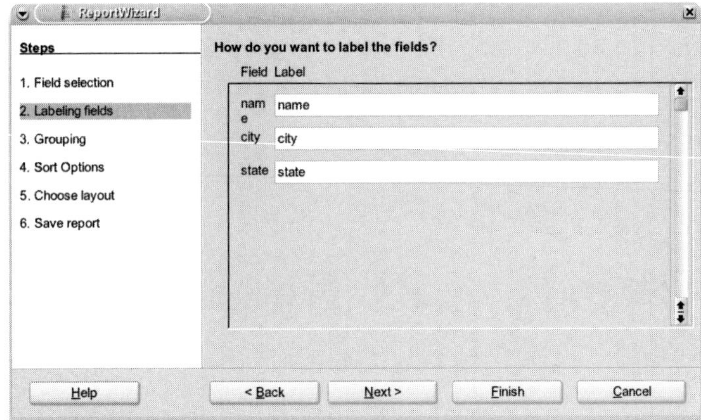

The Labeling Fields screen.

Step 3 groups the fields. Select a field and click Next.

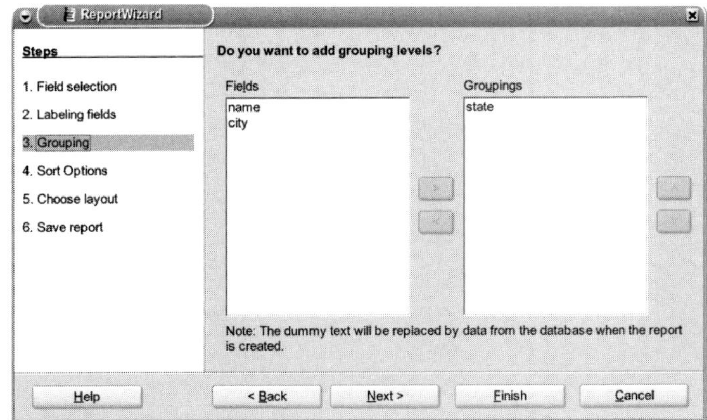

The Grouping screen.

Step 4 sets the sorting order. Select a field and click Next twice.

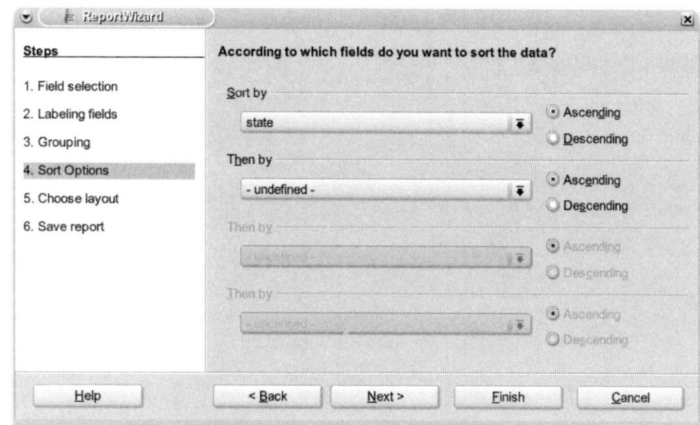

The Sort Options screen.

If you are using the version of OOo on this book's CD, you have to click Next twice because a bug in the software makes the Report Wizard skip to the Save Report step. If you have downloaded a later version, this bug may be fixed. But, if it is not fixed in the version you are using, it's a simple matter of clicking the Back button to get to step 5 (the report layout screen).

Use step 5 to select a canned layout for the report. Click a selection on the Layout of data menu to see how the title block and report author's name text will appear. Click and drag the bar at the top of the Report Wizard screen to move it out of the way for a better view.

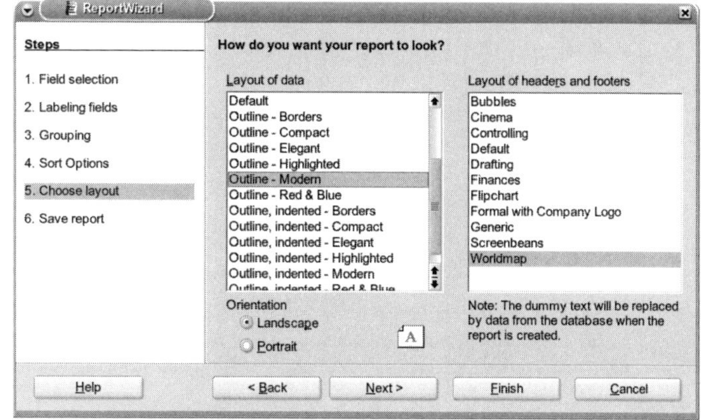

The Choose Layout screen.

Similarly, click an item under Layout of headers and footers to change the background and header/footer images. Experiment with a few layouts to see which ones work best for your data.

Viewing the layout.

After choosing the layout, click Next again to go on to step 6. Give the report a name and click Finish to complete the Report Wizard process.

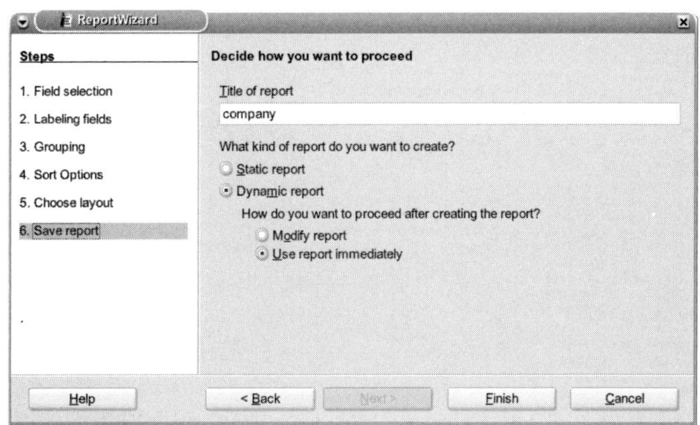

The Save Report screen.

The main Base window reappears with the new report name showing in the Report pane. Double-click the report name to see the Writer (read-only) window with the newly computed report and your MySQL data.

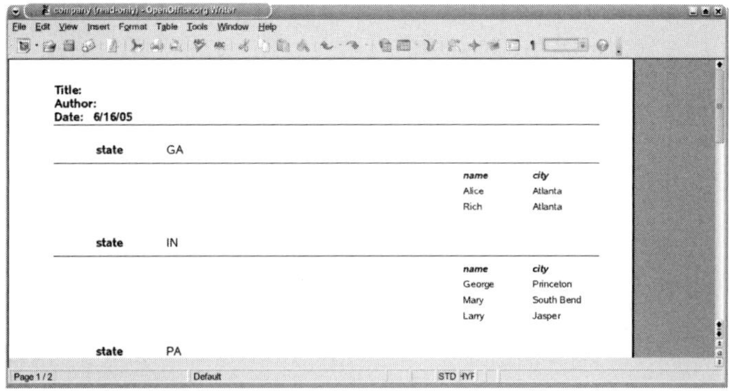

The newly computed report.

Try out several different combinations of data and report formats to get a feeling for what you can do with the Report Wizard.

Printing the report is the next step. Go into Base. Double-click the report name to open the finished report in Writer. Select Print on the File tab. The report is then printed.

Creating Forms for Simplified Data Input—Even if You're Not a Programmer

In the last part of this chapter, we'll create a simple form that you can use to view and edit data in your database.

Start OOo Base, connect to the database, and click the Form icon in the Database pane.

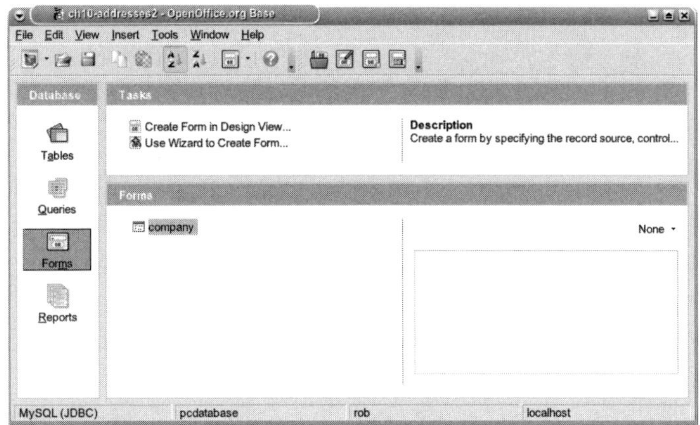

The main Base forms screen.

In step 1 you choose the fields you want to use in the form. Click the double right arrow to select all the fields in the list; they are transferred from the left pane to the right one. Click Next.

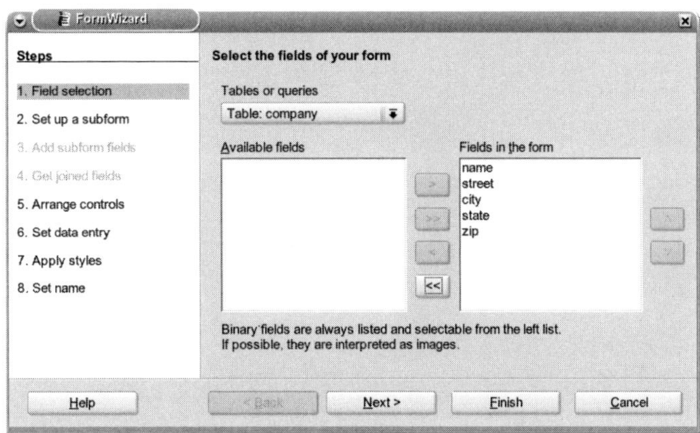

Moving fields from the left pane to the right.

To set up a subform, enable the Add Subform radio button in step 2. In the example, Next was just clicked.

Steps 3 and 4 pertain to subforms. Because you didn't add any, you can ignore them.

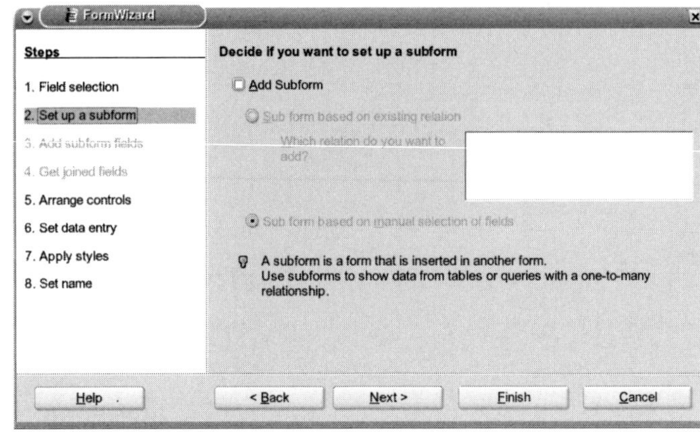

Setting up a subform screen.

Step 5 gives you the option of several form layouts for the labels and fields. They can be arranged in various spreadsheet or columnar styles. Click Next.

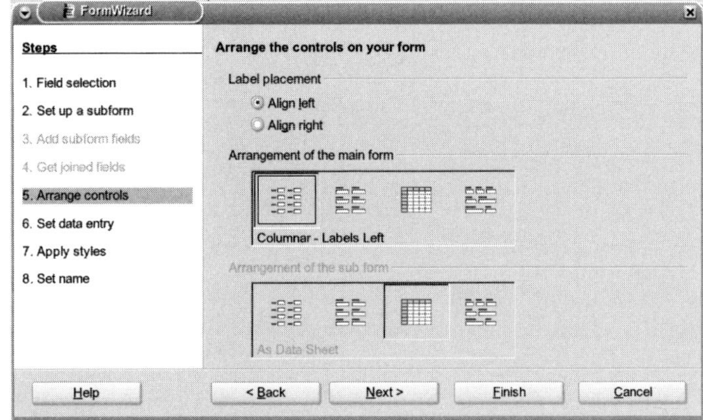

The Arrange Controls screen.

Use step 6 if you want your form to allow only new data input. You can also select how your data will be displayed. Click Next.

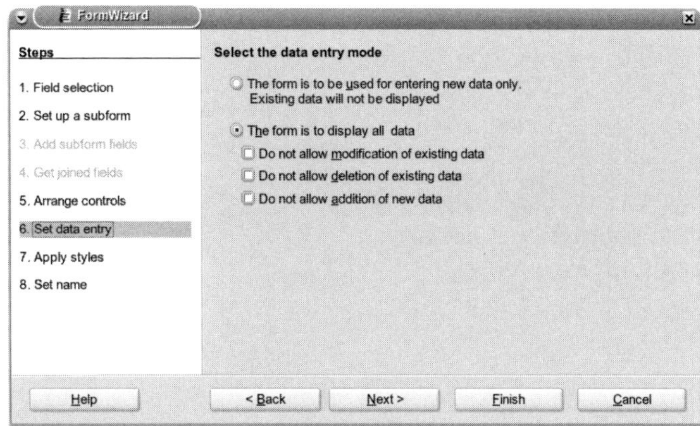

Selecting how the form and data are displayed.

The form's background color and whether it's flat or 3D can be set in step 7. A cool blue color called Ice Blue was chosen for the example and is shown behind the wizard screen. Click Next.

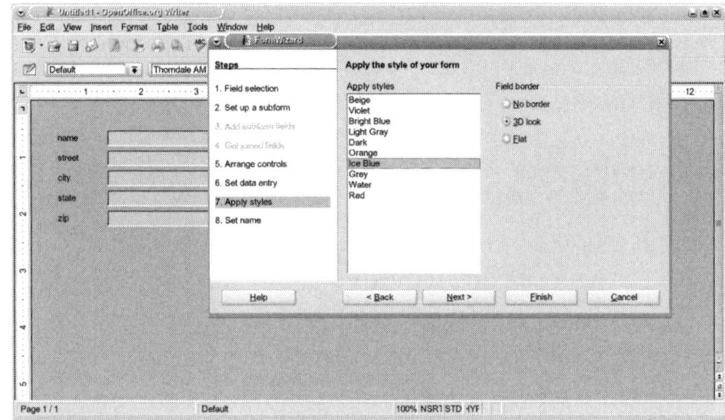

Viewing the sample form with the Ice Blue background.

Finally, step 8 gives you a place to type in a form name. Saving the form lets you come back later and reuse it. Click Finish.

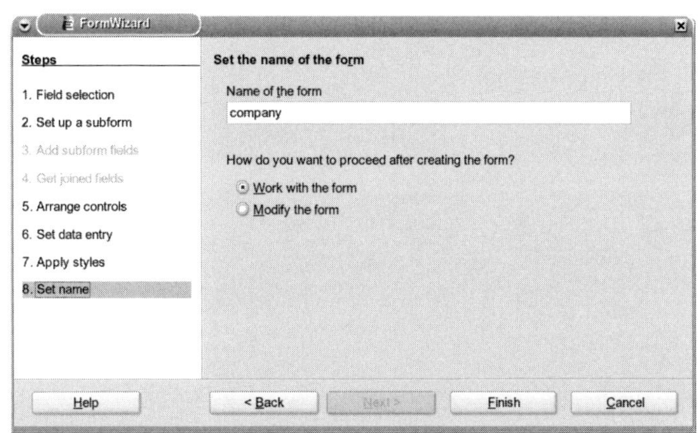

Saving the form with a name.

The form is now complete. If you have write access to the database, you can view and edit data.

You can use the arrow keys at the bottom to move back and forth through the records.

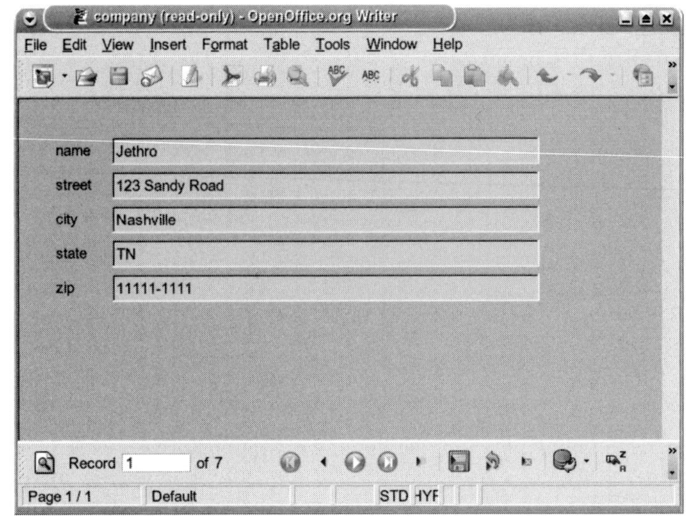

The completed form.

Wrapping Up

Using the database connectivity and creation tools in OOo can help you put some of that valuable company data to work in your Writer or Calc documents. Admittedly, there are a few steps, although the wizard helps you point and click through the basics. A little training in general database use can help, too, if you haven't done much database work before now.

Chapter 11

Sharing Files Between OpenOffice.org and Microsoft Office

By Bruce Byfield

Even if you're the most dedicated OpenOffice.org person in the world, sooner or later you'll be asked to share files with Microsoft Office users. Some free-software advocates refuse to save OOo documents in Microsoft Office formats and suggest outputting to HTML, PDF, or RTF instead, but this isn't always an option, especially if your boss is the one doing the asking.

In OpenOffice.org, you can select File > Wizards > Document Converter to convert all the Microsoft Office files in a folder to OOo format. Or you can open Microsoft Office documents one at a time by choosing File > Open and selecting the appropriate file. Conversely, to save a file in a format Office can read, select File > Save As and pick the appropriate format. If your main concern is content, and you can ignore minor formatting errors, this may be all you ever need. However, you can get better results if you spend a moment or two planning your file-sharing strategy.

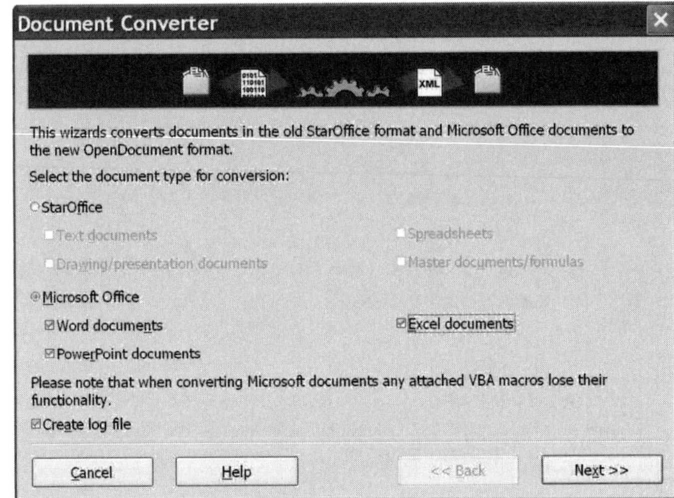

The Document Converter Wizard.

In OOo 2, importing and exporting Microsoft Office files is much easier than it was in earlier versions. Sadly, many features of OOo are still completely or partly unsupported in Microsoft Office. Many of these unsupported features are simply dropped when a file is converted. Your success in exchanging files depends largely on knowing which features are supported.

Preparing for Sharing—Files, That Is

The first step in file sharing is selecting an export filter. OpenOffice.org includes export filters for Microsoft Word 6.0, 95, 97/2000/XP, and 2003 XML. If you don't know what version of Office the person to whom you're sending the files uses, the 97/2000/XP filter is probably the best choice.

Next, if formatting matters, check that the fonts in your file are available to both OpenOffice.org and Microsoft Word. If not, you can expect repagination and possibly even the destruction of complex designs if you open a file made in either program with the other one.

You can sidestep this issue by using only standard fonts such as Times New Roman or Helvetica. If OpenOffice.org is installed on all machines, you can also use the Bitstream Vera fonts that are installed with it. The only drawback to these choices is that they are used so often that they make your documents look like everyone else's. If design is important to your work, the only solution is to install the fonts everywhere they are needed or to share files in PDF format.

If you use nonstandard fonts, be aware that not all fonts that share a name are necessarily identical. For example, literally dozens of fonts are named Garamond, all allegedly based on the designs of the Renaissance typographer of that name, but few of them have much in common besides the name.

Now adjust the settings within OpenOffice.org itself. First, select all the options in Tools > Options > Load/Save > Microsoft Office. These options improve the handling of OLE Objects, but only if you are using Writer in an operating system that supports OLE Objects, such as Windows.

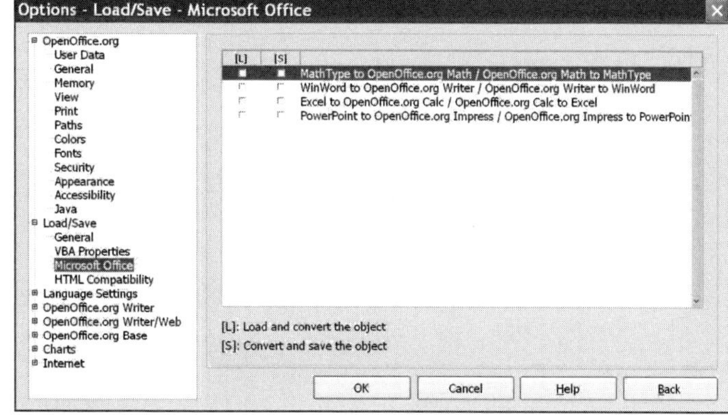

Load/Save Microsoft Office.

Second, check that all the options in Load/Save > VBA Properties are selected. OOo doesn't run Visual Basic scripts, but when these options are selected, they are preserved for later use when a file is opened in Microsoft Office. Otherwise, the person with whom you exchange files will be justifiably peeved to find that their macros disappeared after you opened their files.

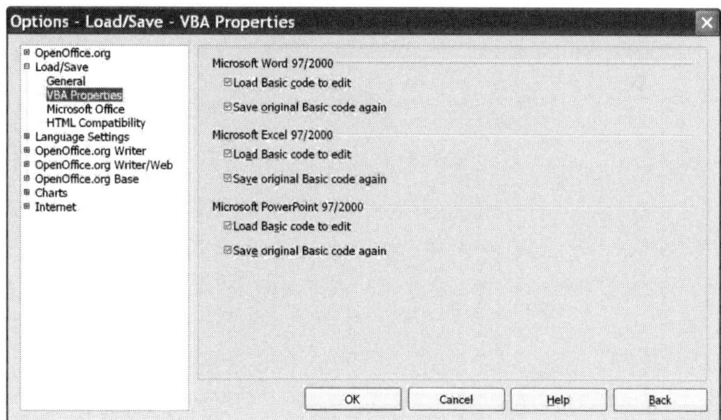

VBA Properties.

Paying attention to these matters takes a lot of the misery out of sharing files. Even so, if you want formatting perfection, you need to tweak your files. That tweaking is infinitely easier if, as a final preparation, you format in both OpenOffice.org and Microsoft Office using character and paragraph styles instead of formatting manually. You can save styles in a template so that you need to set them up only once. More to the point, character and paragraph styles also transfer successfully between Writer and Word, so you can use the styles to speed up your tweaking.

Preparing to Share Files Between Writer and Word

Before sharing text documents, open a blank Writer document and check the options available in OpenOffice.org at Tools > Options > OpenOffice.org Writer > Compatibility. Some of the options in this window are for compatibility with older versions of StarOffice, the proprietary version of OpenOffice.org, but about half are for Microsoft Word compatibility. Several set OpenOffice.org to add spacing between lines and around objects as Microsoft Word does:

- "Add spacing between paragraphs and tables (in current document)"
- "Do not add leading (extra space) between lines of text"
- "Add paragraph and table spacing at bottom of table cells"
- "Consider wrapping style when positioning objects"

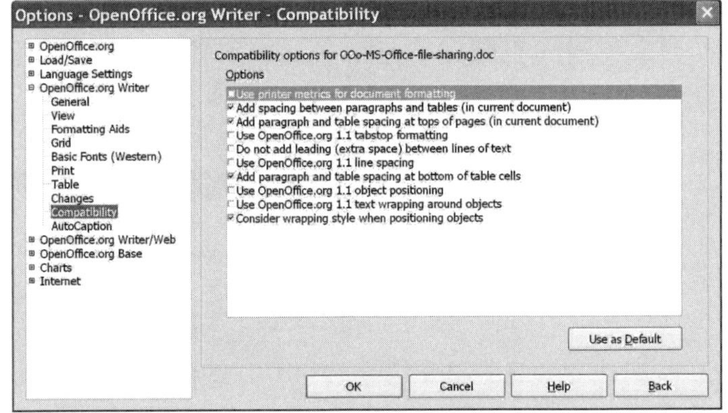

Compatibility options.

If you are importing Microsoft Word files, select "Add paragraph and table spacing at tops of pages (in current document)" as well. Whether importing or exporting, you should also select "Use printer metrics for document formatting" if both the OOo and Word-using machines have access to the same model of printer (or to any PostScript printer). This option provides a common standard independent of the software.

When you have set the options, click the Use as Default button to save your choices as the default settings. Some of these settings are only for the current document, so save the current document by selecting File > Template > Save so that you don't have to adjust the settings each time you start a document that will be opened in Microsoft Office.

Sharing Files Between Writer and Word

With the options for file sharing enabled, you can generally exchange text documents with few problems. The text itself usually translates with only minor problems. The difficulties are likely to be caused by inserted objects or page-level formatting.

Character and paragraph formatting, whether set manually or with styles, usually transfer easily. Provided that the fonts used are available to both programs, characteristics such as font size, effects, and positioning are trouble-free. Even rotation of characters and changes in font width transfer without difficulty. The same is true of basic paragraph characteristics, such as line spacing and tabs. OOo's list styles are not supported in Microsoft Word, but paragraphs associated with a list style in Writer use the same type of list in Word.

The only difficulties with paragraphs show up when you use OOo features unsupported by Microsoft Word, such as custom hyphenation, page breaks, and last lines of justified paragraphs. Word drops these items in favor of its default settings. The result may be minor differences in line and page breaks—usually amounting to no more than a single additional line, if that.

Numbered and bulleted lists were a conversion problem in earlier versions of OpenOffice.org. The main reason was that Writer and Word used different default fonts for bulleted lists. In OOo 2, these problems are greatly alleviated. Even bullets made with special characters and advanced options, such as text before or after a bullet, now transfer cleanly. Only bullets made from graphics, such as the ones in the OOo gallery, do not export to Microsoft Word.

Graphical Bullets in OpenOffice.org

Wild parrot populations in the United States include colonies of:

- Quaker or Monk parakeets
- Cherry-headed conures
- Double yellow-fronted Amazons

Turn into plain bullets in MS Word

Wild parrot populations in the United States include colonies of:

· Quaker or Monk parakeets
· Cherry-headed conures
· Double yellow-fronted Amazons

A bulleted list that didn't transfer correctly.

The greatest problem with lists seems to be the use of Tools > Outline Numbering, which prevents the saving of a file in Microsoft Word format. If you are making a file you expect to share with Microsoft Office users, you should avoid Outline Numbering.

Many fields are trouble-free, including page numbers, cross-references, and tables of contents. In fact, even custom table-of-contents entries, such as ones with the page number first, open successfully in Microsoft Word. A few fields, including those based on file attributes (such as word count) are converted to text. This can cause problems if the file is being passed back and forth for revision. Fields that do not work at all include all of those for conditional text, such as hidden text and hidden paragraphs. Hidden text simply disappears in Microsoft Word, while hidden paragraphs are revealed. Fields as a whole do not import or export well, probably because they are so bound up in the logic of one program that they have no equivalent in the other.

Inserted objects produce mixed results when sharing files. Many common objects transfer without problems. Bookmarks and hyperlinks transfer successfully unless attached to a frame. So do notes and revision changes. Other objects may not do as well. The settings for graphics—including size, anchor, and alignment—jump the gap smoothly except when Align as Character is set in Writer, in which case the graphic simply does not appear in Word.

Complex table and border settings generally transfer smoothly, but a nested table does not survive when the file is opened in Word. Similarly, simple shapes made with the drawing tools carry over, but callouts or complicated diagrams sometimes suffer minor spacing problems. Footnotes are transferred but generally cause repagination, so end notes seem a better alternative for a shared document.

A few objects do not convert at all, including animations and embedded OOo files. And with OOo (or any other program) running on GNU/Linux, OLE objects in a Microsoft Office document do not convert either, because—despite the listing for OLE Objects under Insert > Object—the operating system does not support them.

Other items that do not transfer successfully are mostly concerned with page layout:

- Margins for page styles are maintained, but the page styles themselves are lost. So are all the headers and footers except the first ones, along with borders or shadows given to them.
- Text frames are transferred, but without most of their settings.
- Sections fail even more seriously, being treated as page break markers, and they drop password protection and hidden settings.

- Both frames and sections with multiple columns often display only the first few lines.
- Master documents can be neither imported nor exported.

Given that Microsoft Word has no sense of the typographic page, these problems are to be expected.

Sharing Files Between Calc and Excel

The main compatibility problems between Calc and Excel spreadsheets are functions. Basic functions such as SUM, AVERAGE, and MAX generally cause no problems. However, check the OOo online help before using the more-advanced functions. Although Calc is designed to be highly compatible with Excel, each spreadsheet program has functions that the other lacks. In a few cases, Calc may have arguments that Excel lacks. In other cases, Calc may have two similar functions: one for general use, and a second for Excel compatibility. For example, WEEKNUM calculates the week number of a given datum based on the ISO 6801 standard, while WEEKNUM_ADD does the same calculation in an Excel-compatible format.

Objects in Calc have the same mixed record as in Writer. Page and cell styles usually don't survive the transition, but cell formats that *use* styles generally translate well.

Sharing Files Between Impress and PowerPoint

The PowerPoint filter seems far more reliable in OOo 2 than in earlier versions. In particular, OOo 1.x's frequent inability to transfer a background graphic in a master slide has been eliminated. Slide transitions are also exported more reliably, although you should experiment with them to make sure all the ones you're using work properly. However, animated GIFs created in Impress still do not open in PowerPoint. Similarly, to avoid any small changes in spacing in complex diagrams, you may want to create the diagram in Draw and then export it to Impress in a common graphic format such as .jpeg or .gif.

When importing from PowerPoint, you need to be aware that many of the options for sound cannot be used in Impress. Although OOo 2 supports a larger array of sound formats than earlier versions, Impress still lacks tools for recording sounds and narration or for playing CD tracks with a slide. Sound in Impress remains limited to individual slides. Nor can Impress handle PowerPoint's Pack and Go or Package for CD, both of which bundle a slide show along with all its associated graphics and fonts for easy transportation between machines.

Sharing Draw Files

Microsoft Office does not support Draw's native formats, .odg and .sxd. Fortunately, Draw files export to most common graphics formats, including .png, .gif, and .jpeg. All these formats can be viewed in a web browser or inserted in a blank Microsoft Office document. Keep the original, and export as needed.

Conclusion

This is not an exhaustive list of what works and what doesn't when exchanging files with Microsoft Office. In fact, such a list does not exist. The OOo online help does list potential problem areas, but this list does not take into account the changes in version 2.0, so it is too pessimistic.

Still, if there's a secret to sharing files between the two office applications, it comes down to three words: Keep it simple.

The more basic the formatting, the more likely that the exchange of files will be trouble-free. Objects, page design, and any styles other than paragraph and character styles are especially likely to cause problems.

Understand, too, that, except in the simplest cases, the process is unlikely to ever be perfect. Sharing files has always been a weak side of office programs. Making import and export filters is too expensive for commercial companies and often is too unglamorous for free-software developers. The situation isn't improved, either, by the fact that Microsoft Office formats are proprietary and often are altered between versions, which means it takes constant reverse-engineering to keep up with them.

Under these circumstances, the fact that sharing files raises problems isn't surprising. Often, what's surprising is that you can share files at all.

Chapter 12

OpenOffice.org as a Community Effort

OpenOffice.org is free to use, and you can share it with your friends for free, but it wasn't free to develop. It started life as a commercial program called StarOffice. Sun Microsystems purchased StarOffice publisher StarDivision in 1999 and released OpenOffice.org Build 641—essentially a modified version of StarOffice 5.1—as open source software in 2000.

The original StarOffice was one of the first decent office software packages for Linux. It was included in many major Linux distributions, just as Microsoft Works is often part of a Windows installation. When Sun bought it, renamed it, and "opened" its source code, improvements came more rapidly than they had when StarOffice was closed-source, proprietary software.

StarOffice 5.1.

Open Source Magic

Open source software's rapid pace of development often seems like magic to people unfamiliar with the process, but the reason for this speed is purely mundane: Open source development puts no barriers between the users and the developers. No marketing people or retailers or others are involved in the program's creation and distribution—just you (the user) and the programmers who develop it.

If you have an idea about how a piece of open source software can be improved, or you want to suggest a new feature, you typically can join that software project's email list and make your suggestion directly to the people who can do something about it. This is great for the developers, too, because if you run into a bug, they can ask you directly what you were doing when it happened instead of hearing about users' problems thirdhand from customer service or tech support people.

Besides reporting bugs, open source software users who are programmers themselves can modify their favorite programs however they wish and then share their improvements with others. These modifications can become part of the program if enough other users and programmers feel they are worthwhile. If they are useful to only a few users, they may become "plugins" or optional add-ons that aren't part of the basic software package but that can be downloaded by those who need them.

Nonprogrammers can also contribute to open source projects, including OOo. Artists are always needed to design logos, screens, icons, and the many other graphic details that make a piece of software look good on the user's screen. Writers can help produce documentation. Neither this book nor any other piece of mass-produced printed material can possibly keep up with every advance in OOo or the many plugins for it, so there is always a need for updated "how-to" material that can be published on the OOo Web site.

And then there's translation. OOo and other open source programs can legally be translated into any language you want. There is no need to beg a software company for a localized version. You can write it yourself, either on your own or as part of a group.

In fact, you can modify OOo however you like, for whatever purpose you want. The copy of the software you got with this book (or a more recent version you downloaded) is *yours* in a way no piece of proprietary software hampered by a restrictive license will ever be.

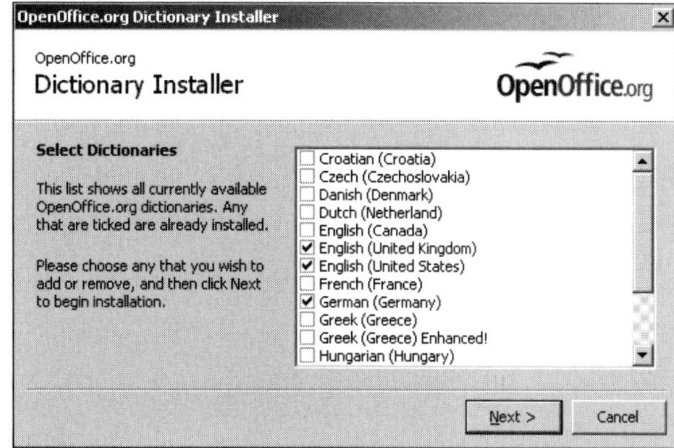

OpenOffice.org in many languages.

Free Tech Support

This is another beautiful part of the open source community. Right now you're an OOo beginner. At some point you'll have questions about OOo that this book hasn't answered for you. Many of us find that the best place to get answers to our OOo questions is the OpenOffice.org forums at www.oooforums.org.

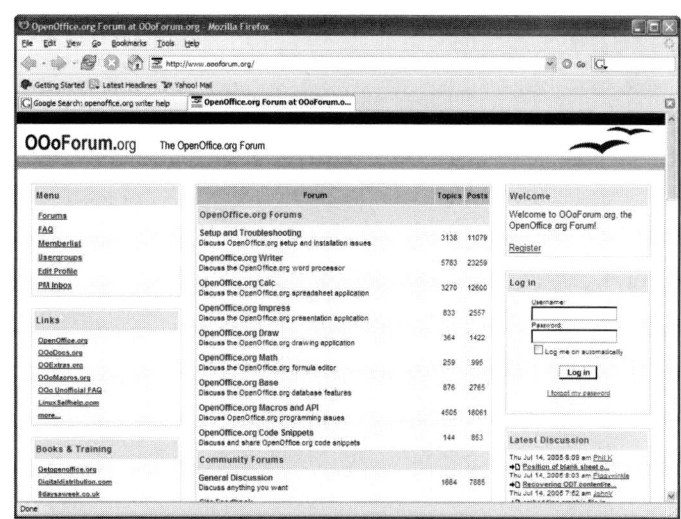

OpenOffice.org help forums.

This is just one of many places on the World Wide Web you can go for free OOo help. Type "OpenOffice.org help" into any search engine, and you'll find many others.

The people helping you on these forums are not paid for their work, so please make sure you are polite whenever you post a question. Also, remember that the biggest courtesy of all when requesting free help online is to search for questions similar to yours that have already been answered before you post your own.

There's another catch to this "users helping users" concept, albeit a voluntary one: Right now you may have plenty of questions and no answers, but if you keep using OOo and keep watching those help forums, sooner or later a question will come up that you will be able to answer. Go ahead and answer it. Then answer some more as you become more proficient with OOo—because while you are learning, more new people will start using it and will ask questions. This will be your payback to the people who helped you, and it will make you a full part of the open source community. You will not only have received but will have given. This is what makes "open source software" a *community* instead of just a way to develop and distribute software.

What Does Sun Microsystems Get by Giving Away OpenOffice.org?

No matter how much time or effort you put into OOo, Sun Microsystems is still OOo's prime benefactor. Sun not only bought StarDivision and gave away its newly-acquired star product for free, but it has paid skilled software developers to work on OOo. This is not charity. Sun uses OOo internally, and it's a large-enough company that purchasing Microsoft Office or another proprietary office software suite for all Sun employees would cost as much as hiring a considerable number of programmers. So, if nothing else, Sun gets an excellent piece of software for internal use. Plus, Sun gets the benefit of volunteer work done on OOo—not only by programmers, but also by artists, usability experts, documentation writers, and even volunteer question-answerers, who function, in effect, as a free help desk.

Beyond all this, Sun actually *makes money* from OpenOffice.org. Not from OOo itself, but from StarOffice, a name Sun reserved for the commercial version of OOo, which it sells as proprietary software to both companies and individuals.

So why buy StarOffice when OpenOffice.org is free?

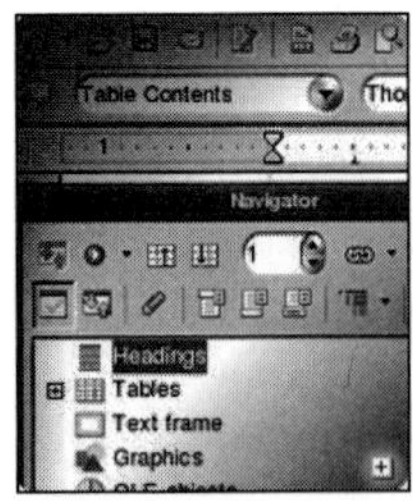

StarOffice 8.

There are a number of reasons, starting with the fact that StarOffice includes an extensive manual, while OOo provides only community-produced documentation. Another factor is clip art and templates. OOo includes only a few pieces of clip art and not many premade document templates, while StarOffice includes thousands of pieces of clip art and hundreds of document templates.

These are not the only features StarOffice offers that OOo lacks. Go to www.sun.com/staroffice, and Sun will tell you about many more, up to and including online training. Because StarOffice is based on OOo—essentially it *is* OOo with some "secret sauce" added—Sun manages to develop StarOffice for much less money by drawing on community resources. It would cost much more to continually improve such a complex program using only staff employees. As a bonus, freely-distributed OOo serves as free (but priceless) advertising for StarOffice.

The reality is that most of us do just fine with OOo and don't need StarOffice's extra features. But some people happily pay for StarOffice—especially companies that want not only the added StarOffice functionality but also the ability to call Sun software engineers directly for support.

(As an additional plug, StarOffice costs much less than most office suites and has fewer licensing restrictions than almost any of its competitors.)

Getting Hooked on Open Source Software

Don't laugh. It's easy to get hooked on open source software, and not just because it's often free to download and use. Freedom can often be more important than free in the "You don't have to pay for it" sense, especially when it comes to software. After you've installed OOo and other open source software packages on a number of computers, the next time you install a proprietary program that puts you through an extensive registration and verification process as part of the installation, you'll wish all your software were open source.

Once you get in the habit of using high-quality open source software like OOo, you might start thinking that maybe, just maybe, an awfully high percentage of the cost associated with commercial software might be going into marketing instead of into the software itself.

The problem with this train of thought is that it's entirely true. Almost every major proprietary software vendor in the world spends more on marketing and preventing "piracy" (a word proprietary software vendors use when they really mean "unauthorized sharing") than on software development. And none of the marking or "anti-piracy" cost does you—the user—any good. It is far more convenient to use software you can install on any computer you want than to use software that forces you to worry about licenses and license keys and all the other proprietary software folderol.

As an individual user, the fact that you can freely share your favorite software with friends and family is good because it allows you to be generous. In a corporate setting, the ability to install as many copies of a program as you need without tracking license keys and purchase conditions is a money-saver that can exceed the savings you get by getting the software for "free" in the monetary sense.

Sooner or later you may even switch to Linux, the free operating system that was used—along with OpenOffice.org—to write most of this book. Linux is immune to virtually all current Internet-spread worms and viruses, and it can't get infected with Windows adware or spyware. In fact, many people consider Linux boring; it just sits there and works, day after day, without a burp or a blip. It takes a little work (but not much) for most users to switch from Windows to Linux. Of course, that switch is easier if you do it the "Point & Click" way, which is why a book called *Point & Click Linux!* is available from the same place you got *this* book.

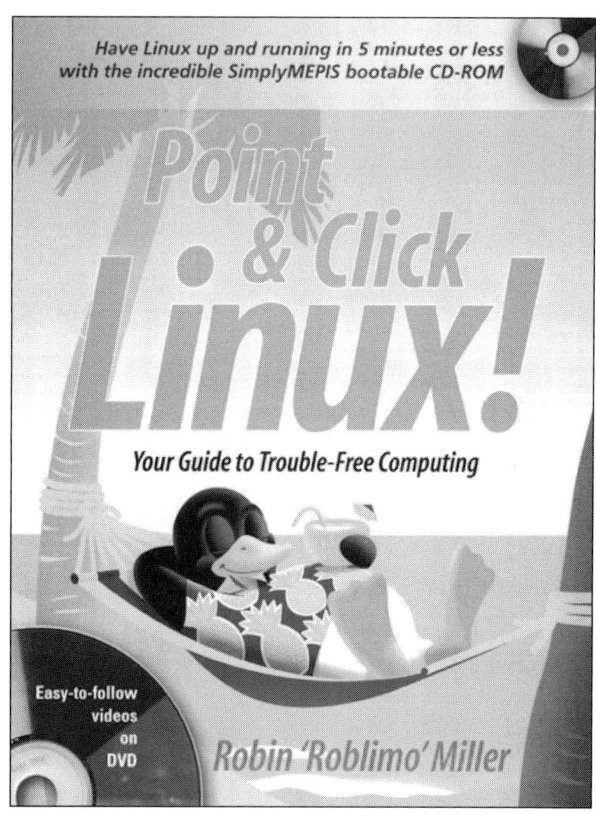

The *Point & Click Linux!* cover.

But you don't need to learn a whole new operating system right now. You might be better off learning how to use popular open source programs one at a time before you contemplate an operating system switch. Two open source programs you probably should try next are the Firefox Web browser and the Thunderbird email client. Not only are they free and open source, but many people consider them *better* and *more secure* than almost all their proprietary competition.

Section III

Bonus Chapters

Chapter 13

About Firefox and Thunderbird

Most people on the Internet use the Microsoft Internet Explorer Web browser to cruise the World Wide Web and use either Outlook or Outlook Express to send and receive email. They use these programs because they came with Windows, not because they chose them for themselves. This is like buying a toaster that comes from the factory set to make toast much darker than you like and leaving it that way instead of trying different settings until you find one that makes toast to your taste.

The only problem with the toaster analogy is that a toaster comes with a knob or other device you can use to change the way it toasts, but Windows doesn't come with a choice of Web browsers or email programs. You need to go get them for yourself, and once you start looking for better ones—and there are plenty out there—it's easy to get confused.

For most people, the best Web browser choice is Firefox, and the best email choice is Thunderbird. They have been favorably reviewed by almost every publication that tests software, not to mention hundreds of newspaper and TV computer reporters.

The Firefox Web browser.

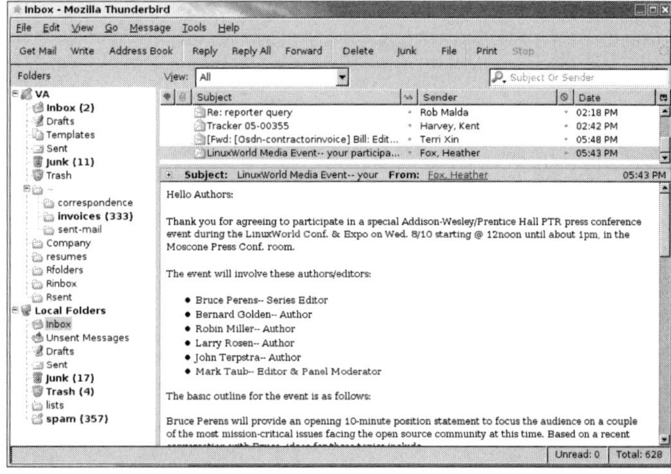

The Thunderbird email program.

Here are some of their primary advantages over their Microsoft equivalents:

- They are immune to virtually all Explorer and Outlook security exploits.
- Firefox has tabbed browsing, a feature you'll never want to be without once you've tried it.
- Firefox has a built-in popup ad blocker, plus an easy-to-add blocker for almost all banner ads.
- Thunderbird has built-in junk email/spam filters you can easily "train" to meet your needs.
- Many customization options are available, allowing you to use the Internet "your way."

These programs are developed and maintained by the Mozilla Foundation, a group originally set up, staffed, and funded by Netscape (now owned by Time Warner) in much the same way Sun Microsystems set up and financed OpenOffice.org. However, the Mozilla Foundation is now totally independent from its original corporate master and, instead, is financed by donations from individuals and corporations that love its products.

A Netscape Web browser is still available, and it is based on Mozilla. It's free in the cost sense, but in many ways it is not as technically elegant as Firefox and Thunderbird. Netscape is a Web browser and email program combined, which means it is cumbersome and slow to load.

Firefox and Thunderbird are available for most major computer operating systems, and they work almost exactly the same in all of them. The Firefox screenshot shown here was taken in Windows. The Thunderbird screenshot was taken in Ubuntu Linux running a Gnome desktop. Both programs take on the characteristics, or "themes," of their surroundings so that they look like all the rest of your programs. But the buttons and icons are all in the same place no matter what desktop you use, which makes moving from Firefox and Thunderbird on one computer to the same programs on another computer a no-brainer.

Mind you, you can change the "look and feel" of Firefox and Thunderbird almost any way you can imagine instead of sticking with the defaults. You can change colors, fonts, and many other display characteristics, and you can add many nifty plugins and extensions to extend the usefulness of Firefox and Thunderbird.

But we won't go into detail here about Firefox and Thunderbird themes, plugins, and other customizations. This is just a brief introduction to these two fine programs. Learning everything about them—and about some of the many fine open source programs available for other Internet tasks—would take another whole book.

Point & Click Firefox! sounds like a catchy title, doesn't it? Hmmmm . . .

Chapter 14

Light up the World Wide Web with Firefox

The first thing to do is download a copy of Firefox. It's available directly from www.mozilla.org. There are no tedious registration forms to fill out. Click on the Free Download link and pick where you want the downloaded file to go on your computer (probably on your desktop if you're running Windows). Firefox will start downloading almost immediately.

The Mozilla home page.

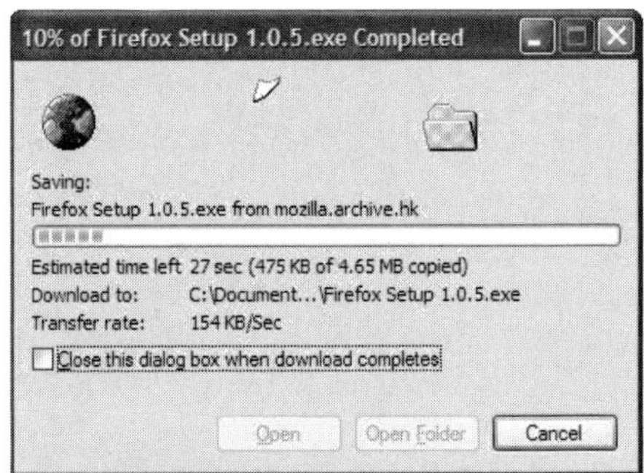

Downloading Firefox for Windows.

Installing Firefox

Once the download is complete (the time it takes depends on your connection speed), install Firefox by clicking Run in the Microsoft Explorer Download Complete window.

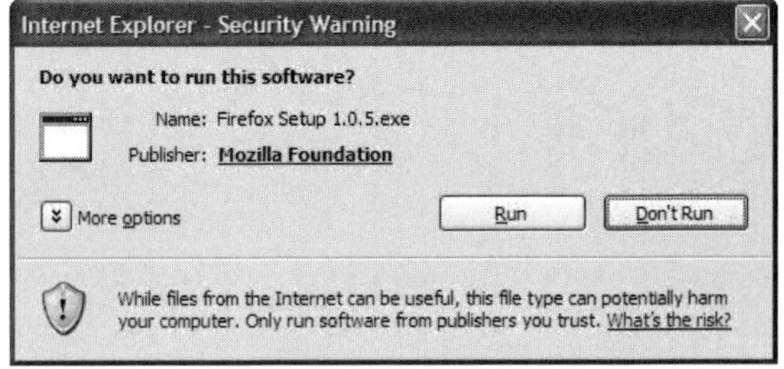

The Explorer Download Complete window.

The rest of the process is entirely automatic. You need to agree to the license terms, but they are not onerous.

The Mozilla software license agreement.

After that, you can safely choose the default installation. In a minute or two you see the Install Complete window. You might as well start Firefox now, so check the Launch Mozilla Firefox now button and then click Finish.

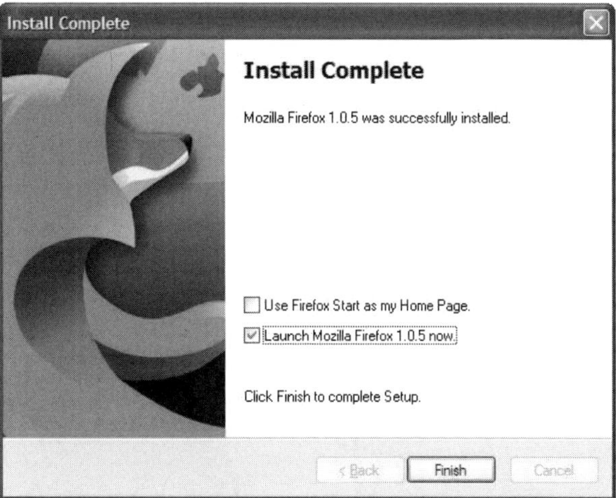

The Install Complete window.

Importing Explorer Settings

The default home page in Firefox is a Google search box. Many people leave this as their Firefox startup page, but you don't have to. In fact, if you already have a home page set in Explorer, you can transfer it, along with all your other Explorer settings and favorites, to Firefox in a few seconds by clicking File in the upper-left corner of the Firefox window and choosing Import from the dropdown menu.

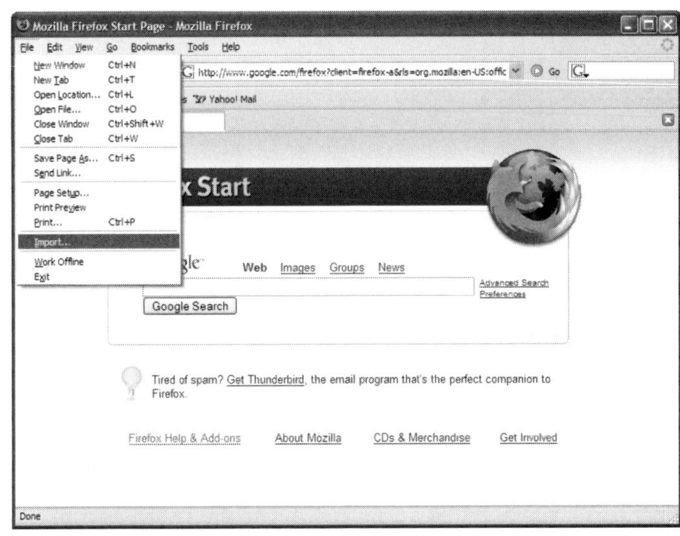

Preparing to import Explorer settings.

The next window has a series of checkboxes. You can select specific Explorer settings, passwords, and favorites to import, or you can just go with the default and import all of them at once.

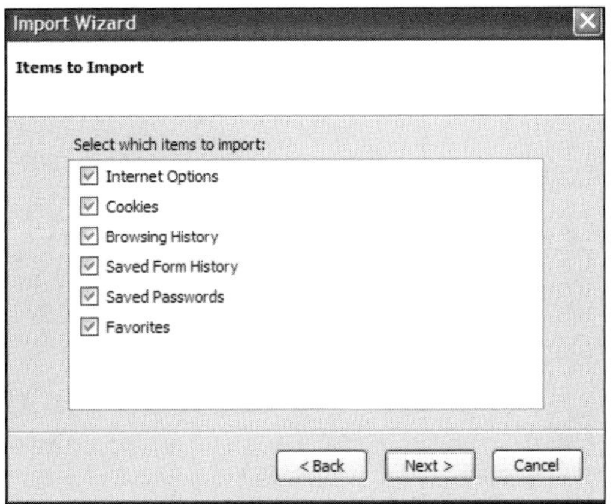

Importing Explorer settings.

Your Explorer Favorites will be called Bookmarks in Firefox, but that's the only major change. You'll still log into your favorite sites automatically, and all your other options will be the same.

Privacy and Other Options

But what if you want to change a setting or two? Select Tools > Options from the dropdown menu.

Selecting Options.

This brings up the General Options window, which is where you can change your home page and several other self-explanatory basic settings.

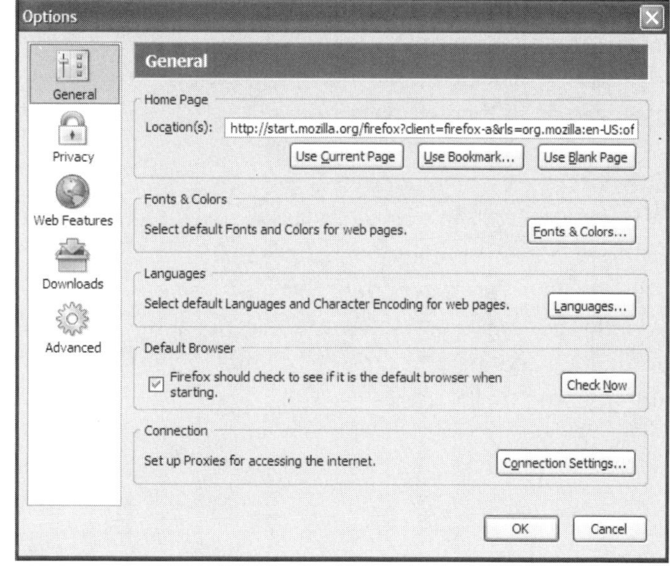

The General Options window.

Another useful Options window controls privacy. Remember when you were shopping online for a surprise gift and it wasn't a surprise because the person to whom you were giving the gift borrowed your computer and saw the page you'd ordered it from? With Firefox you can erase your WWW tracks so that no one can see what sites you've visited. You can clear just the site history, just your download history, or any combination of the available options up to and including all of them at once.

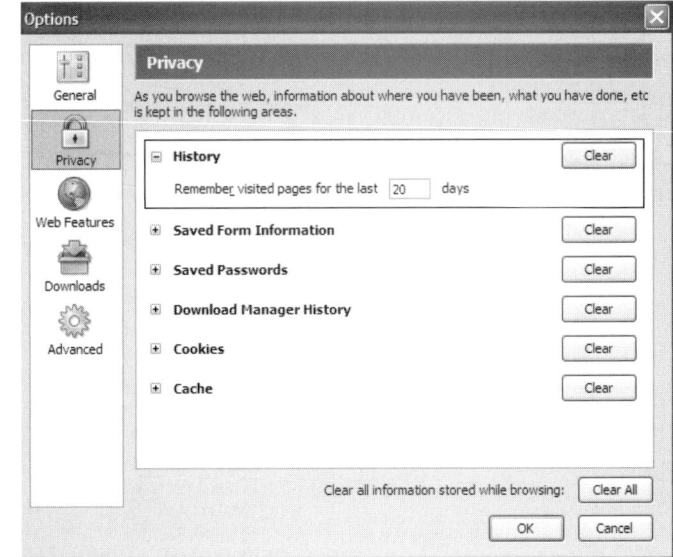

Privacy Options.

The next important window sets Web features. By default it's set to block most popup ads. A few will still get through, because advertisers keep looking for ways to defeat popup blockers, and sometimes they succeed. There's also an option to allow popups from selected Web sites. This is important, because some banking and ecommerce sites rely on popup windows for logins and other vital functions. By allowing popups only on sites where you want and need them, you can block most popup ads and still have your favorite popup-using sites work correctly.

This window is also where you control image loading, Java, and JavaScript, but this isn't necessary for most users, so we won't go into it here.

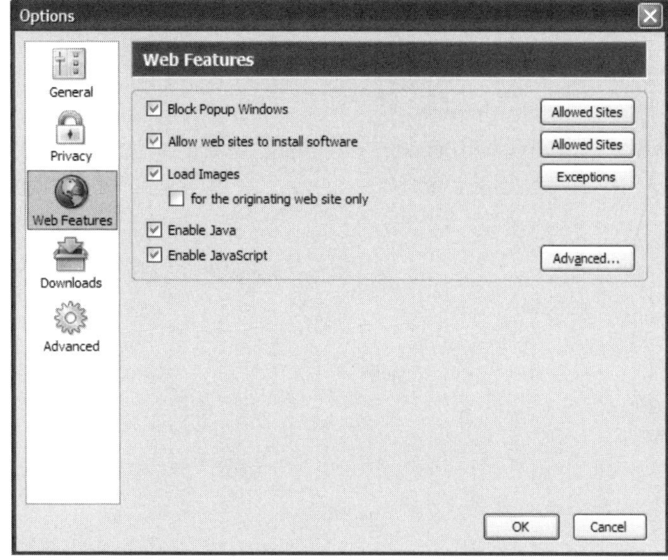

Web Features.

The only remaining window in this group is called Advanced, but it really isn't very advanced. Go ahead and explore it for yourself. If you change a setting and don't like the results, you can undo it in a second or less, so experimenting a little on your own won't hurt anything.

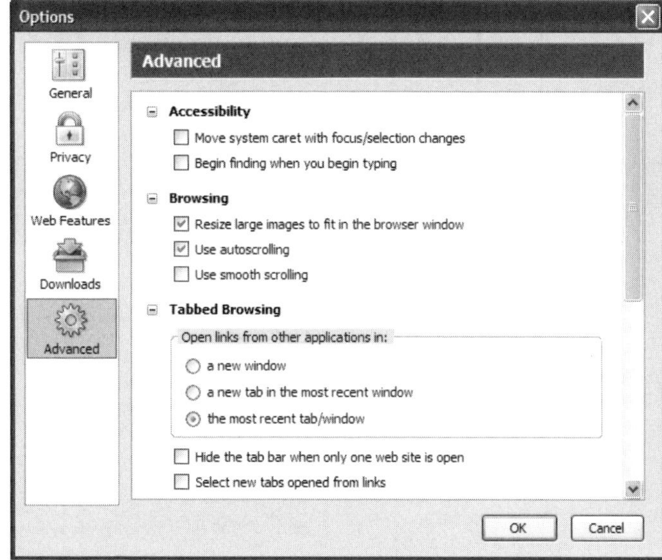

Advanced.

Saving the Best for Last: Tabbed Browsing

This is the feature that sells most users on Firefox, even if they're not concerned about security and don't appreciate its fast, clear rendering of almost all Web sites. It's one of those features that's easier to explain with a video than with text and screenshots, so we'll just touch on it here and leave the rest for the video treatment.

Here's a view of NewsForge.com, scrolled partway down the main page. Several headlines are visible.

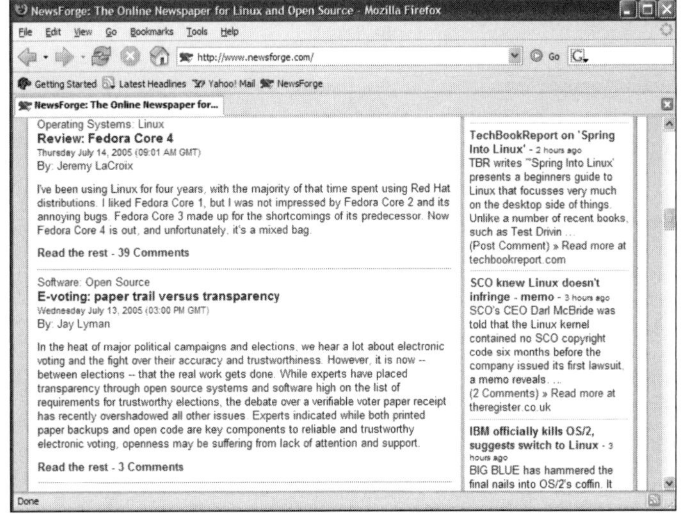

The NewsForge main page (partial view).

You see several interesting headlines. Instead of just clicking them one by one to open them, right-click the first one instead. This brings up a little menu.

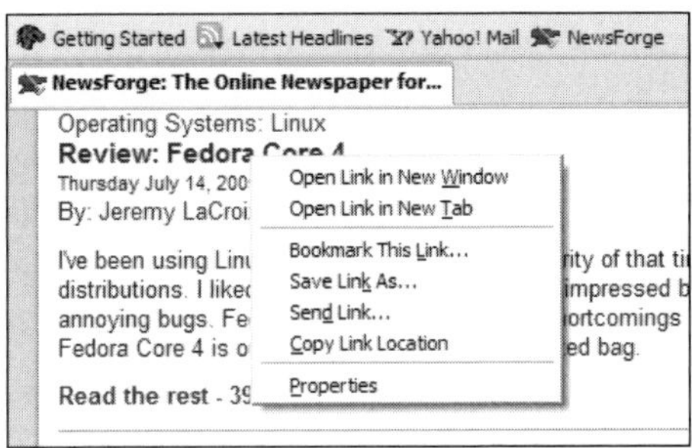

The Link menu.

If you choose the Open Link in New Tab selection, you open the story "Review: Fedora Core 4" in a new tab.

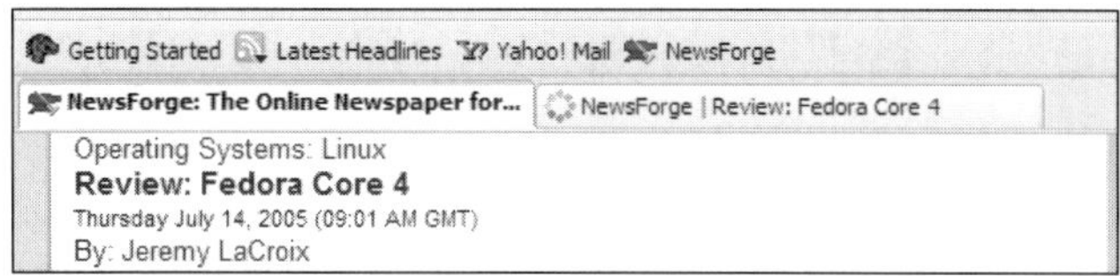

Two tabs are open.

The magic here is that not only can you go on reading the first page—scrolling up and down all you want—while the second page loads, but you can click on to the newly-opened page, read it, and return to the first page right where you left off instead of reopening it.

You can open multiple pages at once, until the tab bar on top of the browser window is so covered with tabs that you can't read the words in any of them.

This is a great convenience, not only when you're reading stories on a news Web site but also when you're doing research with a search engine or comparing a number of items on an ecommerce vendor's site side by side.

Many tabs open, with some still loading.

Microsoft's Internet Explorer (IE) 7 is supposed to have a feature similar to Firefox's tabbed browsing when it comes out, but as of this writing I haven't seen it. Not only that, in the summer of 2005 Microsoft still wasn't sure if IE 7 would be fully compliant with World Wide Web Consortium (W3C) standards for browser displays, while Firefox already met W3C specifications.

Firefox Help, Extensions, Themes, and Other Goodies

The Getting Started tab at the top left of the Firefox browser window takes you directly to Firefox Central. From this page you can find help, the latest Firefox news, plus lots of extensions and plugins, extensions, and themes you can download for free. There are also links where you can buy T-shirts, donate money, and volunteer. Firefox Central is worth regular visits even after you are no longer "getting started" with Firefox. This is where you learn about the latest themes, plugins, and other goodies that make Firefox not just functional, but fun.

Firefox Central.

Chapter 15

Thunderbird Saves the Email Day

Imagine a fast, easy-to-use email program that is immune to Outlook viruses, worms, and trojans. Now imagine one with a built-in filter that keeps spam and other unwanted email from clogging your inbox and that can access email from both POP and IMAP email servers. Except there's no need to imagine this program. It's called Mozilla Thunderbird, and you can download it right now—for free—and start using it immediately.

The download is at www.mozilla.org/products/thunderbird/. It requires no registration.

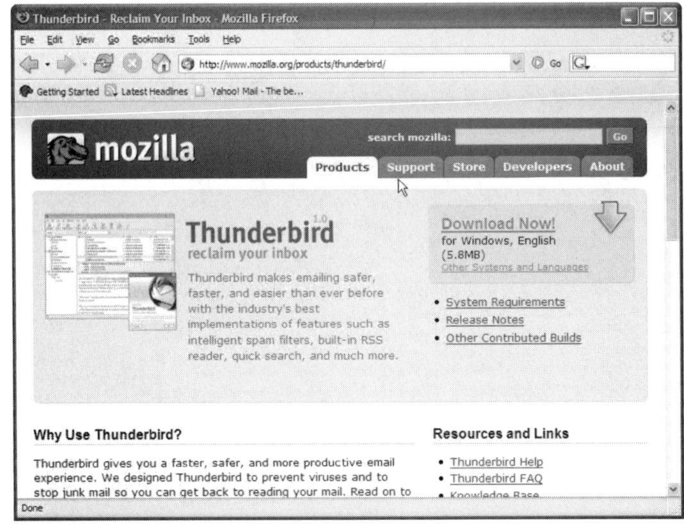

The Thunderbird home page.

Installing Thunderbird

The installation routine is almost exactly the same as the one for Firefox. The first time you run Thunderbird, you are given the opportunity to import settings and other data from Outlook Express, the email program included with almost every copy of Windows.

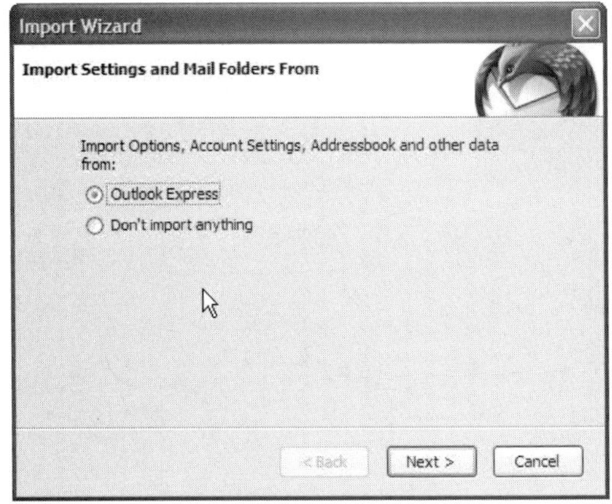

Importing Outlook Express settings.

The next question is, "Do you want to use Mozilla Thunderbird as the default mail application?" You may want to play with it for a bit before you make this

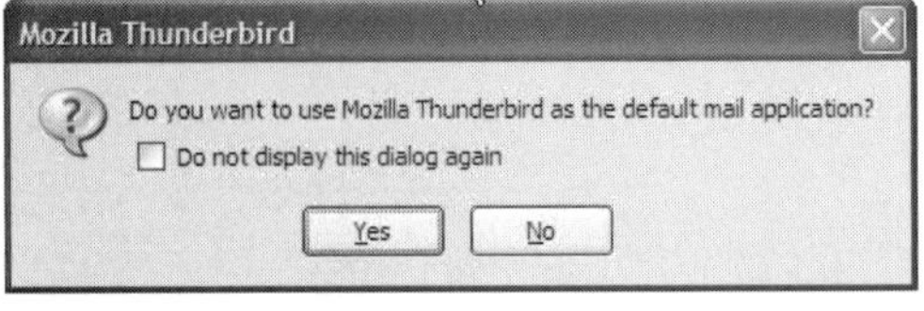

The default email selection.

decision, but it's easy to select it as your email default later, and it's just as easy to switch back to Outlook Express, so this is not a critical choice. But you *may* want to think for a moment about how worms and viruses keep popping up in PCs that run Outlook Express and use this opportunity to say goodbye to them *right now* by committing to Thunderbird.

Here is your first taste of Thunderbird.

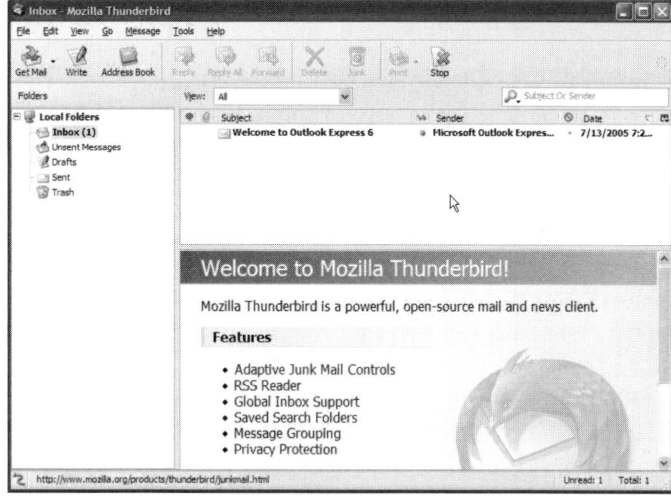

Thunderbird, ready to use.

But what if you don't have any Outlook Express settings to import, either because you don't like the ones you have or—as on the test computer where this book's figures were shot—this is a fresh Windows installation and you don't have any settings to import? Try to do something like download email or write a new email message in Thunderbird. You'll automatically call up the setup utility that helps you set up email accounts.

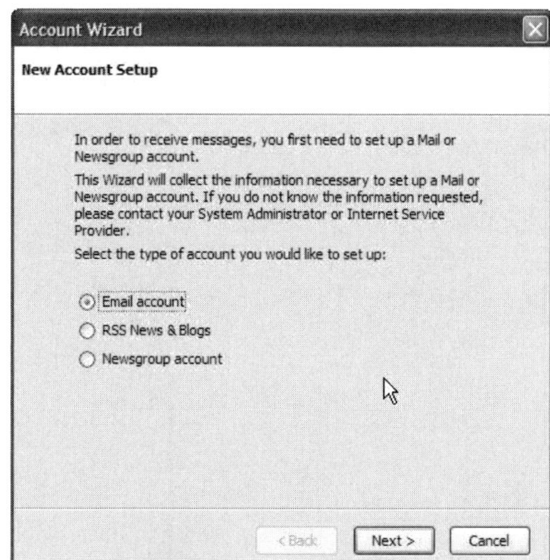

Thunderbird configuration.

Configuring Thunderbird

You can set up email, RSS, or UseNet Newsgroup accounts—or all three, although you need to do them one at a time. Email is the best place to start. You need to know some basic information that you should have handy; if you don't, you can get it from your Internet service provider (ISP) or, if you're on a corporate network, your systems administrator.

The first pieces of required information are your name and email address. The next few bits of information need to come from your ISP or network administrator. As a general rule, if you're not sure what IMAP email is, you have POP. And if you have been using another email program, the server names almost certainly will be listed in it under "account settings" or a similar name. No matter how you get these pieces of information, this is where you type (or paste) them in.

(If you imported settings from Outlook Express, all this has automatically been done for you.)

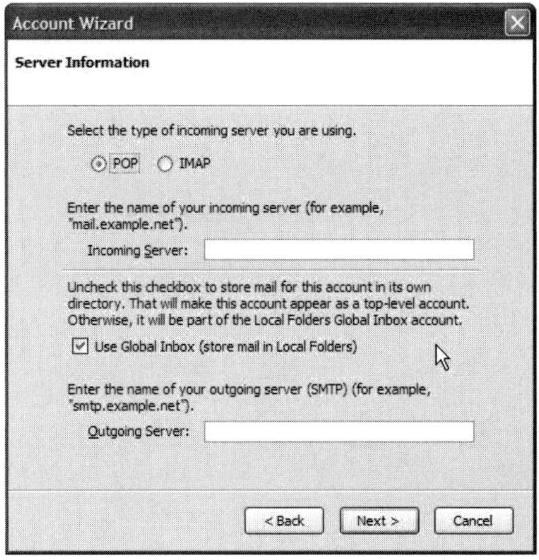

Server Information.

The user name you type into the next screen may or may not be the same as your usual email name. Some ISPs and corporate networks require your entire email address. Others don't. This is one of those pieces of information you may need to get from your ISP or admin if you don't have it handy.

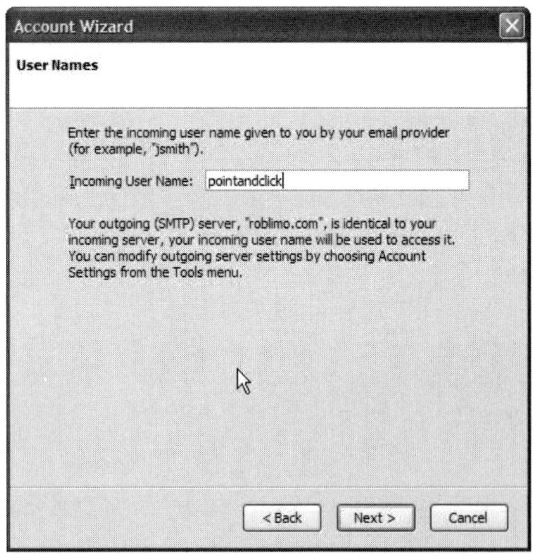

User Names.

The next screen is where you name this account. If you have only one email account, you can call it "email" and be done with it. Or you can get creative. Naming email accounts is important only if you have more than one, and even then you can name them whatever you like.

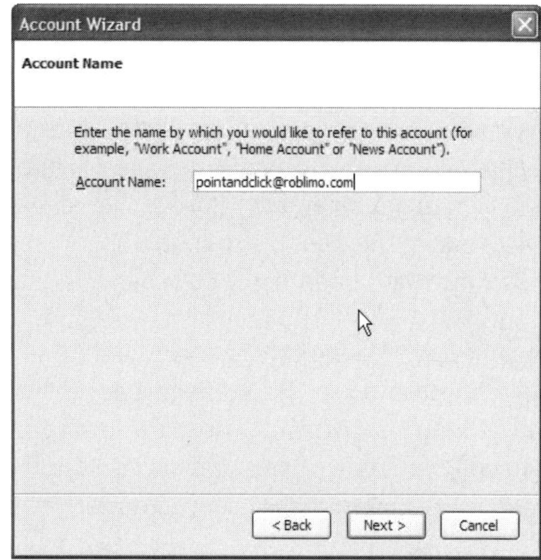

Account Name.

The last screen is a recap where you can check the information you typed in to make sure it's correct. If some of it isn't, you can click Back until you come to the screen where you made the mistake and correct it. If everything's fine, click Finish. You're now ready to use Thunderbird to send and receive email. It automatically launches and starts downloading email as soon as the installation is done.

From this point on, using Thunderbird is so simple that you can figure it out without help. Clicking menu items to see what they are won't hurt anything. Any change you make can be changed back, so feel free to explore and experiment.

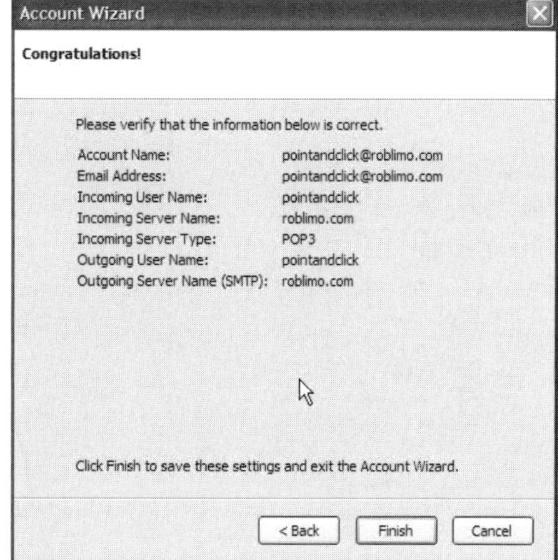

Finish.

Setting up the Thunderbird Junk Email Filter

Thunderbird uses a Bayesian filter, based on a probability theorem developed by the Reverend Thomas Bayes in the 17th century. You can look up Bayes's work and the math behind it at www.wikipedia.org if you like, but in practical terms as it applies to spam filtering, you might paraphrase Bayes's theorem this way: "If an email has more than *x* number of characteristics found in previous spam emails, this email is also likely to be spam. But if it has *y* number of *another* set of characteristics, it is probably *not* spam."

The beauty of using the Bayesian method to filter spam is that you create your own definition of spam—or, as Thunderbird calls it, "junk email." Some people like receiving emails advertising new computer gear, for instance, while they detest getting emails selling weight-loss drugs. Others may be interested in weight loss but dislike pornography offers. Windows users probably want to declare all emails with unexplained attachments—which can easily carry worms, viruses, or other malware— junk, while a virus researcher running Linux (which is not affected by Windows malware) may want to receive those emails.

You train your Thunderbird junk filter to match your personal preferences. This takes no math skills. You download some email and click each one you consider junk. After a few hundred clicks, the program automatically decides which emails are junk and which aren't, based on your input.

Consider the typical email download shown here. You see some email headers. Chances are that at least a few of those emails are junk. Highlight one so that the message body appears. If it's junk, click the dot to the right of the Sender listing, and a trash can appears.

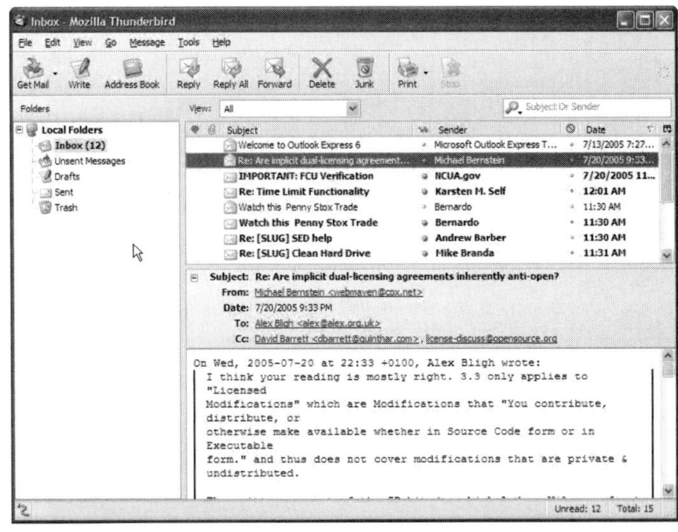

The Thunderbird inbox.

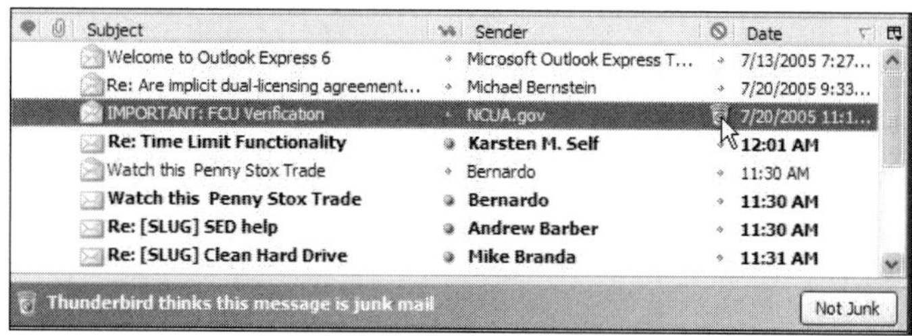

Declaring an email a piece of junk.

This email, which is a phishing scam that pretends to come from a credit union, is now junk in the eyes of Thunderbird's Bayesian filter. You go through your current emails and—no surprise—end up marking more than half of them as junk.

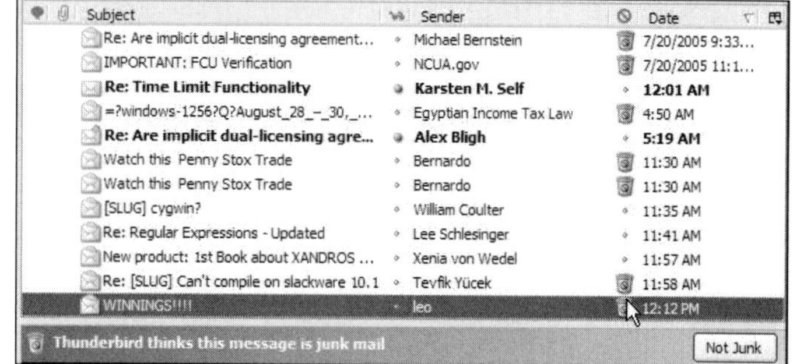

Seven out of 12 emails are junk.

Remember, someone interested in Egyptian income tax law might decide not to mark that email as junk. This is why it's good to "train" your *own* email filter instead of letting someone else decide which email you should and shouldn't receive in your inbox.

But in any case, you *can* decide with Thunderbird. You can also change your mind after you declare an email junk by clicking the trash can or the Not Junk button below and to the right of the list of emails in your inbox to unjunk it.

Once you've decided what is and isn't junk, it's time to decide what you want to do with your junk email. At the very top of the Firefox window, select Tools and then Junk Mail Controls.

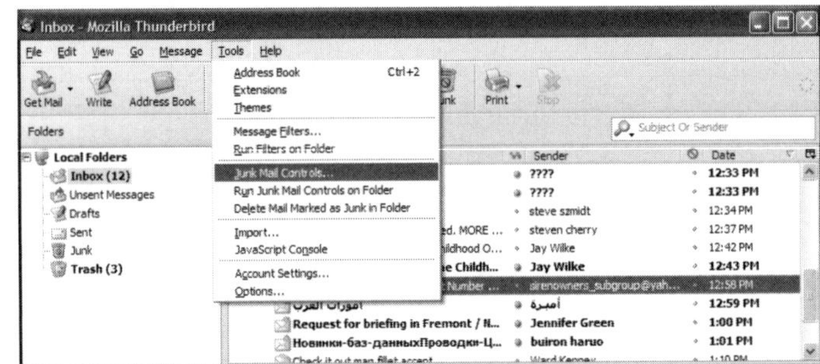

The Thunderbird Tools menu.

This brings up the Junk Mail Controls dialog box. The boxes checked in the figure provide a good set of defaults. As with all Thunderbird settings, you can change them later, so there is no need to agonize over your settings before making your choices.

Now, whenever you mark an email as junk, it will go to the junk folder all by itself, as will the emails that the Bayesian filter decides are junk as it learns your preferences, which usually takes several hundred emails.

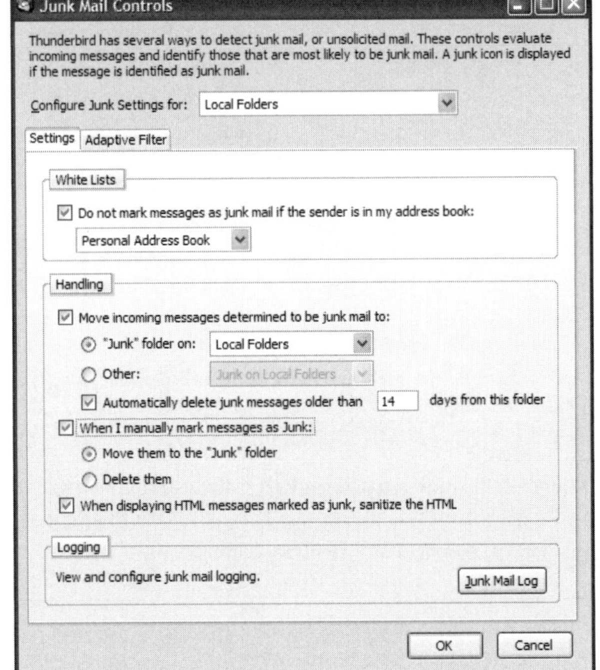

Thunderbird junk mail settings.

The next step in this process is to monitor your junk folder for a week or so and make sure that no emails have landed there that shouldn't have. If you find some, mark them "Not Junk." After a while the filter will stop automatically marking emails as junk that you really want to see.

The last step—and this one is necessary only if you get thousands of emails every week—is to periodically go into your Junk folder and clean it out by selecting Tools > Delete Mail Marked as Junk in Folder. If you used the settings suggested here, your Junk folder will automatically cleanse itself of all junk email that is more than 14 days old. (Yet another alternative is to set it to self-clear after 10 days or three days or any other interval you like.)

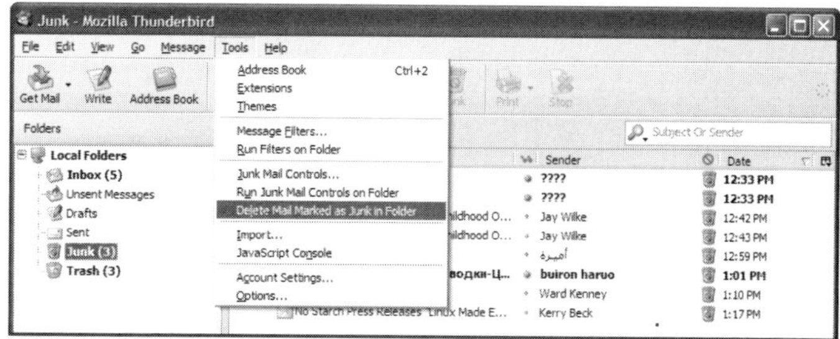

Deleting mail marked as junk.

Some Final Notes

You now know enough about Thunderbird to start using it as your primary email program, but you have barely scratched the surface of what you can do with it. Click around those menus at the top of the window—especially Options under the Tools menu—and you'll discover many other ways you can customize Thunderbird's settings to suit your tastes.

Go to the www.mozilla.org/products/thunderbird/ Web page. You'll find all kinds of downloadable themes and extensions, tips and tricks, and useful advice about how to use, customize, and improve Thunderbird.

You may want to check that Thunderbird page every few months, not just once. New features and tools are always in development, and there are places where you can suggest ones you'd like, too.

And this bears repeating: Feel free to experiment with both Firefox and Thunderbird. Try different settings. These are rugged programs. You won't break them by messing around, and you can undo any changes you make as easily as you made the change in the first place, so there is no reason not to play with different settings, themes, and extensions whenever you're sitting in front of your computer and have a few moments to spare.

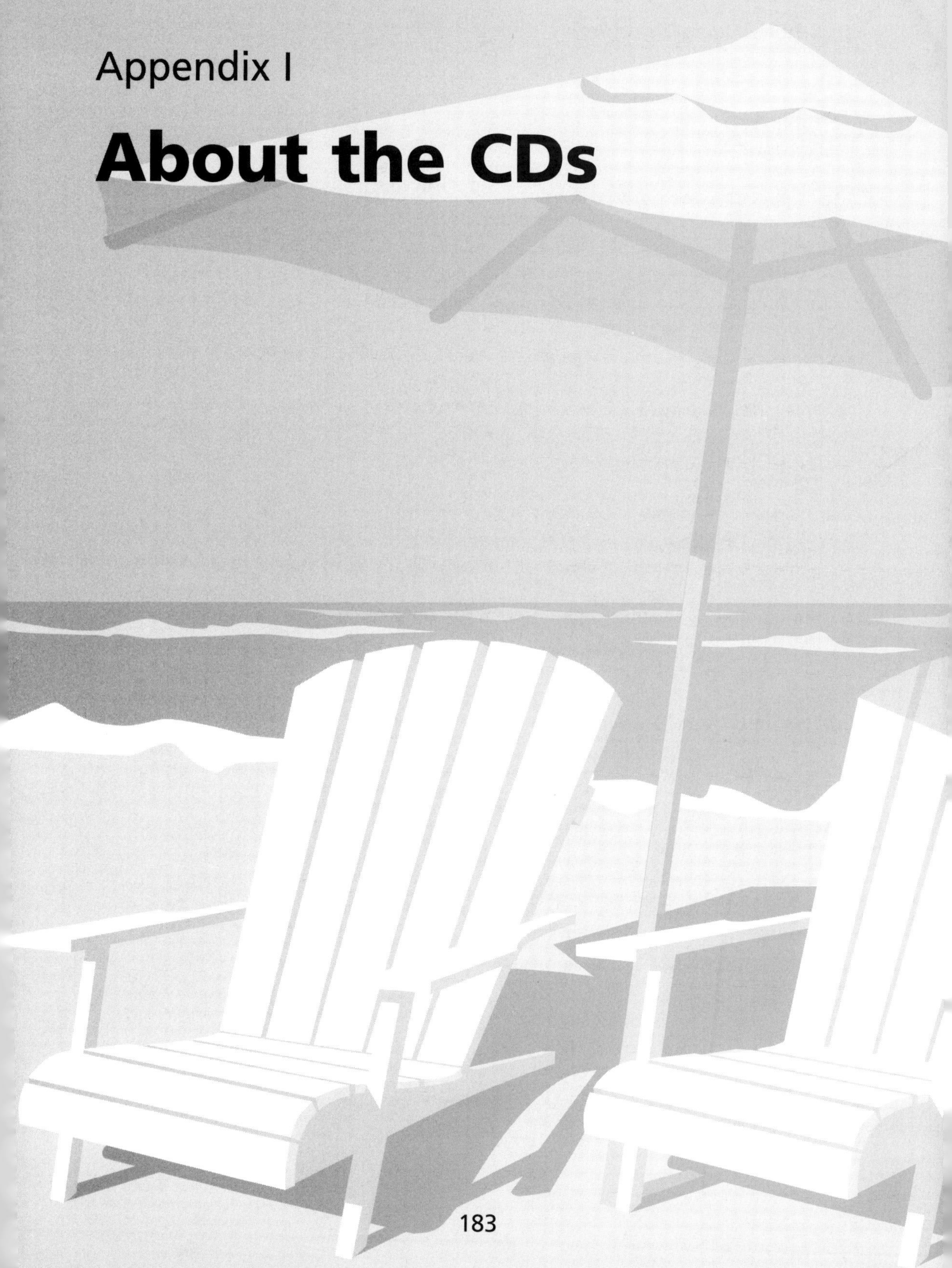

Appendix I

About the CDs

The Program CD

The program CD included with this book contains Windows and Linux versions of OpenOffice.org and Windows versions of Firefox and Thunderbird.

When you open the program CD you will see two folders. The Windows folder contains three files: OOo2.exe, Firebird.exe, and Thunderbird.exe. Clicking on one of these files while running Windows should automatically install the program that shares the file's name. If this does not work, copy the program you want to install from the CD to your Desktop folder and open it by clicking on the program icon that will be automatically created there.

The Linux folder contains OOo2 as a series of RPM files that will install correctly on most RPM-based distributions but will need to be repackaged through the "Alien" utility to install correctly on a computer running Debian or a Debian-derived Linux distribution.

Ideally, you should use the programs on this CD only for testing purposes. Once you decide to make OpenOffice.org, Firefox, and Thunderbird part of your day-to-day computing life, you should download the latest versions of these programs from their respective Web sites:

- You can find OpenOffice.org at www.openoffice.org.
- Firefox and Thunderbird downloads are available at www.mozilla.org.

Note for Linux Users

Before you install the versions of OpenOffice.org, Firefox, or Thunderbird that are on this book's CD or download the latest versions from the programs' Web sites, you should check your Linux distribution's software repository to see if it contains a version that is already integrated with your favorite Linux packaging and menu system. Almost all major Linux distributors include these three programs either as part of their base offerings or as downloadable add-ons. You will find installing distribution-specific versions of them easier than installing the "generic" versions you find elsewhere.

Note for Mac Users

When this appendix was written, there was no current Mac OS X port. However, a set of "build" instructions was available for using OOo 2 as an X11 program within Mac OS X. Up-to-date information on OOo for Mac OS X can be found at http://porting.openoffice.org/mac.

Another alternative for Mac OS X users is NeoOffice, the "Neolithic Office" version of OOo for Mac OS X whose development lags behind development of OOo itself. You can learn more about NeoOffice (and find the latest downloadable version) at www.neooffice.org. NeoOffice integrates well with the Mac OS X desktop and has most or all of the same features as its Linux/Windows counterpart.

Java Note

All versions of OpenOffice.org depend on Java for some of their functionality. Most computers have recent versions of Java installed. If yours does not, you can learn more about Java from your operating system supplier (Microsoft, Apple, or any Linux distributor) or directly from www.java.com.

Software Licenses and Source Code

All software on the program CD is licensed under terms approved by the Open Source Initiative (www.opensource.org), which means you are free to copy and redistribute all or part of the Point & Click OpenOffice.org! program CD however you wish. License terms and source code for the programs on the CD are available from the programs' respective Web sites, listed at the beginning of this appendix.

The Video CD

The video CD will play on any computer that has a Web browser and Flash player installed. To view the videos, open the CD on your computer (if it does not open automatically) and click the file named "Click Here." This automatically opens your Web browser and, on most computers, automatically plays the first video.

Each video has a control bar that tells you how long the video is in minutes and lets you start, replay, pause, fast-forward, and rewind it.

The videos are 800 pixels wide and 600 pixels high. This size gives them maximum clarity in most Web browsers on most monitors. If the videos are too large for your screen, you can select View > Full Screen in most browsers to expand your browser's viewing area. If your toolbar occupies the left side of your browser window, which is common in Microsoft Explorer's default configuration, you may want to close that toolbar to give the video more room to display.

Perhaps you follow these steps and still can't see the videos full-size. This usually occurs because you have a very old monitor or one set to 800 × 600 screen resolution instead of the 1024 × 768 size that has become the minimum standard monitor resolution in recent years. Instead of using the menu to open the videos, you can click the movies folder icon and view the videos individually by right-clicking their titles and selecting your Web browser as the program used to open them. This automatically scales the videos to fit your browser window. They will not be as clear as when they are shown at their full 800 × 600 size, but they will still be legible enough that you can learn from them.

If you do not have a Flash player installed on your Windows or Mac computer, you can download it for free from www.macromedia.com/go/getflashplayer. The download site automatically detects your operating system, so you get the version that is right for you. A Linux version is available at that Web site as well, but if you run Linux, you will almost certainly find it easier to install your Flash player if you obtain it from your Linux distribution's download repository instead of directly from Macromedia.

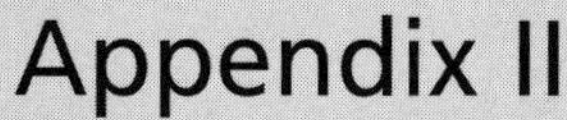

Appendix II

OpenOffice.org Resources

The main OpenOffice.org Web site is, of course, www.openoffice.org. That's where you get the latest OOo downloads and information.

http://documentation.openoffice.org is the official source of OOo documentation and advice.

Excellent (free) OOo help and advice are available at www.oooforum.org.

www.kaaredyret.dk/openoffice.html is a privately maintained collection of OOo training materials and other information.

www.ooomacros.org is all about OOo macros—how to use them and how to create them.

A book that takes you deeper into OOo is *OpenOffice.org 2.x Resource Kit* by Solveig Haugland and Floyd Jones (ISBN 013148205X, published by Prentice Hall Professional Technical Reference).

The best place to go for help with an OOo problem, whether it's a simple "How do I . . . ?" question or a major frazzle that's driving you up the wall, is http://support.openoffice.org. This Web site also has links to many other OOo resources, including a worldwide list of commercial OOo training and support providers.

Index

C

D

I

J

K

L

M

N

O

T

U-V

W

X-Y-Z

Prentice Hall Professional Technical Reference
http://www.phptr.com/
Prentice Hall PTR InformIT InformIT Online Books Financial Times Prentice Hall ft.com PTG Interactive Reuters
TOMORROW'S SOLUTIONS FOR TODAY'S PROFESSIONALS
PRENTICE HALL PTR
Prentice Hall Professional Technical Reference
Browse
Book Series
What's New
User Groups
Alliances
Special Sales
Contact Us
Search | Help | Home
Quick Search
PTR Favorites
Find a Bookstore
Book Series
Special Interests
Newsletters
Press Room
International
Best Sellers
Solutions Beyond the Book
Shopping Bag
Keep Up to Date with
PH PTR Online
We strive to stay on the cutting edge of what's happening in professional computer science and engineering. Here's a bit of what you'll find when you stop by www.phptr.com:
What's new at PHPTR? We don't just publish books for the professional community, we're a part of it. Check out our convention schedule, keep up with your favorite authors, and get the latest reviews and press releases on topics of interest to you.
Special interest areas offering our latest books, book series, features of the month, related links, and other useful information to help you get the job done.
User Groups Prentice Hall Professional Technical Reference's User Group Program helps volunteer, not-for-profit user groups provide their members with training and information about cutting-edge technology.
Companion Websites Our Companion Websites provide valuable solutions beyond the book. Here you can download the source code, get updates and corrections, chat with other users and the author about the book, or discover links to other websites on this topic.
Need to find a bookstore? Chances are, there's a bookseller near you that carries a broad selection of PTR titles. Locate a Magnet bookstore near you at www.phptr.com.
Subscribe today! Join PHPTR's monthly email newsletter!
Want to be kept up-to-date on your area of interest? Choose a targeted category on our website, and we'll keep you informed of the latest PHPTR products, author events, reviews and conferences in your interest area.
Visit our mailroom to subscribe today! http://www.phptr.com/mail_lists